Leading in Law

Leading in Law

Leadership Development for Law Students

Donald J. Polden

Barry Z. Posner

CAROLINA ACADEMIC PRESS

Durham, North Carolina

LIBRARY OF CONGRESS CATALOGING-IN-PUBLICATION DATA

Names: Polden, Donald J., author. | Posner, Barry Z., author.
Title: Leading in law : leadership development for law students /
by Donald J. Polden, Barry Z. Posner.
Description: Durham, North Carolina : Carolina Academic Press, LLC, [2022] |
Includes index.
Identifiers: LCCN 2022002555 (print) | LCCN 2022002556 (ebook) |
ISBN 9781531021009 (paperback) | ISBN 9781531021016 (ebook)
Subjects: LCSH: Law--Study and teaching--United States. | Practice of law--
Study and teaching--United States. | Leadership--Study and teaching--United States.
Classification: LCC KF273 .P65 2022 (print) | LCC KF273 (ebook) |
DDC 340.071/173--dc23/eng/20220208
LC record available at https://lccn.loc.gov/2022002555
LC ebook record available at https://lccn.loc.gov/2022002556

Carolina Academic Press
700 Kent Street
Durham, North Carolina 27701
(919) 489-7486
www.cap-press.com

Printed in the United States of America

We dedicate this book first to our spouses, Susie and Jackie, who have been our partners, advisors, and loving critics for decades, with more to look forward to.

Second, we're quite appreciative of the many students over the years who have shared their experiences and through their challenges have sharpened our thinking—we hope that we have made them proud.

Third, we are grateful for the support and encouragement of our colleagues in believing that leadership matters in the education of law students and who have graced us with their feedback and insights on drafts of this book.

Finally, we dedicate this book to the next generation of lawyers, with the anticipation that behaving like a leader will enhance their contributions as lawyers and move us forward to a more just and humane world.

Contents

Part II

INTRODUCTION

Leadership Development for Law Students

Developing leadership in lawyers should be as important a part of the law school curriculum as property or torts, and those leadership skills are what young lawyers need to distinguish themselves in today's complex legal profession.

—Donald J. Polden

Developing leadership in lawyers is more important than ketchup on French fries.

—Barry Z. Posner

Regardless of whether you want to think about the issue from an academic or a gastronomic perspective, suffice it to say that developing leadership in lawyers is critically important. This book is about leadership—but, in particular, it is targeted at students who will be lawyers who will lead others. We also believe that a more comprehensive treatment of leadership in the legal world will inspire lawyers who are asked to lead or would like to lead to become more capable and skilled at leadership.

Of course, lawyers as leaders are important to social, economic, and political systems; after all, leadership matters in nearly all areas of life, and there is no shortage of opportunities for leadership to be exercised. However, the specific focus of this book is about learning to be leaders within the legal profession and the roles and responsibilities of lawyers as leaders in the ways that they serve others in their profession.

In addition to preparing students to be leaders—regardless of their eventual titles, roles, or positions—through the exercise of the behaviors associated with leading (leadership), this book also addresses the need for students to develop their professional identity and to exercise the same by providing leadership in a number of dimensions, circumstances, and settings. Furthermore, lawyer leadership is considered across a variety of aspects of the legal profession including the practice of law.

Law schools have been expected to develop their students for the demands of a profession that is ethically based and complex, and often volatile, and one in which a broad array of skills, behaviors, and attitudes are necessary to be successful. Increasingly, law schools are turning to leadership development courses and programs to strengthen the formation of attitudes and abilities that are needed for success in today's legal profession. Law schools play an important "gatekeeper" function for the legal profession and strengthening, through leadership education and development programs and curricula, the capability of their graduates to provide leadership for their firms and society.

Granted, there are lots of books on leadership, but few of them focus on lawyers and even fewer still focus on preparing students to lead versus teaching students about leaders. In other words, there is a dearth of books that provide a method and approach for developing leadership skills, attitudes, and behaviors in law students and budding lawyers. Providing a method and approach to developing leadership skills, attitudes, and behaviors is the "secret sauce" that this book brings to leadership education for law students. Our philosophy in writing such a book is that doing is more important than knowing: knowing has little value without action. To put it another way, consistent with the Jesuit philosophy of Santa Clara University, to know and not to do is not to know.

Contents and Organization

Our answer to the public need for lawyer leaders (and law-educated experts who are called on to lead) is through sound instruction in leadership. This book provides a framework for and approach to educating lawyers, in particular law students, to lead in today's rapidly changing environment. Producing lawyers who are prepared to be effective leaders in the legal profession will yield more competent representation in law firms, public defender and legal aid offices, and other legal service delivery organizations if those organizations are effectively run by people well versed and skilled in leadership. Effective leadership in these organizations produces better outcomes, including, but not limited to, significantly improved case management, greater justice, and hardier and healthier lawyers.

We do more, though, than mount the case for more leadership education in law schools and an increase in professional development programs for lawyers.

We identify and describe the key aspects of effective leadership by lawyers—not only for lawyers with a firm or legal office, but also for lawyers as public servants, in nonprofit organizations, and in many other "callings" where lawyers function. We also articulate an approach and operating system for developing exceptional leadership abilities in students who are intent on becoming lawyers and practicing law: The Five Practices of Exemplary Leadership®. In doing so, we continue the recent important progression of lawyer education and training that was invigorated by the MacCrate Report and subsequently advanced in the Carnegie Foundation report, *Educating Lawyers*. Furthermore, we build on a foundation of research and information gathered from surveys, interviews, and empirical information to provide an opportunity to both reflect on the challenges that law students face in law school (and that lawyers face in the practice of law) and to practice approaches for taking a leadership role.

The Five Practices of Exemplary Leadership® and Lawyer Leadership Education

Barry Posner, one of the authors of this book, and his coauthor Jim Kouzes, created The Five Practices of Exemplary Leadership framework, which is described in detail in Part II of this book. The framework emanated from qualitative and quantitative research conducted over nearly four decades, and it eventually led to the book *The Leadership Challenge*, which has won numerous awards (including being named as one of the ten best books on leadership of all-time), has been translated into twenty-two different languages, and has sold over three million copies.

Donald Polden, the other author of this book, when he arrived at Santa Clara University to serve as dean of the School of Law in 2003 met Barry (who was then dean of the Leavey School of Business). After a discussion about the prevalence of leadership education in business schools and why law schools were not teaching leadership, Barry gave Don a copy of *The Leadership Challenge*, and Don immediately saw the relevance of teaching leadership to lawyers.

In the mid-2000s, Santa Clara University's School of Law offered what Don believes is the first leadership course taught in a JD program at an American law school. Shortly thereafter, he began regularly teaching the leadership course himself. Due to his duties as dean, he didn't have a lot of time to spend in the classroom, but he taught the course because of the importance he placed on the subject matter. One of the greatest challenges was finding materials on leadership in the field of law, so he began developing his own materials using the central lessons of *The Leadership Challenge*, as well as materials from business, politics, government, and medicine.

Law Student Insights

This book contains numerous anecdotes and quotes from law school students, mostly in leadership classes, and from numerous guest speakers, interviews, and conversations with both young and veteran lawyers over the years. Some of the student input is derived from responses to a survey that we conducted with law school students from several universities to glean knowledge about their perspectives on leadership and leaders.

The survey responses are supplemented by classroom conversations, student presentations and papers from the many years of Barry's experience teaching a leadership seminar to law students in the JD/MBA program, along with Don's many years of experience teaching a leadership elective in the law school, and considerable service in this area to the American Bar Association. All of the quotations from students in this book are real, even though we've kept their names and specific circumstances confidential.

Parts and Chapters

This book is divided into four parts.

The first part, consisting of one chapter, addresses why leadership development and training are important in preparing law students for the roles and responsibilities they will have in their careers. The chapter identifies nine skills, behaviors, and attitudes required by lawyers to do their work competently and ethically.

The second part, in six chapters, describes The Five Practices of Exemplary Leadership, an operational system for leadership and five practices that, research has shown, matter to personal as well as organizational productivity and stature. This framework and these practices form an accessible and practical basis for learning to lead and becoming the best leader that you can be.

The six chapters in the third part address the context for lawyers to exercise leadership—for example, thinking about leading in client relationships, in internal relationships (such as within the law firm or corporate legal office), and in public roles. Examined are key issues regarding professional identity, ethics, decision making, emotional intelligence, diversity, and handling conflict and adversity.

The final part, consisting of one chapter, serves as a bookend to the first part. It focuses on achieving a mindset for leadership development, leading in challenging times, and being a lawyer leader who impacts the legal profession and the world in a positive way.

The individual chapters present current research findings, case studies provided by law school students, and practical guidelines for thinking and behaving as a lawyer leader. Each begins with a roadmap of key ideas in the chapter ("The Lead-In") and concludes with a summary section ("Following Through") that highlights the main points in the chapter. At the end of each chapter are a set of questions ("Reflections"), meant to stimulate you to think more deeply, and often personally, about the materials presented in the chapter. Reflection questions can be discussed in a group setting with your colleagues and put into written form as exercises to advance your appreciation and understanding of what it takes to be a lawyer who provides leadership and makes a difference.

Go Forth and Learn to Lead

Nonlawyers often jokingly ask, "Lawyers say they 'practice law'; why don't they 'do' law?" In fact, lawyers both practice to become better lawyers and also do the work of lawyers. Similarly, lawyer leaders both practice to become better lawyers *and* leaders *and* also do the work of lawyers *and* leaders—and this book endeavors to assist them in this undertaking.

Donald J. Polden
Barry Z. Posner

Part I

This first part, which consists of one major chapter, addresses why leadership development and training are important in preparing law students for the roles and responsibilities they will have in their careers. The chapter identifies nine skills, behaviors, and attitudes required by lawyers to do their work competently and ethically.

ONE

Educating Lawyers for Leadership

Developing the leadership abilities and potential of law students, lawyers, and people leading legal institutions is essential to their careers and to the legal profession.

THE LEAD-IN

- Leadership: A Learned Skill
- Lawyers in Leadership Positions
- Conventional Law School Education
    - Learning to "Think Like a Lawyer"
    - State Bar Exams and Optional Leadership Courses
- Insufficiency of Law School Education
    - Lack of Leadership Development in the Legal Profession
    - Ethics and the Need for Leadership Development
    - Foundational Reports
    - Recent National Discussion
- Critical Leadership Skills, Behaviors, and Attitudes
    - No. 1: Credibility
    - No. 2: Ability to Lead Change in a Complex Environment
    - No. 3: Good Judgment
    - No. 4: Persuasiveness
    - No. 5: Creativity, Entrepreneurship, and Innovation
    - No. 6: Ability to Build and Sustain Relationships
    - No. 7: Inclusiveness
    - No. 8: Resiliency
    - No. 9: Personal Responsibility for Development
    - Linking with Individual Leadership Development
- Following Through
- Reflections

With over 1.3 million lawyers in the United States[1] (or approximately one lawyer for every 255 people, and just behind Israel as the country with the most lawyers per capita in the world[2]), most people would agree that law schools have few challenges with enrollment or with populating the legal profession. However, while many lawyers are in—or aspire to be in—leadership positions, many people would contend that the legal profession hasn't done much to educate lawyers for those leadership positions. For most, leadership is left for lawyers to learn "on the job" and generally quite late in their careers. Law schools have taken a fairly lackadaisical effort toward leadership education for students, and all too many students have the viewpoint (reinforced by their instructors) that "if it isn't on the bar exam, why bother." This shortsighted perspective has damaged the reputation of what was once the most respected of all professions, and it shortchanges the success of individual lawyers, their clients and firms, and society in general, because of the critical value-added role that leadership offers. Taking for granted competence in understanding the statutes, policies, precedents, and rules of law, leadership is the variable which differentiates high performance from average and mediocre productivity and profitability.

Leadership: A Learned Skill

Some people believe that leaders are born, not made. This couldn't be further from the truth. Leadership is not a position in an organization or a status that one inherits, and it is not necessarily a case of "either you have it or you don't." Rather, it is the product of a process by which a person employing certain skills, behaviors, and attitudes influences others to achieve positive and ethical change. And these skills, behaviors, and attitudes associated with exemplary leadership can be learned, honed, and developed.

Developing the leadership abilities and leadership potential of law students, lawyers, and people leading legal institutions is essential. In a country of laws and a society devoted to the rule of law, the roles that lawyers play are critical to the success of the nation's political and economic regimes. Performing those roles well demands exceptional leadership, and those leadership abilities must be taught to and developed in lawyers, beginning with their law school experience.[3]

Lawyers in Leadership Positions

The need for developing the leadership competence of lawyers is due, in no small part, to the important roles they play in communities, government institutions, and significant commercial, business, and interpersonal transactions.[4]

Lawyers act and serve in many leadership roles and capacities. They lead in their firms and government law offices, in political and public sector roles, in their community work for nonprofit organizations, and in private practice—guiding and counseling their clients to resolve disputes, seeking justice, and crafting collaborative and durable transactions.

While lawyers make up an extremely small percentage of the population—less than only four-tenths of 1 percent of the American population[5]—they are overrepresented in leadership positions, including elected officials, judicial officers, members of numerous civic and community task forces and teams, in senior positions in private and public organizations, on boards of directors of corporations and nonprofits, and in small businesses and private practices. Consider that twenty-seven of the forty-six presidents of the United States were lawyers, and in the most recent Congress (117th Congress), one hundred and forty-four members of the House (32.7 percent) and fifty senators (50 percent) hold law degrees.[6] Furthermore, thirty-four percent of state governors have law degrees,[7] and fourteen percent of all state legislators indicate "attorney" as their occupation.[8]

The fact that lawyers serve in many important leadership positions is actually not a recent revelation. As early as the nineteenth century, British commentator Alexis de Tocqueville observed that, in America, "lawyers consequently form the highest political class"[9] and are essentially the keepers of the rule of law.[10] Perhaps this explains why only about 5 percent of Americans have ever thought about running for political office, yet 58 percent of lawyers have considered the idea.[11]

Conventional Law School Education

A great deal of the educational program in law school focuses on traditional notions of how best to educate lawyers for the roles they play in society and the law practice settings in which they function.

Learning to "Think Like a Lawyer"

The core law school curriculum has been essentially the same since Blackstone, and innovations to the basic program of study have happened infrequently. The standard first-year curriculum consists of a smattering of topical areas—civil procedure and tort law, for example—and some discipline-specific skills, like performing legal research and marshaling arguments into a brief or memorandum. The chief educational approach of the first-year curriculum is developing students' abilities to deduce how past legal precedent should apply to future law cases or controversies and to figure out how to approach and solve legal problems. This methodological form of analysis is an essential tool for lawyers in common law jurisdictions (such as the United States) and, as taught in law schools, is often referred to as "learning to think like a lawyer."

This approach has demonstrated efficiency, as schools can educate large cohorts of students by having them experience the process of learning through the questions and answers of a few students.[12] Through the use of hypotheticals to test out various legal doctrines, students can learn legal reasoning in large classes and without much individual instruction. This approach is in sharp contrast with other professions, like medicine, that teach essential knowledge and clinical skills in small classes often with "hands-on" professional development and practice. The growth in the number and types of clinical courses and programs in American law schools suggests that legal education is attempting to provide more student-focused development of key skills and abilities.

State Bar Exams and Optional Leadership Courses

The first-year curriculum creates a foundation of legal doctrines and principles that are subsequently built on in advanced courses in those subject areas. Courses such as these are the gist of state bar examinations, which notoriously test for subject matter knowledge rather than professional skills development.

This is precisely the major reason in our surveys of law school students* that they gave for *not* taking a leadership elective while in law school: "The course doesn't count when it comes to passing the bar exam." This shortsightedness

* We will refer throughout the book to our surveys of hundreds of law school students, as well as examples and quotations from law school students. The latter come both from the open-ended statements from the surveys, as well as comments both in class and on written assignments from law school students over the years. The surveys were conducted at a number of law schools, providing diversity in admissions selectivity, enrollment size, geography, and student gender and ethnicity.

comes back to haunt law school graduates when they are faced with the challenges of leading a law firm, a team of associates, a corporate board, or even their child's Parent–Teacher Association.

Of course, some students do take elective leadership courses. When we surveyed those students about why they felt that enrolling in a leadership course was worthwhile, they gave several forward-looking responses, including "I wanted to gain more knowledge regarding leadership skills so that I can feel more comfortable with my future job and advance my career," "I felt this would give me real-world insight into the work attorneys do and ways to approach leadership," and "I plan to obtain a leadership position upon finishing my law degree."

Insufficiency of Law School Education

Learning how an automobile engine works doesn't necessarily result in being able to drive a car, to drive one safely, or to race competitively with maximum efficiency and speed. Similarly, while knowledge about the law, and thinking like a lawyer, are necessary, they are actually insufficient for the effective practice of the law (and they won't be the chief factors in building your reputation as a lawyer). The information and knowledge provided in law school doesn't fully prepare lawyers to perform professionally and ethically in the complex world that they will encounter. What lawyers are being asked to do and the skills they need to be effective in doing those things go far beyond information—and, often, even the law as presently constituted. The skills required are simply not addressed in law school curricula. What are the skills necessary for the twenty-first-century lawyer, functioning in highly volatile and unpredictable environments as a lawyer and public servant? They can be captured in a single word: *leadership*.

Lack of Leadership Development in the Legal Profession

Leadership development has been a core tenet in many professions and viewed as essential for those in business, education, medicine and health care, the military, and even the clergy. Leadership education courses, programs, and academic scholarship are abundantly evident in business education curricula and in schools for public policy, management, political science, and military training. What has been missing for too long, though, is a similar commitment by the law profession. Only about one half of American Bar

Association–approved schools offer leadership education, training, and development courses and programs.[13] Similarly, although most employers believe that leadership development opportunities should be a part of every student's educational experience,[14] legal firms themselves rarely offer such opportunities. Fortunately, much of this myopic view of what law students and young lawyers need to be able to do to be successful is changing, and there is increasing emphasis on the development of leadership abilities and opportunities.

The fact that lawyers are an outsized presence in leadership positions makes it all the more remarkable that legal education in America has long neglected formal training in leadership. Considering the long-standing prominence of people with legal education and training in national, state, and local governmental leadership roles, it is both surprising and disappointing that the introduction of leadership into law school curricula has only been a recent phenomenon and at that not particularly widespread. In fact, the first law school JD leadership course only materialized in 2005. Currently there are approximately ninety-eight law schools, or about forty-eight percent of all the American Bar Association (ABA) law schools, that offer a leadership program, elective course(s), or certificate, and the number is increasing.[15] In 2017, the Association of American Law Schools recognized a new Section on Leadership, and more than 250 law faculty, staff, and administrators are members.

Still, the growth of leadership studies in law schools has been slow and has often failed to gain traction. Some legal academics are dismissive of leadership studies as a "soft" skill, whereas they view the skills taught through the substantive law and legal methods of the first year as "harder" and more intellectually rigorous. This feeling is echoed by many students who indicate that they don't need a course in law school because it is "not on the bar exam." We make the case that leadership is essential for sustaining both individual and organizational excellence, and the behaviors associated with leadership are both accessible to everyone and highly relevant to the effective practice of law.

Ethics and the Need for Leadership Development

As lawyers, you will be asked to answer or advise others on many critical questions, and many of your answers can't be found in textbooks or legal precedents alone but are questions that require your judgment in responding. They are less about "Can we get away with doing this?" and more about "What should we do?" They are less about "What is correct?" and more about "What is right?"

Understanding more about leadership, and about yourself, will address and rectify the perception of the vast majority of the public that most attorneys are more interested in "winning than in seeing that justice is served" or in "making money than in serving their clients."[16] An online poll found that lawyers are perceived as high on competence but low on warmth (friendliness and trustworthiness), which is problematic because this combination erodes credibility.[17] Even law students, whether in the United States or elsewhere (England, Scotland, Germany, Australia, and Argentina), *on their first day of class*, rate lawyers as not altogether honorable (that is, trustworthy and ethical), ratings that are even lower than those from the general public.[18]

Foundational Reports

The significance of the lack of lawyer leadership training is not a new observation. The MacCrate Report (1992) and the Carnegie Foundation report (*Educating Lawyers: Preparation for the Profession of Law*, 2007)[19] considered what lawyers are taught to do and what lawyers are asked to do when they begin to fill their roles in the practice of law. They posed the following question: "Is law school education fully preparing prospective lawyers for the skills, tasks, attitudes, and abilities they need to be successful in client representation, public and private service, and a faithful commitment to the legal profession?"

Both reports concluded that (1) lawyers perform many roles for which they are not fully educated or prepared in law school, and (2) the training that law students receive in contemporarily important practical and interpersonal skills is insufficient. This is especially true, they asserted, when it comes to law students forming their "identity" as legal professionals.

Preparing lawyers for the roles that they play in today's volatile, uncertain, complex, and ambiguous (often referred to as VUCA) world requires both better and more training. The legal profession, in its time-honored tradition of assuring access to justice, has an essential role in addressing these VUCA challenges, and legal education has a critical role to play in enhancing the leadership skills of would-be lawyers who can take charge in this regard.[20]

Recent National Discussion

The current national discussion, reflecting and expanding on the discourse in these two previous reports about what lawyers in training should be taught to do in order to handle the current challenges of the profession, focuses on two essential questions:

- "What do lawyers do in their law or legal organizations and in their communities?"
- "What are the skills and competencies they need to do that work?"[21]

The impact of the 2008 financial depression and the COVID-19 pandemic created great urgency for meaningful responses to these questions. Are law schools and other professional education programs training and educating law professionals, especially newer entrants to the legal profession, with the skills and attitudes they need to perform effectively?

The ongoing discussion about what lawyers do is important because it attempts to contemporaneously pinpoint the roles that lawyers play in society and then draw definitive conclusions about what skills, behaviors, and attitudes lawyers need in order to effectively perform those roles. We hear from experts in law and legal education that lawyers need a complex set of skills and abilities and that they should be able to perform them in a fast-changing society and economy.[22] What they are *not saying* is that lawyers need to know more tort law or how to draft better motions for summary judgment. Rather, they are indicating that lawyers need to be more flexible and adaptive in terms of demonstrating new abilities and behaviors in the many roles they will perform as lawyers.

What are these essential qualities, abilities, and behaviors that today's lawyers require? They can be summed up as leadership. Becoming an exceptionally skilled and respected lawyer rests on learning about and practicing essential leadership behaviors. In other words, it is necessary to enhance leadership capabilities as applied to building and leading teams, creatively problem solving and thinking, influencing others through highly effective communication abilities, entrepreneurial abilities, and first-rate decision making and professional judgment.[23] The discussion among thoughtful commentators and experts has concluded that *without enhancing leadership capabilities, the legal profession will become increasingly narrow in its focus and irrelevant in the broader societal sense.*[24]

Critical Leadership Skills, Behaviors, and Attitudes

The most recent industry statistics[25] indicate that nearly forty-nine percent of the more than 1.3 million lawyers in America practice law in law firms, and of that group, about ten percent are solo practitioners. Eighteen percent of lawyers practice law om government, 6.2 percent in nonprofit organizations, 2.9

percent in legal services and public defender offices, and one percent in public interest law offices. Finally, nearly thirteen percent practice within a corporate setting (e.g., in-house legal counsel or lawyers who are employees of their client, such as for compliance and risk management). Finally, more than seven percent work in a business setting but are not practicing law (and 3.5 percent do not report their employment).

Although lawyers' work environments are diverse, much of their work is performed collaboratively, within their firm or through interactions with other lawyers and, of course, judges. Lawyers solve problems, applying their skill of "thinking like a lawyer" and their subject matter knowledge, but there is more involved in achieving personal and professional success.

What are these skills, behaviors, and attitudes that lawyers need in order to perform their core areas of work professionally, expertly, and ethically in today's challenging practice of law? Among the most essential are credibility; ability to lead change in a complex environment; good judgment; persuasiveness; creativity, entrepreneurship, and innovation; ability to build relationships; inclusiveness; resiliency; and personal responsibility for development. These skills, behaviors, and attitudes need to be part of every law student's education. They are clearly all about developing strategies to lead oneself and others—and the next part of this book will link them to specific leadership strategies. The final chapter will return to their importance in the contemporary work of lawyers and encourage a career-long commitment to successfully engaging those strategies.

No. 1: Credibility

Lawyers must be credible.

Credibility rests on your ability to keep promises and follow through on commitments. "Honest," "competent," and "inspiring" (being energetic, enthusiastic, and expressive about the matter at hand) are the three characteristics that are the components of what social scientists refer to as *credibility*.[26]

Global studies, involving hundreds of thousands of people in all walks of life and commerce, have asked about the characteristics, traits, and abilities that are most central to people in their *willingness* to follow someone. "Honest," "competent," and "inspiring" are at the top of the list and, along with "forward-looking," are the only characteristics consistently chosen by more than sixty percent of those surveyed, regardless of demographics, settings, or circumstances.[27] These findings parallel the results from our survey of law school students.

Lawyers, like any other professionals, function in a world in which their honesty and candor, along with their subject matter expertise, are front and center. Fundamentally, lawyers who are not seen as credible don't have much sway with people in general and, more specifically, with their clients, associates, opposing counsel, judges, and juries, among others. Judges need to be able to believe the representations and statements of lawyers appearing before them, in large part because lawyers appear in court as "officers of the court" with the attendant integrity of a judicial appointment. Furthermore, opposing counsel rely on the candor of the other team's lawyers where it doesn't conflict with their duty to clients. Moreover, credibility is absolutely essential to the lawyer–client relationship. Credibility impacts clients' willingness to follow their counsel's advice. After all, how likely are clients to follow the advice of a lawyer who is untrustworthy or who has lied to clients about the representation of their interests? Unlikely, at best. And be aware that your reputation for credibility is the major determinant of whether as a lawyer you receive referrals, generating new clients as a rainmaker.

You have to demonstrate your credibility every day. The never-ending list of lawyer jokes is evidence of the public's view that lawyers are deficient in credibility, so you have to be proactive about negating this perception. When asked to think about the character of individuals based on their chosen field, Gallup pollsters found that only twenty-one percent of US adults rated lawyers as very high or high for honesty and ethical standards.[28] In our survey of law students, clearly a biased sample, still only about seventy-five percent agreed with the statement that "lawyers are highly respected and trusted"—so work is needed to improve the general credibility of the profession and those within it. Credibility takes time to build and acquire, but it can be lost quite quickly, even in a single exchange, engagement, action, or angry outburst. When you don't do what you say you will do, people will consider that you haven't been truthful, don't know what you are talking about, or don't really care all that much—and hence render the verdict that you are not someone who is credible or worthy of following and paying attention to. When you are honest, competent, and inspiring, people will take you at your word and hand down a judgment of "credible."

No. 2: Ability to Lead Change in a Complex Environment

Lawyers must be able to lead change in an environment that is highly complex, both for them and for their clients.

For many years, the principal role of lawyers was to support and sustain the status quo. They helped clients maintain or hold onto their freedom, their wealth, and their status in society. However, increasingly with social unrest and demands for greater sharing of "the American dream," calls for racial and gender equality, antipathy to the status quo, and ventures into unpopular wars, there is an awareness that a law degree and knowledge of the law are more than a route to greater financial security—they are a way to make society fairer, more inclusive, and more just.

Enrollment in law school, especially by women and underrepresented members of society, has increased dramatically over the years, as have courses in poverty law, gender and the law, and clinical programs engaging law students in representation of marginalized clients and communities. Increasingly, legal education is seen as a way to change humanity and many of the perceived problems in American society. Many people study law and become a lawyer expressly for the purpose of making society more just, humane, and inclusive because it provides the tools to achieve these civic and society goals. Leading these changes requires leadership abilities as well as the legal tools to implement change.

No. 3: Good Judgment

Lawyers must exercise good judgment, which creates outcomes appropriate and responsive to their clients' needs.

Over three hundred and fifty attorneys within the nation's largest law firms and corporate legal offices were asked, "Aside from legal knowledge, which attribute is most important for a law firm or legal department leader to possess?" Their most frequent response was "good judgment."[29]

In most cases, lawyers are retained by clients because they have developed a reputation for being successful in achieving favorable outcomes. After all, who would knowingly hire lawyers who lose most of their cases? The ability to craft a strategy or approach to a case or transaction is a product of a lawyer's knowledge and judgment of what is appropriate and necessary in the circumstance. Sound professional judgment is essential to creating a strategy or vision for addressing a client's needs, whether through a business transaction, a court case, or a negotiation on the client's behalf.

"Thinking like a lawyer" is about how to interpret a statute, a contract, or relevant court decisions, but the practice of law is all about judgment. Lawyers make "judgment calls" all the time—about people, about strategy, in litigation or transactional work, and in crisis situations. Lawyers have to provide sound professional judgment, especially in "bet-the-company" situations where their clients could lose it all. As leaders well know, there is no freeway to the future; their ability to envision the future comes from being forward-looking and capable of seeing beyond the horizon—that is, using their judgment to pick up on the clues that abound today, which predict what tomorrow will bring.

No. 4: Persuasiveness

Lawyers must effectively persuade and influence others. Conceptualizing leadership as "the ability to persuade others to embrace your ideas and to act upon them, then lawyers are remarkably well-suited to be leaders… [as they] learn the art of persuasion the very first year of law school."[30]

In the course of their everyday activities, lawyers persuade others toward shared, necessary, or consequential outcomes. The chief "product" of lawyers is their advice and the ability to persuade others as to the validity of that counsel. Importantly, the ability to influence others is directly related to credibility and the lawyer's vision for action.

In our survey of law students across several campuses, nearly all of them (99 percent) agreed with the statement that "the ability to persuade or influence others is particularly important for lawyers." Clearly, these lawyers-in-training already appreciate and understand the critical importance of persuasion to their craft.

Surveys about the psychological characteristics of lawyers have shown that, compared with professionals in other fields, they tend to be highly analytical, more skeptical, more autonomous, and less collaborative.[31] Contrast these characteristics to the behaviors required for effective leadership and persuasion, in particular, which necessitate high degrees of collaboration, a positive outlook, and an experimental perspective. The lawyer-leader challenge is in being able to navigate the paradoxes between thinking like a lawyer and thinking like a leader in order to best serve their clients, themselves, and their professional obligations. The tensions between leading others and thinking like a lawyer should be grappled with in order to embrace the paradoxes inherent in these roles of lawyer and leader.[32] The ability to navigate paradoxical thoughts, arguments, and roles enables lawyers to arrive at innovative solutions to problems and, indeed, to reimagine legal and political institutions while functioning within them.

No. 5: Creativity, Entrepreneurship, and Innovation

Lawyers must think creatively, incorporating entrepreneurship and innovation to address complexity and uncertainty.

Because most of their work requires exercising judgment, lawyers, as we just indicated, must think like leaders in imagining the possibilities and be willing to create alternative perspectives as professional problem solvers. The 2020 twin pandemics of coronavirus and economic discontinuities, along with widespread demands for racial justice and unsubstantiated claims of voter fraud by politicians, highlighted the need for lawyers to bravely and competently face volatile change head-on and adapt to uncertainty and economic and societal disruption. The future of the legal profession and the work of lawyers will continue to be fundamentally more complex and uncertain in the coming decades than in the last few.[33] Increasing globalization of law practices, growing competition from alternative legal services providers (such as online legal services companies and automated and lawyer document reviewers), persistent client demands for lower costs and better-value work products, technological changes (e.g., artificial intelligence and smart machines), and accumulative costs of obtaining and retaining high-quality talent are all challenges that firms are already experiencing, but these challenges will accelerate into the future. The only real choice in responding to these challenges, according to David Susskind, "futurist" and expert on the business of law, is leadership. The other two alternatives, he noted, are not particularly enticing or viable: firms can invest just enough to be ready to respond if they are in fact pressed by the competition, or they can commit "commercial suicide" by attempting to resist the movements that the business of law is experiencing.[34]

Unfortunately, those law organizations without effective leadership are not stepping up to these challenges with a clear vision for change through innovation. From 1987 to 2018, more than thirty large, corporate law firms failed in the United States alone. For example, in 1987, Finley, Kumble, the fourth-largest law firm in the United States, collapsed. In 2013, Dewey LeBoeuf went bankrupt, and criminal charges were filed against it. And in 2018, Sedgwick filed for bankruptcy.[35] The common factor in all of these instances was poor leadership, as reflected in bad investments, inability to retain human talent, and failure to control firm costs. One legal industry consultant, who has been a trustee on at least eight law firm dissolutions, put it more bluntly: "You have to lay a dissolution pretty much at the feet of the people leading the firm."[36]

No. 6: Ability to Build and Sustain Relationships

Lawyers must be able to build and sustain relationships through excellent interpersonal skills, high ethical standards, and professional competence.

Face it, law is a "retail" business where personal and professional relationships are critical and necessary. This is true about the work of lawyers whether the lawyer is advising a client on a business deal or a plea in a criminal case, managing a legal firm or functioning as corporate counsel, or serving as a volunteer director of a community-based nonprofit organization.

Furthermore, this observation is true about the work of lawyers whether the lawyer is in a relationship with formal directing authority or one in which the lawyer has no formal hierarchical or official authority. Lawyers need relationship skills, as well as the legal skills and knowledge that clients require, because law is essentially a business that serves people.

Social science research shows that being effective in the workforce requires more than just being smart and having strong technical skills, which is generally the focus of most law school curricula. In addition, being effective in the workforce requires those characteristics that bolster the ability to build and sustain relationships. For example, one study found that what is most critical for those in the workforce are behavioral abilities and attitudes such as personal awareness and self-regulation, ability to manage relationships with others, and empathy for others.[37] Related studies, concerning lawyers' ability to successfully interact with others and maintain a professional status, have added that "character" is an essential attribute, perhaps even more important than legal skills, for an attorney. This was the conclusion of a study involving more than twenty-four thousand lawyers, which found that the most important skills for successful work as a lawyer were all related to character, such as integrity, resilience, work ethic, common sense, grit, and diligence.[38]

These critical skills are not routinely taught in law schools. However, curricular changes adding leadership development courses and programs on professional identity formation are moving legal education in this direction. This is a positive change as interpersonal skills and professional character development are important for law students entering the legal professional in these complex times.

No. 7: Inclusiveness

Lawyers must be able to lead their organizations, clients, and institutions toward a more diverse and inclusive environment.

Just as leadership matters in today's law practice settings, so too does diversity matter.

American society and its communities, businesses, and consumers are increasingly diverse along multiple lines (e.g., race, gender, ethnicity, sexual identity, etc.), and these changes demand that legal firms be more representative and responsive to these demographics. Individual clients, as well as corporate legal departments and government law practice units, are more than ever expecting more inclusive workforces. In addition, studies show that diversity improves firm performance, enhances a positive workplace culture, and addresses many generational challenges that organizations face.[39] More fundamentally, creating and maintaining equality of opportunity is the right thing for organizations to do, especially those charged with advancing the rule of law and the spirit of a just and fair society.

To create a more diverse workforce and practice setting, leadership is required—in particular, conscious efforts and actions to bring about a more inclusive organizational culture. Recent research has put the spotlight on inclusion as a necessary ingredient to successful diversity.[40] Rather than simply hiring diverse employees and expecting them to fit into the existing culture, the focus of inclusion is actively embracing diverse perspectives and changing the firm's culture to reflect them. Studies have found that when attorneys consider their leaders committed to inclusion, they are more likely to remain with their firm. More specifically, levels of engagement and creativity increase when women and lawyers of color feel that they are treated fairly and belong in the firm, rather than feeling like outsiders.[41]

No. 8: Resiliency

Lawyers must be hardy, able to ensure long hours and competing demands, persevere both in the moment and over time, continue to learn from experiences (both positive and negative), bounce back from adversity, and deal with uncertainty and ambiguity in a positive way.

The way you cope with the challenges that your classes, and eventually your job, throws at you will determine your long-term mental and physical vitality. More than one in five associates report regularly feeling unable to cope, and nearly half of all lawyers report experiencing negative mental health effects stemming from their work.[42] Resilience is particularly important for women and people of color who are often the object of significant pushback when they are put in leadership positions within law firms or other legal organizations. You can't internalize that pushback, and you need to be prepared for both implicit and structural racism and sexism (or the intersection of the two). Those in the majority culture can promote resilience, not just for others, but for themselves by becoming "allies" as resilience is built on helping and advocating for others, creating support networks, expressing gratitude, and focusing on what's working rather than dwelling on problems. Leadership is demonstrated when you hold yourself and others accountable when mistakes are made, listen to understand, and share growth opportunities with others. Learning to lead yourself, building your personal and professional skills, and holding yourself accountable for your successes and shortcomings are fundamental attributes of excellent leaders and lawyers and foster resiliency.

No. 9: Personal Responsibility for Development

Lawyers must take charge of their careers and take greater responsibility for development of their professional skills.

The volatile and complex law practice environment is changing much about how young lawyers develop and advance within their law organizations and throughout their careers.[43] Increasingly, individuals, rather than their employers, must take responsibility for self-improvement. Lawyers need to take much greater personal responsibility than in the past for developing the skills and abilities that they need to be successful in law. These include sophisticated competence with using networks, both technology-driven and informal; greater flexibility in spanning the boundaries within the law and between law and other disciplines; more creative thinking; and stronger resiliency. The development of these competencies, among others, is quite consistent with the demands for developing leadership abilities in these times of ongoing and continual change in the legal profession, what in rafting is referred to as "perpetual whitewater."

Researchers have shown that there is a strong link between learning and leadership, with those most actively engaged in learning demonstrating the greatest utilization of leadership behaviors.[44] Taking personal responsibility for self-improvement requires you, like any leader, to have a personal vision of the future, specifically, a sense of both what you want and where you want to be going forward—that is, what you want out of your career and crafting a life that matters.

Linking with Individual Leadership Development

Law schools have yet to fully offer the kinds of personal and professional development that emerging lawyers and social and community activists need to develop these nine key skills, behaviors, and attitudes and fully change the legal and economic landscapes. In short, leadership has not been an essential part of the legal curriculum, and law schools have been deficient in providing a systematic approach to lawyers' leadership development.[45] More than foundational legal knowledge is needed to provide high-quality client service. The ensuing conversation has focused attention on the question of how well legal education is advancing the formation of critical lawyering abilities from the first day of law school. The clear conclusion has been that law students need, beginning with law school orientation, a thoughtful, well-constructed curriculum that encompasses the skills and abilities needed to carry out their professional duties—and these skills and abilities extend beyond mastery of subject matter material education. One important reason that law students are calling for more courses in personal and professional development is that they have seen what the future of law practice looks like and what lawyers will need if they are to make a difference. That future requires their mastery of those skills and abilities, and leadership education is a pathway to that mastery.

Students also need a place to reflect on a more human and humane approach to their profession and thinking like a lawyer. Too many students, as echoed by practicing attorneys, exclaimed that the law school curriculum teaches how to assign blame and break things down, not build them up. Too often we heard a variation of this story: "I had an evidence professor who asked the class what is the most important principle of the case? A classmate responded 'to find the truth?' The professor in a raised voice said: 'The truth! The truth! I don't care about the truth, I only care about what you can prove.'" Law students want more from their law schools' curriculum, including lawyering skills development that is consonant with their values and morals.

A leadership course is a possible respite from learning to think like a lawyer. An opportunity to be reminded about why you came to study the law, and what you aspired to accomplish as a result of being a lawyer. A balance from learning the content required to pass the bar exam to focusing on who you are, what you care about, and why the law and a legal career is an opportunity for you to find meaning and purpose in your life.

FOLLOWING THROUGH

- Leadership is not something that you either have or you don't. It is a learned skill—and you, too, can learn it.
- Lawyers comprise an outsized role in leading the country, so it is essential to educate them in leadership skills, behaviors, and attitudes.
- Traditional law school curricula, which focus on "thinking like a lawyer," are necessary but not sufficient for educating law school students to be the most effective in the practice of law.
- Law schools need to educate students about the skills necessary to think and behave like leaders.
- The nine most critically important skills, behaviors, and attitudes that law students and lawyers—especially those just starting their legal careers—require in today's increasingly complex legal profession are: credibility; ability to lead change in a complex environment; good judgment; persuasiveness; creativity, entrepreneurship, and innovation; ability to build relationships; inclusiveness; resiliency; and personal responsibility for development. The key organizing element is the role of leadership.

REFLECTIONS

1. Based on what you have learned in your law school classes, what do you think are the critical competencies required for success as a lawyer? How are these different from the requirements for success in life?

• Knowledge of the law
• Understanding what you know & don't know

2. What do you already know about leadership, and how did you learn whatever it is you know when it comes to leadership? Who have been your role models for learning how to be an effective leader?

• True leaders are bold & humble
• I learned this by observing leaders in my own life (e.g. mentors, church leaders, friends)

3. What have you done to take charge of your own personal and professional development? What more do you need to do? How do you handle those situations when you feel that you're not up to being a lawyer?

• Doing things that make me afraid → either through opportunities or positions

• Take a step away and say a prayer

4. How strongly would you rate yourself on the nine critical skills, behaviors, and abilities? Which ones do you feel that you need to work on, and what do you think you can do toward that end?

• Need to work on resiliency, ability to lead change in a complex legal profession, and professional responsibility for development

Part II*

This second part, in six chapters, describes The Five Practices of Exemplary Leadership®, an operational system for leadership and five practices that, research has shown, matter to personal as well as organizational productivity and stature. This framework and these practices form an accessible and practical basis for learning to lead and becoming the best leader that you can be.

The Five Practices operational system will form the basis for their application to the work of lawyers and law students in Parts III and IV.

* The leadership operating system articulated and validated by James M. Kouzes and Barry Z. Posner in their books *The Leadership Challenge* and *Everyday People, Extraordinary Leadership* forms the basis for this section and Chapters 2–7.

TWO

Leadership: What It Means to Law Students

Leadership is a relationship between those who aspire to lead and those who choose to follow.

THE LEAD-IN

- Definitions of Leadership
    - Intricate Definitions
    - Leaders and Followers: Relationship
- Law School Basics and Lawyer Leadership
    - The Ethics of Lawyer Leadership
    - Thinking like a Lawyer versus Thinking like a Leader
- The Foundation of Leadership: Credibility
- The Five Practices of Exemplary Leadership®
- Following Through
- Reflections

Do those in positions of authority always exhibit leadership, and are those who exhibit leadership always leaders? The word *leader* typically conjures up an image of someone with a title or a hierarchical position in a firm or company, such as managing partner, CEO, chief legal counsel, director, or senior associate. More often than not, the title carries with it some authority (position of power) and generally assumes that one or more people report to that individual. The dictionary definition of *leader* conveys this same idea: "a person who manages or controls other people."[1]

Yet, it is readily apparent that while an organization can give someone a title, that doesn't necessarily make that person a leader in the sense of exercising leadership. Look up the word *leadership* in a dictionary, and you won't find it capitalized or referring to a position or place in an organization.

So, if *leadership* is not synonymous with *leader* in the sense of a person with a title, what is it exactly? Leadership is a set of qualities, abilities, and behaviors—and these are available to and accessible by anyone regardless of title, role, or authority. In fact, in the most high-performing firms everyone feels like they are a leader, and can make a difference no matter where they are located in the organization. In other words, there are no shortage of opportunities for everyone to provide leadership.

Definitions of Leadership

Pinning down a specific definition of *leadership* is a good place to start in understanding the concept of leadership.

Intricate Definitions

Academic literature on the matter has more than forty distinctive theories of leadership and over two hundred definitions of *leadership*, more similar than different in their emphases.[2]

One of the more robust and nuanced definitions is this one: "Leadership is the art of mobilizing others to want to struggle for shared aspirations."[3] Another definition, one that is particularly apt in the context of lawyer leadership, is that it is "a process by which an individual or a group influences others to achieve positive and ethical change."[4] Consider these important distinctive characteristics in defining leadership:

- Leadership is an *art*. Contrast art with science, and you get an appreciation for the artistry associated with being a leader. It is the difference between understanding the science of colors and their combinations and being able to use color to be a painter across multiple mediums. Artists, like leaders, have their own unique style, meaning that leaders can employ the science of leadership according to their own personality, preferences, and circumstances (i.e., they each paint the canvas differently, and uniquely, while using the same brushes and palettes).
- Leadership involves *mobilizing others*. Leadership involves action—getting people up and moving from the status quo to some place they have never been before. Moreover, let's acknowledge that leadership involves motivating others into action because leadership is not a solo enterprise.

- Leadership means getting *others to want to*. This phrase signals that people will be acting because of their intrinsic or internal motivation rather than based on a hierarchy of command and control. Leadership involves influencing others to action through reason and persuasion.
- Leadership necessarily involves *change*. Change may be necessitated because of a crisis or because of threats to the organization or because the group has lost focus and ambition. Change may be required, as well, to take advantage of new circumstances and opportunities. In all instances, responding to the need for change requires leadership. For lawyers, change is directed at achieving positive and ethical outcomes.
- Leadership necessitates *struggle*. If you are going to ask people to do something they have never done before, you have to admit that, realistically, it will require more effort than is currently being expended. Often people will have to make some sacrifice, by giving up something on which they are currently spending time and effort in order to take on this new challenge.
- Leadership encompasses *shared aspirations*. For leaders, the goals are always beyond the horizon, in the future, and something that they hope to achieve (without any guarantees). Moreover, this dream has to be not only in the mind of the leader, but also in the minds of those who would want to struggle to achieve that desired state—in other words, the vision is embraced by all.
- Leadership is *a process*. It is neither a static nor a one-and-done effort. There are a series of behaviors and actions necessary to achieve a desired end, and it seldom resembles a straight line. Moreover, this process can be learned, demonstrated, taught, and, like any other skill, improved through deliberate practice. This reinforces the notion that leadership can be exercised by anyone, regardless of their title, position, rank, or authority.

The lengthy definition above does tease out some important tenets of leadership, but what would be an even simpler definition? Try filling in the blank in this sentence: "This person is a leader because________________."

You could fill in the blank with many ideas and actions. However, the simplest and most all-encompassing response to this statement would be "...this person *has followers*." The point is that it is hard to imagine that someone can be a leader without followers. If you accept this premise, then what most "defines" leaders, or what makes someone a leader, is that they have followers. The relationship between leaders and their followers is often complex and contextual, but, nonetheless, both parties need each other, and when the relationship works well, everyone benefits.[5]

It is also useful to compare and distinguish managers from leaders because it is a common error made by many to treat them as synonymous, and they are not. Leaders inspire action by others through a vision for change or innovation. Managers take the status quo and attempt to maintain it for the good of the organization. Consider a leader like Dr. Martin Luther King Jr., who inspired his followers toward great achievements in civil rights. But he had staff in his organization who managed, controlled, and administered the day-to-day operations of his organization. Surely, the two "titles" or concepts are not mutually exclusive, and, in fact, the very best managers are generally effective leaders, and often the best leaders are not particularly adept at management.

Leaders and Followers: Relationship

What naturally follows from the "requirement" that leaders have followers is that there is a relationship between the two. Specifically, leadership is a relationship between those who aspire to lead and those who choose to follow.[6] This is true regardless of whether the relationship is one-to-one or one-to-many. And this is true across many fields, occupations, and settings—including law, lawyers, and law practice. When clients seek out a lawyer, they are looking for not only a person with abilities to help them deal with their legal, business, and personal difficulties, but also a relationship with someone who cares about them.[7] If you are going to be a leader whose guidance others want to follow willingly, there needs to be a human connection—something that binds you and others together.

Many movies have recognized the importance of this kind of relationship. In *Jerry Maguire*, for example, a sports agent, disillusioned by dishonesty in his industry, starts his own company, focusing on personal relationships—and it is personal relationships that lead to his success as a leader. Lawyer movies, too, portray relationships as a critical element of good leadership (lawyering). For example, in *The Client*, lawyer Reggie Love takes a personal interest in her eleven-year-old client, Mark.

Regardless of the setting, the quality of the relationship will determine over the long term whether others will follow your lead or not. A relationship between people characterized by fear and distrust will seldom produce anything of lasting value. A relationship characterized by mutual respect and confidence will overcome the greatest adversities and leave a legacy of significance.

Law School Basics and Lawyer Leadership

In the recent survey of "Law Firm Competency Expectations for Associate Development" the most common competencies could be grouped into three distinct categories:[8]

- Traditional Legal and Communication Skills: Legal analysis, written advocacy, communicating clearly, legal knowledge/expertise, judgment/common sense, and oral advocacy
- Character Traits and Relationship Skills: Responsibility/reliability, teamwork/collaboration, initiative, and attention to detail
- Client Focused Orientation: Responsiveness to client and understanding of the client's business/ circumstances

While the first competency reflects the bread-and-butter of legal education, the survey authors noted that the "competencies related to Character Traits/ Relationship Skills and Client-Focused Orientation—not traditionally focused on in legal education—were emphasized by firms in the study and that might be surprising to some."[9] Not surprising at all to us, and underscoring the need for leadership development as a necessary component of legal education. In point of fact, 88 percent of the survey firms singled out "leadership" specifically as one of the desired competencies.

The Ethics of Lawyer Leadership

Definitions clearly show that leadership is a positive attribute. But can it be problematic from an ethical perspective? The ABA's *Model Rules of Professional Conduct* governs the lawyer–client relationship, which implicates leadership issues. Thus, before embarking on a path to leadership, it is wise to ask whether there is any ethical reason not to do so. The answer is no, but, as with every other aspect of being a lawyer, it is important to explore potential ethical issues.

Do lawyers lead their clients? Are clients "followers" of their lawyers, whether the client is a corporation or a person facing criminal charges? These are frequent questions in leadership classes and in academic discussions about lawyer leadership, and they deserve serious consideration. While law students often dream of a world without hypothetical questions, they also learn quickly in law school that hypothetical questions train them to deal with real-life ambiguity and paradoxes, and this is one of the most persistently paradoxical areas in law practice.

The *Model Rules of Professional Conduct* articulate the relationship between attorney and client. Rule 1.2 provides in part:

> (a) Subject to paragraphs (c) and (d), a lawyer shall abide by a client's decisions concerning the objectives of representation and, as required by Rule 1.4, shall consult with the client as to the means by which they are to be pursued. A lawyer may take such action on behalf of the client as is impliedly authorized to carry out the representation. A lawyer shall abide by a client's decision whether to settle a matter. In a criminal case, the lawyer shall abide by the client's decision, after consultation with the lawyer, as to a plea to be entered, whether to waive jury trial and whether the client will testify.[10]

Note that the rules provide that lawyers must abide by the decisions made by the client, especially in terms of decisions to settle or enter a plea and other forms of final outcome of the proceeding or legal matter. Moreover, the lawyer shall "reasonably consult with the client about the means by which the client's objectives are to be accomplished."[11]

However, this does not mean that the client is the leader and the lawyer is the follower. In fact, a thorough look at the *Model Rules of Professional Conduct* shows that although lawyers must allow their clients to have autonomy, lawyers would be derelict in their duties if they didn't make every effort to guide clients toward the best decisions by giving them clear direction on how the clients should exercise their authority to make the final decisions. For example, according to Rule 1.2, lawyers must be competent in the advice they provide to permit the client to make an informed decision—leaving, of course, the final decision to the client.[12] And Rule 2.1 states that lawyers must provide independent, professional, and candid advice and that in giving this advice, lawyers "may refer not only to law but to other [relevant] considerations such as moral, economic, social, and political factors."[13]

Clients hire lawyers because they do not possess or cannot learn the information needed to make decisions in their best interests. We live in a highly complex world with many sources of sometimes conflicting responsibilities and rules that require careful study to understand so they can be acted on.

Legal systems have complex rules of procedure and jurisdictional requirements and complicated access points to have a case heard and resolved. The modern growth of myriad regulatory agencies adds a layer of forums for adjudication of rights and duties. Many people believe that we live in a highly litigious society where having access to legal counsel is almost as important as access to competent medical care and advice. In short, clients need attorneys to work through these complicated situations and, as a result, rely heavily on the advice and assistance provided by their lawyers. The old adage is that smart clients rely on their lawyers to get legal problems solved.

Lawyers serve in multiple ways other than by direct representation in legal proceedings: they serve as mediators; advocates in litigation or other proceedings; policy advisers; governmental officials; and, of course, legal advisers for clients. Accordingly, there are many avenues through which lawyers inspire their followers toward a shared goal or vision—often toward resolution of a difficult challenge or need for change. In nearly all of these situations, lawyer leaders move others toward shared goals through persuasion or influence; they guide others toward these goals, and that guidance is willingly accepted and followed. Lawyers lead their clients through shared objectives (for example, a favorable outcome in a trial, a successful negotiation of a real estate transaction, or approval by the Securities and Exchange Commission of a major transaction), by candid discussions, their zealous commitment to the client's best interests, and exercise of their best professional judgment and advice.

Thus, the concept of the lawyer as the "leader" in the relationship with the client is not contradictory to the ethical rules, or the received "model" of the attorney-client relationship under the Model Rules, or the description of lawyers' duties to the client, or the fiduciary nature of the relationship between attorney and client.

Thinking Like a Lawyer versus Thinking Like a Leader

Is "thinking like a lawyer" the same thing as "thinking like a leader"? The two concepts overlap in some respects, but in other apects, are, in fact, diametrically opposed.

At an early stage in their careers, in the first year of law school, would-be lawyers are introduced to the notion that they must learn how to "think like a lawyer." For many students, this notion conjures up a perception of a secret recipe or acumen-imbued insight that enlightens only some students, who, by reason of education or intelligence, are especially adept at it. The rumors persist that the law school entrance examination tests for this ability and that "you either have it or you don't."

The reality is that intelligence or cognitive thinking skills are important to success as a lawyer, but much of the 1L "thinking like a lawyer" is actually a deductive reasoning ability that is useful in the US (and English) common law system, where a judge deduces the correct (or best) outcome in a case from precedent established in prior cases with similar factual predicates. Many lawyers still marvel at the time that was devoted in their first-year contracts law class to study a case involving a lengthy definition of what constitutes a "chicken."[14]

But there is more to the notion of thinking like a lawyer than the ability to reason from prior cases. An important part of how a lawyer presents to clients, other lawyers, and judges is their character and essential personality traits. Empirical studies of lawyers' personality traits tend, with some uniformity, to describe people who are particularly strong in certain traits or attributes and less so in others.[15] For example, some of the comparisons between the personality characteristics of lawyers versus the general population reveal that lawyers are:[16]

- *Introverted.* Fifty-seven percent of lawyers are introverts compared to forty-three percent who prefer extroversion. Introverts generally prefer to work alone and tend to be somewhat quiet and reserved, taking questions under consideration and processing them internally rather than through discussion with others.
- *Analytic.* Seventy-eight percent of lawyers score as "thinkers" versus forty-seven percent of the general population. Lawyers tend to use logic and expertise, rather than their feelings, in reaching decisions.
- *Skeptical.* Lawyers score considerably above the average, compared to the population at large, in skepticism. They tend to view the glass as half-empty and question people's comments and motives.
- *Autonomous.* Lawyers have a strong preference for being in control and not being subject to anyone telling them what to do and how to do it.
- *Inflexible.* Lawyers score considerably below the general population on resilience, or the ability to handle criticism and setbacks.

- *Unempathetic.* Lawyers generally don't score very high on their ability to be empathetic; they often fail to pay attention to or consider others' viewpoints and feelings. As the joke goes, "lawyers have feelings too... allegedly."

Some of these traits are helpful in the practice of law; others, not so much. For example, skepticism and autonomy are helpful propensities for creative problem solving, independent thinking, and finding flaws or potential problems in a client's case. Analytical thinking and dexterity in considering opposing arguments are also helpful characteristics for practicing law. On the flip side, low levels of resilience make it more difficult to trust others and more prone to overthink actions and exaggerate negative consequences. Low levels of empathy can adversely affect the ability of lawyers to understand the client's needs and concerns. Some of these traits are reflected in the joke about a lawyer summarizing his client's criminal case to a jury this way: "Could my client be innocent? Probably not, but it is interesting to think about."

However, it is important to remember that these traits are just generalizations—not every lawyer exhibits these traits to the same degree, or even at all. Furthermore, as psychologists will point out, these traits are not immutable, and as a budding lawyer you can address, enhance, or ameliorate them in various ways, for instance, through training and a conscious commitment to other, more desirable approaches to your legal work.

The ability to alter these traits is important because these same traits of lawyers can also present challenges for lawyer leaders—those who lead their firms and organizations, for example. Leadership requires a certain skill set, which is not necessarily the same skill set needed to be an effective lawyer. Effective leaders tend to be collaborative and inclusive.

Leaders generally, in contrast to lawyers, for example, often score above the median on empathy and in their ability to connect with others through persuasive influence and shared values.

Leaders tend to be out and about—"walking the halls" and talking with their constituents, inspiring them in ways that shape and communicate shared goals and aspirations. In sum, leadership is primarily about interpersonal behaviors and building an authentic relationship with followers.

Thinking like a lawyer is an important skill in the practice of law, and some of the attributes of those who think like a lawyer are also important for leaders. Building a toolbox that includes more than thinking like a lawyer is a necessity for lawyers who aspire to be leaders.

The Foundation of Leadership: Credibility

What sort of person would you listen to, take advice from, find influential, and *willingly* follow? In other words, for people to want to follow an individual over the course of a project or the course of a career, what do they most want to see in that person's behavior?

Following the lead of other researchers,[17] we surveyed hundreds of law school students about the personal values, traits, and characteristics that they feel are most important to them in an individual they would willingly follow. The key word is *willingly*: it is one thing to follow someone because you think you have to "or else"—and yet another to follow someone because you want to.

The results not only were strikingly similar across different law schools and demographics, but also consistently correlated with normative data from over 125,000 people from around the world.[18] Essentially, the top characteristics that law school students look for in someone they would willingly follow are no different from what other people across industries, functions, fields, nationalities, ages, and genders desire.[19] People, especially clients, law firm associates and interns, bar association members, and others, follow lawyers because of their credibility—an attribute that encompasses character and competence.

Our survey of law school students showed that the number one trait that they wanted from an individual that they would willingly follow is *honesty* (being truthful, having integrity, demonstrating trustworthiness), selected by nearly four out of five respondents. Other traits selected by law school student respondents included *competent* (capable, proficient, effective, gets job done, professional), *inspiring* (uplifting, enthusiastic, energetic, cheerful, optimistic, positive about future), and *forward looking* (visionary, foresighted, concerned about the future, has sense of direction). You earn the designation of leader when other people *perceive* you as having these essential characteristics. You may believe you exhibit these characteristics but leadership, like art, is in the eye of the beholder, and may be dependent on contextual factors as well as both implicit as well as explicit biases.[20] Still, lawyers who are seen as lacking integrity, having less than exceptional competence in their work, being tired and boring, or lacking a big-picture perspective will not be followed with the fullest commitment and internal drive.

These survey findings have a solid conceptual foundation in what social psychologists and communications experts refer to as "source credibility."[21] In assessing the believability of sources of information—whether lawyers, newscasters, salespeople, physicians, priests, business executives, military officers, politicians, or civic leaders—researchers typically evaluate them on three criteria: their perceived trustworthiness, expertise, and dynamism. People considered to be credible sources of information rate highly in these areas. This is particularly true for lawyers because of the personal and professional obligations they have toward others.

Credibility elevates leaders because of the ideals of not only clients, but also other lawyers: character and competence. Client demands drive law organizations (across the spectrum of law firms, district attorneys' offices, etc.), and clients are motivated by attorney track records and their counsel and perspectives. Clients want successful outcomes and sound professional advice and therefore seek to retain highly skilled advisors and representatives. Moreover, lawyers in firms select their outstanding colleagues to lead the firm because of their trustworthiness, commitment to the common good, and capabilities. Law firm colleagues want their leaders to tell the hard truth and to put the truth out there, on the line. People follow individuals who have skills that those people value, and lawyers only follow leaders who are themselves good lawyers. "Good" is, of course, a subjective belief, but colleagues' selections of leaders always reflect their judgment about character, competence, inspiration, and vision.

Clearly, the characteristics that law school students, lawyers, and clients generally want from those they would willingly follow are the same as what scholars have conceptualized as constituting credibility. To follow willingly, people must believe that the leaders' words can be trusted, that they are personally passionate and enthusiastic about their work, and that they have the knowledge and skill to make a difference. Credibility is the foundation of leadership.

The Five Practices of Exemplary Leadership®

So, what is it that leaders do to build and sustain credibility? What do they do that makes others see them as capable and trustworthy leaders? What are the behaviors that people exhibit that engage and mobilize others to want to follow? What are people actually *doing* when they are leading and making extraordinary things happen?

To answer these questions, Jim Kouzes and Barry Posner, leadership scholars and authors of more than a dozen leadership books, collected thousands of case studies over the years from people about what they were doing when they were at their "personal best" as leaders. These were times when individuals excelled at leading, when they were getting others to operate at peak performance—and the examples cut across a wide variety of settings, nationalities, organizations, levels, ages, genders, educational backgrounds, and the like.[22]

Two prevailing lessons emerged from these cases. The first was that *everyone had a story to tell.* Regardless of who was asked, people were able to identify a time when they did their best as a leader. The second was that despite differences in settings, circumstances, and individual or organizational demographics, the actions and behaviors of people when they were at their best were *more similar than different.* People demonstrated a common set of behaviors when they functioned at their personal best as leaders.

Kouzes and Posner grouped these behaviors into a *leadership operating system* that they referred to as The Five Practices of Exemplary Leadership® (The Five Practices). When making extraordinary things happen, leaders Model the Way, Inspire a Shared Vision, Challenge the Process, Enable Others to Act, and Encourage the Heart. Hundreds of studies have validated this framework, documenting how The Five Practices make a significant difference in people's levels of well-being, commitment and motivation, and work performance, and the success of their organizations.[23]

Those people who most frequently use the behaviors associated with The Five Practices are viewed as considerably more effective, across a variety of outcomes, than their counterparts who use them less often.[24] The same relationship is true even for those who indicate that they are "individual contributors" (as opposed to people in hierarchical positions).[25] Net Promoter Scores are a widely used market research metric employed by companies around the world to assess customer and employee loyalty and predict business growth[26] and can be applied to leadership. Instead of asking "how likely would you recommend this product (or company) to a friend" consider what happens when you ask an individual's managers, peers, coworkers, and direct reports: "How likely would you recommend this person to your colleagues as a good leader?" Figure 1 shows that the percentages of those strongly agreeing with this statement *dramatically* increases with greater frequency of The Five Practices of Exemplary Leadership.

In terms of the legal profession, the viewpoints of the hundreds of law school students whom we surveyed affirmed the viewpoints of the general population. These students, who were interns or clerks in law offices, reported on their perceptions of leadership by attorneys, staff, and other supervisors in those settings. The students' analyses and insights documented that where a managing partner, law firm lawyer, corporate counsel, or district attorney

FIGURE 1

Likelihood of Being Recommended as a Good Leader by Peers Increases with Greater Frequency of The Five Practices of Exemplary Leadership®

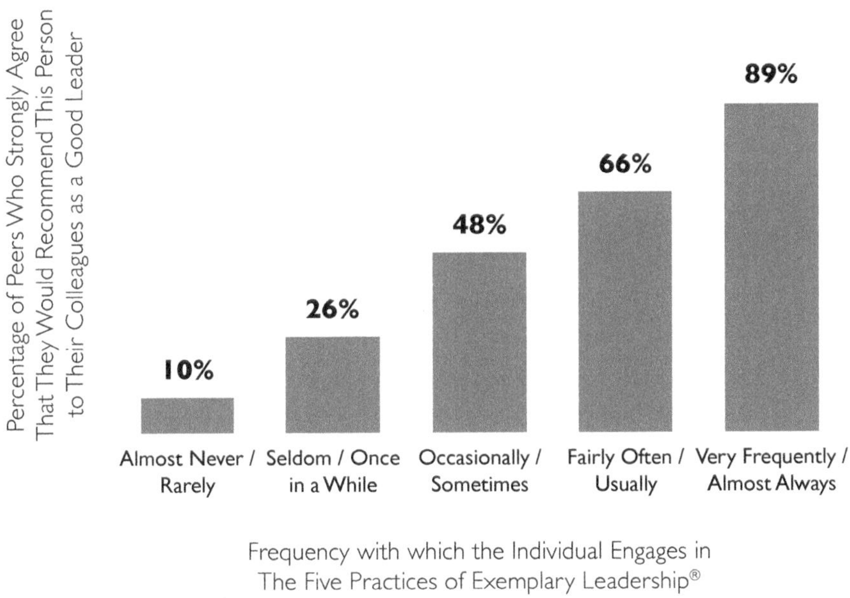

demonstrated The Five Practices, these junior "lawyers in training" had more positive professional experiences and perceived the organization as more successful in meeting its responsibilities. Equally important, the law school students reported a much higher likelihood of replicating these same positive behaviors in their own careers.

The bottom line is that, regardless of whether or not you are in a leadership position, the more you utilize The Five Practices, the more likely it is that you'll have a positive influence on other people and the organization. To have a significant impact on the people around you and the organizations with which you are involved, you must invest in learning the leadership practices and behaviors that will enable you to become the very best leader you can. This is exactly the aim of the next five chapters in Part II.

FOLLOWING THROUGH

- Being a leader involves more than being a person with a lofty title.
- There are many definitions of *leadership*. A simple, all-encompassing definition is that leadership is a relationship between those who aspire to lead and those who choose to follow.
- The ABA's *Model Rules of Professional Conduct* governs the lawyer–client relationship, and lawyers can be leaders without violating ethical boundaries. In fact, a strong sense of professional ethics will strengthen a leader's reputation as credible and competent.
- Thinking like a leader entails more than thinking like a lawyer because leaders exhibit traits that lawyers may not necessarily exhibit.
- Credibility, which encompasses both character and competence, is the main characteristic in a leader that inspires others to follow that leader.
- The behaviors that build and sustain credibility are encapsulated in The Five Practices of Exemplary Leadership® (The Five Practices): Model the Way, Inspire a Shared Vision, Challenge the Process, Enable Others to Act, and Encourage the Heart.

REFLECTIONS

1. To what extent are the skills necessary to be an effective lawyer the same as or different from those necessary to be an effective leader?

2. When you think of lawyers that you know, how credible would you say they are? What factors make them more or less credible? Do you think that lawyers need to be viewed as more or less credible in their professional lives than, for example, business executives? Stockbrokers or financial planners? Ministers or family counselors?

3. Credibility is earned through your behavior as seen by others. What evidence would you say is available that indicates you are honest? That you know what you are talking about? That you have commitment and passion for the law and justice? That you have a sense of direction and point of view about the future?

4. Mentally construct a discussion with a client—for example, one charged with a serious felony—that includes a clear statement by you on how decisions are going to be made between you and the client, considering situations involving (1) a request for extension (thereby waiving speedy trial rights), (2) a plea bargain deal offer by the prosecutor, and (3) whether or not to appeal from an adverse jury finding of guilt. How do you describe your role as the attorney in each of these situations?

THREE

Model the Way

Unable to find your voice, you will end up mouthing other people's words and thoughts, using a vocabulary and adopting a perspective that doesn't represent you at all.

THE LEAD-IN

- Clarifying Your Values and Finding Your Voice
    - Clarify Your Values
    - Find Your Voice
- Lead by Example
    - Lead by How You Allocate Time
    - Lead by Teachable Moments
    - Lead by Storytelling
    - Lead by the Words You Choose
    - Lead by Focused Questioning
    - Lead by Soliciting Feedback
- From Model the Way to Inspire a Shared Vision
- Following Through
- Reflections

Leaders Model the Way.

Law school students, when asked what they perceive to be the critical attributes of the most effective leaders they have worked with, frequently identify those lawyers who model the way for others. Students have noted, for example, that if the firm's leaders punctually submit time reports, then others, including law student clerks, are likely to do so as well. Students recognize that the right actions flow from the examples demonstrated by those in charge.

Modeling the way includes *clarifying your values and finding your voice* and *setting an example for others*. Leaders set an example for others by their actions. In order for their actions to have authenticity, however, they must first clarify their values and find their voice. By doing so, they will build a firm foundation of credibility for their actions because they will do what they said they would do; they will keep their promises. Empirical data shows that leadership effectiveness increases in direct proportion to how often others observe leaders engaging in the Model the Way leadership practice.

Clarifying Your Values and Finding Your Voice

When you take a class in law school, what is one of the first things you want to know about? While you might not have been able to select the instructor, you do want to know a little bit about this person. You might wonder about their experience and what makes this person qualified to teach the class. You might be interested in knowing why this person is teaching rather than practicing law. Or, what is this person's classroom style? Even, how would this person prefer to be addressed?

Similarly, what is the first question people have of any individual who is going to be their supervisor or manager? Whether as the leader of a classroom or a firm, or as an attorney in any new attorney–client relationship, the first question you can expect from your audience (of one or many) is some variation of "Who are you?"

Before you can provide another person, a group, a client, or even a jury an answer to that question, though, you have to be able to answer it for yourself. You have to be able to answer, "Who am I?" To do this, you have to be able to clarify your core values, because only then can you give voice to those values and feel both comfortable and confident talking about and sharing your values with others.

Since leadership is a relationship, you can't expect to build a connection with someone else without being both able and willing to share information about who you are, what you care about, and why you do what you do. After all, people are unlikely to either respect or trust someone—much less willingly follow someone—they don't know. Few people tend to hang around very long in a relationship with someone they can't figure out or make sense of. Indeed, you can expect that much of the conversation you have in an initial meeting with a client comprises talking about and sharing information about who you are, your background and experience, and your standards, beliefs, and expectations for the relationship and case.

If you take a moment to think about people you most admire, whether in history or in your own life experiences as a student or employee, it should be evident that one of their common characteristics is that they are individuals with strong beliefs about matters of principle. They are passionate about their cause, demonstrating an unwavering commitment to a clear set of values and being willing to speak out on matters of principle and conscience.

This is what people expect of their leaders. Like them, if you are going to speak out or step forward, then you need to know and be clear about what is important to you, what you care about deeply.

Clarify Your Values

We've asked hundreds of students in law leadership classes to clarify their values: "Take a moment to reflect about what you believe in and what you stand for. Then, write out a series of 'I believe...' statements."

We have found that most of the students had never been directly asked questions about their values. However, they find that this exercise, while at times challenging, is rewarding and helped them clarify and come face-to-face with their guiding principles. One student even had his values subsequently printed on a coffee mug so he could keep them front and center on his desk, while another student framed and mounted her values on the wall in her study.

Values are your moral guides, your personal bottom line. They supply you with an internal moral compass by which to navigate the course of your daily life. Clarity of values is essential to discerning which way is north, south, east, and west. The clearer you are about your values, the easier it is to stay on your chosen path. Guidance like this is especially critical in difficult and uncertain times. When daily challenges throw you off course, it is essential that you have signposts that tell you where you are and keep you on the right path. And an added bonus: researchers have consistently demonstrated a significant relationship between leaders' clarity and commitment to a set of core values and their likelihood of being effective.[1]

For lawyers especially, having a moral compass is considered "a central constituent of all legal practice,"[2] requiring a clear-eyed understanding of their own values, personal and professional ethics, and sense of duty to others. In law schools, law firms, and many legal workplaces, attorneys demonstrate their values on multiple levels and across many constituencies.[3] Even though at times much of the practice of law is data driven and even mundane and routine, it is still very much a value-driven profession, involving questions about right and wrong actions, clear or questionable motives or intent, and "doing the right thing." Without a clear sense of your own values, beliefs, and moral compass, advising and representing others effectively and ethically is extraordinarily difficult. While law is a profession that is value driven, not all practitioners are value driven; but you can ensure that your best values animate you in your work.

Values serve as guides to taking action. They inform your decisions about what to do and what not to do. They help you know when to say yes and when to say no, understand why you made this or that choice, and make decisions in a consistent manner. If, for instance, you believe that "heated debate" can stimulate thinking and creativity, such as in 1L law school study groups or in litigation strategy meetings, then you know that you need to speak out or do something when people with differing viewpoints challenge the conversation and are ignored. If you value collaboration, then you will act to make sure that your most experienced colleague doesn't write off meetings, but instead comes to them and shares information with others. If you value independence and initiative over conformity and compliance, you will be more likely to speak up and challenge a policy when you think it is misguided.

You cannot effectively exercise leadership without being clear about your values. Clarity brings about an internal sense that something is grabbing hold of you and won't let go and requires taking initiative—that is, leadership. In essence, you care enough about an issue or situation to act. Many people find it easy enough to look around and find something to complain about or point to something that is not working properly; it is only leaders, however, who are willing to grapple with such issues by getting out of their comfort zone and doing something about them. Leaders journey into their hearts and souls to discover their values. They must wrestle with what is inside of themselves long enough to determine what's really important to them, what's underlying their choices, what boundaries and standards they need to set, and what motivates them to step up and speak out.

Find Your Voice

Through an exploration of your inner territory, you will discover what you are about, both figuratively and literally, and you will find your voice. By finding your voice, you will express just who you are and what you stand for, which is absolutely essential to becoming an authentic leader. If you are unable to find your voice, which is extremely unfortunate for a lawyer, you will end up mouthing other people's words and thoughts, using a vocabulary and adopting a perspective that doesn't represent you at all, which significantly damages your credibility. There is the message you want to deliver, and then there is the expression of that message. You need to both *have* a voice and *give* voice.

This can be difficult for lawyers because of the temperaments of many people who practice law. For example, as noted in chapter 2, lawyers are significantly above their professional peers in introversion and analytic thinking.[4] They tend to internalize their thought processes, taking questions under advisement rather than engaging in discussion with others. Indeed, in general, these lawyers tend to be quiet and don't feel the need to be around people all the time, preferring to work alone in their offices. Their analysis of problems or situations is often abstract, unemotional, and sometimes devoid of much empathy. These attributes are often helpful to much of the work that lawyers do, and, alternatively, they may result in some people being left behind in fast-moving collaborative activities or situations that call for sympathetic responses.

This doesn't mean that there is something wrong with the people who are lawyers. However, while some of these characteristics may be helpful in practicing law, many of them can be a hindrance to the exercise of leadership. The most successful lawyers and leaders are those who strive to listen empathetically to what a client or colleague is saying, take into consideration a broad range of feelings and emotions, and communicate thoughtfully and expressively.

To lead yourself and others, you have to understand, appreciate, and fully own the values that drive you. No matter what you are doing or where you are in an organization, you have to freely and candidly choose the principles that you will use to guide your actions. But it is not enough to be clear about the message you want to deliver—you also have to clearly communicate that message in a variety of ways.

Lead by Example

When you are sure you *mean* what you say, you are prepared *to do* what you say. While it is essential that you are able to forthrightly articulate the principles for which you stand, words themselves are insufficient. Leadership happens when you put your values into action. You enact the meaning of your personal values (beliefs, assumptions, and principles) in how you behave, in the decisions you make, and in the steps you take to move toward the future you envision. You bring your values to life across a variety of settings—in team meetings; one-on-one discussions; tweets; emails; social media; informal conversations over breaks and meals; and visits with clients, associates, partners, legislators, judges, and the like.

Leading-by-example illustrations abound in terms of lawyers who volunteer their time for pro bono work. Some high-profile examples include: Sid Wolinksy, who left his "second-choice" job as an entertainment industry lawyer to pursue public interest law opportunities focused on disabilities, veterans, and the poor because he "went to law school... to make a contribution";[5] Todd Belcore, whose public interest work was inspired by the struggles of growing up in a poor family with a single mother and paraplegic brother;[6] and the WilmerHale law firm, which donated $17 million of hours to represent six Algerian terrorist suspects, resulting in a Supreme Court decision that granted habeas rights to Guantanamo Bay detainees.[7] Law students often begin to lead by example in professional life by mentoring new 1L students, volunteering to take a leadership role in a student organization, serving as a student representative on a school committee, or canvassing a political district for a candidate for office. Many continue this inclination to serve others into their professional lives, thereby enriching the legal profession and their communities.

When you lead by example—when your actions are consistent with your words and the values you espouse—then people will consider you credible. People first listen to your words, and then they observe your actions. They take note of the talk, but they pay great attention to how you "walk the talk." They listen to your promises and then look for evidence that you keep your commitments. When people do not see consistency, their verdict is that you are at best unreliable and at worst an outright hypocrite; the price is a loss of trust. When your words and deeds are congruent, the judgment handed down is "credible."

There is not just one particular method of developing such leadership credibility. Several powerful methods of leading by example include leading by how you allocate time, leading by teachable moments, leading by storytelling, leading by the words you choose, leading by focused questioning, and leading by listening.

Lead by How You Allocate Time

Take a moment to think about how you spend your time. This is important because time is a finite commodity and how you expend it is the most significant signal you can send about your priorities and what is important to you.

Time is a lawyer's most valuable resource. Time is finite; an hour spent on one task necessarily means that hours cannot be spent on something else. You will often find yourself making tradeoffs in how you allocate this precious resource, and be challenged to find creative ways to juggle multiple tasks and relationships. What lawyers spend their time paying attention to and working on, and the people with whom they spend time, speaks volumes about their actual priorities, as compared to what they might say they care about.

Visibly spending time on what you have said is important because it shows that you are putting your "money where your mouth is." It's about being the first to do something that you believe everyone else should value and do. Whether the value involves family, teamwork, hard work (arriving early, staying late), timeliness, or even camaraderie, the truest measure of what leaders deeply believe is how they spend their time. People use this as a measure of whether a leader lives up to espoused principles and standards.

Furthermore, if others are to believe that your values are important to you, those values have to show up on your calendar. Calendars never lie when it comes to broadcasting your priorities to others and demonstrating how your allocation of time aligns with your values and priorities. You have to make sure that your distribution of time is in sync with what you say is important and consistent with what you and your colleagues have agreed on as priorities.

Law students tend to be highly receptive during their internships to leading-by-example signals from supervising and managing attorneys about what is important. For example, are the firm's attorneys willing to put in the time and offer their expertise to mentor the students they were responsible for recruiting for an internship or position? To what extent is the workload on the project or case equitably shared? Are interns asked to do things that the attorneys are not willing to do? Leaders who are both conscious and conscientious about how they allocate time in leading by example will gain willing followers. As one second-year student reflected, "the concept of 'modeling the way' goes hand in hand with the importance of earning and sustaining credibility as a leader."

Lead by Teachable Moments

Choosing to spend time on core values is essential to send the message that you are serious about them. Nevertheless, you cannot plan everything about your day. Even for the most disciplined leaders, things can happen beyond your control. However, just as with orchestrated events, unplanned and unexpected occurrences can create teachable moments about how to solve problems and resolve disputes in ways that are consistent with shared values.

Chance occurrences, particularly during times of stress and challenge, can become opportune moments to model and teach others valuable lessons about appropriate norms of behavior. You can't plan them, but you can think about how you will handle these critical moments and interruptions should they occur. As with any hypothetical, you can envision how to be direct and realistic without being blunt or mean-spirited, and shaping the event as a way, for example, to develop others. How you link your actions and decisions to your values conveys a great deal about what really matters to you. By stepping up and confronting an unplanned situation, you show what it looks like when actions and decisions are taken based on values. By standing up for guiding principles under adverse circumstances, you demonstrate that shared values require a mutual commitment to keep words and deeds in sync. The civil rights lawyers who risked personal harm by traveling to the Deep South in the 60s to protect the rights of Black citizens to vote inspired a subsequent generation of young lawyers who sought to achieve an even greater set of social and economic goals for underrepresented communities.

For example, during the 9/11 terrorist attacks, real-life heroes emerged. A group of passengers on United Flight 93 banded together to confront the terrorists and prevent the plane from hitting a major US government building; the plane ended up landing in a Pennsylvania field, killing all aboard. And at the Twin Towers, numerous people risked their own lives to save others from the burning buildings, such as an equities trader who helped over a dozen people escape.[8] Such heroism is not required to be a good lawyer, but it is important to act with your best instincts, shaped by a desire to serve others.

Lead by Storytelling

Another powerful way to lead by example is by telling stories and, through those stories, calling attention to what's important and what is not, what works and what doesn't, what is and what could be.

Stories are important because they translate intangible ideas into tangible actions. You can't just order people to do something like "follow the rules" because most people don't actually read the rule book (assuming that there even is such a thing). However, people will listen to or read a story about an individual fired for breaking a rule, or alternatively about someone who followed the rules and received a raise, and they get the message.[9] Stories serve as mental maps that help people make the connection between what is important and how to put important ideas into practice in a particular context. When people hear a story about how people like themselves enacted a value, they are much more likely to envision themselves doing the same.

Lawyers are inveterate storytellers, most often about their prior cases, clients, successes, and, yes, failures in court or in deals. Many exceptionally talented lawyers credit the stories they heard from mentors for "learning the ropes" and successfully developing their acuity and practice skills. Although "war stories" can get old, stories about how a complicated point was explained to a jury or how a unique reading of the Federal Rules of Civil Procedure gave a client an advantage in litigation—that is, stories with a learning point—almost never get old, are worth repeating, and are always very useful to law students and young lawyers alike. For example, an antitrust trial lawyer told a story about how he educated a federal court jury on a complicated issue regarding the definition of *competition* by using the local state university football team as an example of competition; his point was the importance of making complicated issues easier for jurors to understand, and his story endured in the minds of his audience for years and certainly for the duration of the trial.*

Research shows that storytelling is not a "soft" way of getting the hard stuff done; rather, it is an effective way. If you are trying to communicate the values of your organization, what do you think would have more of an impact: a policy statement that reads "Thou shalt provide timely services to our clients," or a story about how an associate took it on herself to go directly to the client's site to nail down some crucial information? Similarly, what would be more persuasive: seeing statistics about how much stress criminal lawyers experience, or hearing a story about a local prosecutor who, suffering from a severe stress disorder, committed suicide? Stories are generally more effective than policy statements or statistical charts alone. Information first presented in the form of an example or story is more accurately and quickly remembered than are facts, figures, and formal policy pronouncements.[10] Storytelling is an effective leadership practice because stories are generally simple, straightforward, and timeless and appeal to almost everybody regardless of age, gender, or race.

Storytelling comes naturally to many lawyers, and they know that it is essential in a jury trial to weave a story to help the jury understand their party's case.

* The lawyer was attempting to explain the difference between inter-brand competition and intra-brand competition and used team practice and competition between first- and second-string quarterbacks to get the starting role in Saturday's game against another team (or brand). He reported that the analogy was very effective to jurors, even those who were not avid football fans. Sharing creative moments among trial and deal lawyers is an important learning opportunity for young lawyers.

They often present the beginning of the story in opening arguments and then conclude it during closing argument, with the purpose of sending the jurors to the jury room to figure out what happened and which side had the story that most aligned with the facts presented in the trial.

Law students and young lawyers often comment about experiencing the "imposter syndrome"—that is, the feeling of a sense of vulnerability after stepping into a complex, demanding, and uncertain workplace (or courtroom). Women, first generation and LGBTQ law students and students of color often report that they have a heightened sense of "not belonging" in law school and in the practice of law. The fear of making an error of great magnitude or appearing insufficient to the task of being a "perfect" lawyer can be paralyzing, especially for women and people of color.[11] One way of dealing with this is to hear stories from your professors, recent graduates, and practicing lawyers describing their honest reflections about navigating through these fears. Time and experience will eradicate the imposter syndrome; still, the process will be easier if leaders model the way for others through storytelling.

Lead by the Words You Choose

The language that leaders use also sets a tone for action. The phrase "watch your language" takes on an entirely different meaning in the context of leading by example than in the context of being scolded by a teacher for using an inappropriate word in school. In terms of leading by example, it is about setting an example for others in how your language frames the context for thinking and talking about events and ideas, as well as focusing attention on certain aspects of the subject.

Your choice of language affects others' perceptions of you as a leader. The words you choose give voice to your mindset and beliefs. They evoke images about what you aspire to create and how you expect others to behave. Just think about the impact of changing the expression "I have to do this" to "I choose to do this," or "They want me to do this" to "I think this is the best way to do this." It's obvious that the latter expressions put you in the driver's seat, signaling a sense of personal responsibility and accountability—establishing credibility in the eyes of your followers for your actions.

Your choice of words also has a powerful effect on how others see themselves and those around them, as well as the events that they experience. Consider, for example, experiments in which researchers told participants that they were playing either the Community Game or the Wall Street Game.[12] In both scenarios, people played the same game by the same rules, with the only difference being that experimenters gave the game two different names. Of those playing the Community Game, seventy percent started out playing cooperatively and continued to do so throughout. For those told they were playing the Wall Street Game, however, the reverse happened: seventy percent did not cooperate. Of the thirty percent in this scenario who did cooperate, they quickly stopped after noticing that others were not cooperating. Again, it was the name of the game—not the game itself—that changed! Clearly, you can influence people's behavior simply by giving the task or the team a name that evokes the kind of behavior implied by the name. If you want people to act like a community, use language that evokes a feeling of community. If you want people to act like citizens of a village, then you have to talk to them as if they were citizens of a village, not subordinates in a hierarchy.

Would you want to join a law firm that likens itself to a hospital, a factory, a plant, a hot air balloon, a carnival, a university, or a clinic? What words and images best resonate with you? Words matter to lawyers, and they matter to the people that lawyers are attempting to influence.

Lead by Focused Questioning

In a similar way as with language, the questions that you ask and the issues that you raise force attention on the connections, or gaps, between espoused and enacted values. In the course of everyone's daily lives, many questions are raised. The point of most of these is to gather more information, get clarification, or reach a greater understanding. From a leadership perspective, however, the questions you ask should do more than this. The substance of your questions should reveal the values that warrant attention and the amount of energy that needs to be devoted to them. Well-phrased questions present opportunities to teach and reinforce values—and thus constitute another measure of how serious you are about your espoused beliefs. Let's face it: some lawyers are not good listeners, but great lawyers are great listeners. They have honed that skill though thoughtful commitment and practice.

A key to asking good leadership questions is to think first about the *quest* in your questions. Where do you want to take this person (group or organization) with your questions? What value or values are you trying to reinforce with your questions? To what extent do the questions you typically ask ensure commitment to collective values? What evidence do you want to ask about that will illustrate whether decisions being made are consistent with values?

Challenge yourself to identify a routine set of questions that will get people to reflect on core values and what they have done and can do each day to act on those values. Such questions should be somewhat predictable because you want the people you are working with to be thinking about them well before you ask them. As a leader, you should expect people to have your questions in their minds as they make decisions. In one way or another, the questions you ask should all be a variation on a single theme: What are we doing to live out our values and shared commitments? The point is not to ask rhetorical questions (ones that have obvious answers or responses) but to get people to think about how their own actions are consistent with shared values. Your questions should help keep people focused and paying attention to what really matters. Watch a skillful cross-examination of a witness by a very good lawyer and you will understand the tremendous importance of listening as a prelude to thoughtful, effective questioning.

The quantity and quality of your questions are important. Interestingly enough, studies suggest that the more questions you ask, the more your emotional intelligence improves, which in turn makes you a better questioner.[13] Research generally shows that people who ask the most questions, relative to their peers, are perceived as both smarter and more interesting than those who do not ask questions or seek advice and input from others.[14] There are, however, definitely differences in how men and women communicate, who gets heard and how.[15] Keep in mind that not all questions are equally important, though; rather, the ones that solicit more information have special power. Follow-up questions in a conversation, for example, signal that you are listening, care, and want to know more, and this makes your conversation partners feel respected and heard.[16]

Of course, sincerity must underlie the asking of questions. In other words, you must honestly want to listen to the answers. Listening to what others have to say requires that you give their opinions and feedback serious consideration in subsequent decisions.

Lead by Soliciting Feedback

How can you know that you are doing what you say if you never receive feedback about your behavior? How can you be sure that your words and actions match if you do not get information about the extent to which others see them aligned? Asking others for feedback gives you a perspective about yourself that only others can see. With their insights, you have the opportunity to make improvements, as well as determine if your actions are being perceived in ways that you intended. Most people are not used to providing feedback, however, even when solicited, but unless you ask, people are unlikely to tell you what they think. One way to start is by asking for advice about a specific way you could improve, rather than a general request to know "how am I doing?"

Initially, you might not like the feedback that you receive. Many lawyers who solicit post-verdict jury surveys are disappointed in how their message didn't resonate with the jury or at the jurors outright hostility toward the lawyer or the client. However, the more that request for feedback becomes part of everyday conversations, the easier it will be to listen to the information and learn from it, especially when everyone involved shares similar values and aspirations. The point is not to affix blame but to exercise curiosity about what happened and focus on what can be learned. In this way, any problems, mistakes, misunderstandings, and the like that may have occurred are not repeated. One student told us how the managing partner asked all the summer interns about their experiences and how "the partner showed a real interest in what the interns had to say, and actually took notes. He got back to us again before we returned to school and asked us how we felt about the proposed changes that were based on our feedback. This made me realize that a good leader seeks feedback and then does something with the information received."

And the good news is that researchers have found that people who seek out disconfirming feedback (that is, feedback contrary to their self-perceptions) perform better than those who only listen to people who see their positive qualities.[17] Self-reflection, the willingness to seek feedback, and the ability to engage in new behaviors based on this information are predictive of future success in managerial jobs.[18]

Remember, though, that if you do nothing with the feedback you receive, people will stop giving it. They are liable to believe that you are arrogant, or worse, and do not care about what anyone else has to say. But if you incorporate feedback from others, it is more likely that others will accept straightforward feedback from you, which, in the end, is beneficial for everyone.

From Model the Way to Inspire a Shared Vision

Law students frequently explain that their understanding of leadership is based on their observations of how attorneys behave, especially how they interact with their colleagues and clients. These observations provide them with lessons about what it means "to be a lawyer"—and through these observations, they come to understand, embrace, and adopt the customs, mores, and expectations associated with being a *professional* lawyer.

Similarly, one "first-generation" student told us that she began law school with much fear and uncertainty about her first-year classes. But some upper-level students modeled behaviors (such as study and examination techniques) that were instrumental to her first-year successes. She then founded a student organization at her law school to provide support for other first-gen law students. It was, to her thinking, a leadership legacy that she paid forward.

Both of these examples are good illustrations of the transition from Model the Way (leading by example based on your values) to Inspire a Shared Vision (motivating others to share your values and join you in your goals), the focus of the next chapter.

FOLLOWING THROUGH

- Leaders Model the Way by clarifying their values and finding their voice and then leading by example.
- The path to becoming an exemplary leader begins by discovering and owning your personal values and beliefs and then finding your voice by developing the capacity to express "who you are" in unique ways.
- Setting an example is how you demonstrate that you truly mean what you say. Walking the talk, doing what you say, and being consistent in word and deed are how you build credibility.
- How you spend your time; the way you deal with critical, unplanned incidents; the stories you tell; the language you use; the questions you ask; and your receptivity to feedback provide tangible evidence that you are "the real deal" and worthy of being listened to and followed by others.

REFLECTIONS

1. Think about someone in the legal profession whom you admire (e.g., a managing attorney or associate district attorney) and ask yourself

why. Which of this person's behaviors do you find admirable? How would you emulate these key behaviors?

____

____

____

____

____

____

2. What are your four or five key values (i.e., those beliefs or principles that you believe in most strongly)? How do you see these values playing out in your daily life at home or law school or the law firm? On what basis would you claim that you are sufficiently conveying them?

____

____

____

____

____

____

3. What is your leadership philosophy? That is, complete a series of "I believe" statements. "As a leader, I believe______." "And, as a leader, I believe______." and so on.

____

____

____

____

4. Take a look at your calendar over the past two or three weeks and determine how strong the connection is between how you spend your time and what you tell yourself and others is important to you. What does this analysis tell you?

____

____

____

____

____

____

FOUR

Inspire a Shared Vision

Every endeavor begins in the mind's eye with the belief that what's now only an image can one day be made real.

THE LEAD-IN

- Envisioning the Future
    - Look Ahead
    - Look Behind
    - Incorporate the Present
- Getting Others on Board
    - Craft a Compelling Mental Image
    - Listen Deeply
    - Show How Followers Can Make a Difference
    - Tout the Unique Aspects of the Vision
    - Exhibit Energy and Positivity
- From Inspire a Shared Vision to Challenge the Process
- Following Through
- Reflections

Leaders Inspire a Shared Vision.

Law school students, as well as practicing attorneys, seek inspiration and guidance from many exceptional leaders. In classroom discussions designed to help understand the roles that lawyers play in seeking justice and serving those who need legal expertise and advice, students often refer to public role models such as Martin Luther King Jr., Michelle Obama, Malala Yousafzai, Thurgood Marshall, Ruth Bader Ginsburg, as well as local role models such as lawyers staffing legal clinics and those involved with social justice organizations and movements. What these leaders have in common is a dream of what might be, with an end in mind that serves more than themselves—and the ability to enlist people in that shared vision by appealing to their aspirations and envisioning together a future of exciting and ennobling possibilities.

Inspiring a shared vision involves *envisioning the future* and *getting others on board*. From surveys of people around the world, including our own with law school students, the findings clearly show that leaders are expected to be forward looking—to describe what can be, not just what is. Like the role models recognized by students, the challenge is how you take your vision to others in such a way that they are as inspired and determined as you are to make something extraordinary happen. To be compelling, visions have to be less about you and more about others; indeed, others (be they colleagues or clients) have to see themselves squarely within the vision and find common ground in order for them to enlist and commit, not merely comply. According to data from both managers and coworkers, leadership effectiveness assessments are strongly correlated to the frequency with which people engage in the leadership practice of Inspire a Shared Vision.

Envisioning the Future

In the exercise of leadership, you have to be able to visualize a positive future and to give the work that is being done a sense of meaning and purpose.[1] The ability to be forward looking is one of the key expectations that people have of their leaders.

Before you can inspire others, though, you have to inspire yourself. Remember our discussion of values in Chapter Three? Before you can model values for others, you have to clarify those values for yourself, and, similarly, before you can expect to enlist others in a shared vision, you must clarify for yourself your vision of the future. Your inner passion is a good indicator of what you feel mostly deeply about and find worthwhile in and of itself. It's a clue to what is *intrinsically* motivating. If you don't care deeply for and about something, then you cannot expect others to feel any similar sense of conviction. How can you expect others to suffer through the inevitable long hours and hard work if you're not similarly inclined?

Every endeavor begins in the mind's eye with the belief that what's now only an image can one day be made real. No matter what you call it—*vision, purpose, mission, legacy, dream, calling,* or *burning agenda*—the intent is the same. There is something greater than what is happening today that infuses life and work with meaning and importance—something that transcends the here and now and draws people forward.

Look Ahead

The capacity to be forward looking can be developed by spending more time thinking about the future. The future is the domain of leaders, and this means regularly carving out opportunities and time to peer into the distance and imagine what might be out there. You simply have to put in the time today in order to have perspective on tomorrow.

Just because you can't predict the future doesn't mean that you should not, or even cannot, imagine a better one. Otherwise, why would people invest money for their retirement, or parents save for their children's education, or youth activists speak up for racial and social justice? The same reasoning can perhaps even be applied to your own decision to attend law school and pursue a legal career. These are all forward-looking actions, which are undeterred by all of the uncertainties of the present.

Lawyers who represent forward-looking, visionary clients must similarly possess those attributes and qualities. Lawyers representing young climate change policy activists were instrumental in getting their clients to turn ideas into action. The youth activists were puzzled as to why more people were not composting; the lawyers refocused their question into action and created a strategy to seek more systemic changes to the government's inaction on climate and environmental challenges.

Knowing that a vision is essential, though, doesn't make one magically pop out of your head like a bright light bulb, but it does shine some light on the need to be forward looking. When people first begin to exercise leadership, they typically don't have a *clear* vision of the future. After all, there's no map or interstate highway or case law book to serve as a guide to the future. Envisioning the future is a process that begins with an inspiration, a feeling or sense that something is worth doing. Your vision of the future may initially be fuzzy—the feeling that you might have experienced in law school as you first dealt with hypotheticals—but the important thing is that you're focused on forward momentum.

For example, the vision could involve imagining what it would be like to be a lawyer—what people and interests you would be serving in a large or boutique law firm; within a corporate or government setting; as a corporate attorney negotiating complex intellectual property contracts; as an assistant district attorney or public defender trying criminal cases (which side do you want to be on?); in private practice handling wills, contracts, and small claims; or on the staff of a legal services law office helping low-income tenants. These, and many others like them, are among the common dreams and aspirations of law students. Your belief that you could be a lawyer, and that you would enjoy the practice of law, is often what gets you through the hard work demanded of you right now while in law school; you believe that the present situation is a pathway to a better future. As you begin acting on your instincts, you will find that the vision gets a little clearer. You do something, take some action that moves you forward, and the vision gets a little clearer still. You pay attention to it, experience it, immerse yourself in it. You get the process started, and over time you see more detail in your dream. It's an iterative process, one that eventually results in something that you and others can articulate and literally see as a possibility.

What leaders eventually realize about their vision is that it is an elaboration, interpretation, and variation on a "common thread," or theme. And, in fact, the process of envisioning the future is much like composers finding a musical theme from all the notes that swirl in their minds. Think about the fundamental beliefs and assumptions that keep recurring in your life. Equality, justice irrespective of race or gender, fairness, and helping others are beliefs and aspirations that are shared by most law students before they go to law school and, for many, that continue after graduation. Consider what causes you contribute to and those to which you don't. What are the issues that keep popping up on your radar? What things keep you up at night or get you jumping out of bed in the morning? What are the "I wish..." statements that you find yourself echoing?

More than likely, these reflections will reveal that your central theme has been with you for a long time. For example, surveys have shown that people are motivated to go to law school for public-spirited reasons, including public or government service (44 percent), to be helpful to others or useful to society (35 percent), and to become an advocate for social change (32 percent).[2] Service to others is a compelling value, or theme, for law students and for lawyers.

Thus, although visions might be a bit fuzzy at first, what leaders clearly have (and what you have, too) are concerns, desires, hypotheses, propositions, arguments, hopes, and dreams—core concepts around which you organize your actions and aspirations as you look ahead to the future.

Look Behind

In imagining the future, ironically enough, you also need to look back into your past. Looking backward can actually enable you to see farther than if you only stare straight ahead.

Understanding your personal history can help you identify themes, patterns, and beliefs that underscore both why you care about particular issues or circumstances now and why making them better in the future is such a high priority. Recalling the richness of your past experiences deepens your sense of what might be.

In recalling the past, you also appreciate how long it can take to fulfill aspirations and accept that the path to the future will not be a straight line. Just like in sailing upwind, because you can't control everything around you, you have to tack, zigging back and forth as you make your way forward. No doubt there will be ups and downs in any worthwhile pursuit, and you'll veer into territory that you haven't traversed before, which is all the more reason why you need to have a firm picture in your mind of where you were in order to get where you are going and remember why it is important to keep going in order to get there.

Lawyers can benefit as leaders by looking backward as inspiration for continually looking forward and creating new visions. Think about why people go to law school and what they hope to accomplish in their lives as a result of graduating and passing the bar exam. Studies of lawyers have found a relationship between their dreams and goals in deciding to go to law school and the worlds they experience in practicing law, representing clients, and solving problems.[3] Many of the primary motivations to attend law school—for example, interacting with smart people, working on complex issues, and helping others by solving problems—are among the major activities that lawyers enjoy in their law practices. Certainly, achieving a level of economic security is an important factor in attending law school; however, attaining personal satisfaction in the work is just as compelling, or more so, for many lawyers—and surveys show lawyers are generally satisfied with their decision to attend law school. In many cases, the purposes of obtaining a legal education meet with their dreams of being a lawyer.[4] Looking backward, lawyers should feel inspired by such successes to continue being forward looking in envisioning the future, shaping the goals and aspirations of their constituents.

Incorporate the Present

None of this is to say that the past *is* your future. There is still the reality of the here and now, and visions are influenced by what's going on around you. For example, during the coronavirus pandemic, applications for new businesses went through the roof, at their fastest pace in more than a decade. You can increase your ability to conceive of new and creative solutions to today's problems by being present in the present. Only when you understand the current challenges will you be able to imagine a better tomorrow. Immersing yourself in the present, apart from the work that you are doing, however, means getting yourself off automatic pilot, not believing that you know everything you need to know, not viewing the world through preestablished categories, and paying attention to the subtle clues around you about what's happening in the world.

In other words, you have to stop, look, and listen. If you are like "most people," and certainly if you are one of the vast majority of overscheduled law school students and attorneys, you need to start noticing more of what's going on around you right now. For example, ask yourself, what are people doing now that they didn't do a few years ago? What are people wearing, using, and discarding? How are people interacting? How do workplaces and communities look and feel different now compared to how they once did? What trends are popular these days? Why? What are people talking about? What are their hot topics of conversation? What are they saying they need and want? What are they saying gets in the way of them doing their best? What do they think should be changed? Listen not only to these clues but also to the weak signals as well—that is, to what's not being said, such as what people are no longer talking about or paying attention to. Listen for things you've never heard before. What does all this tell you about where things are going? What's it telling you about what lies just around the corner or just beyond the horizon? How can all of this inform your visions as a leader?

Getting Others on Board

Leadership requires more than just having a vision. You need, of course, to imagine the end result, but you also must be able to sell your personal view of the world to others. In other words, you must be able to enlist others to get on board with you.

When you envision the future that you want for yourself and others and when you feel passionate about it, you are much more likely to take that first step forward; the same is necessarily true for others. In global case studies of personal-best leadership experiences, leaders frequently talked about the need to get buy-in from others on the vision.[5] This was similar to what we learned from law school students. Nearly all of them explained that their personal-best leadership experience required being able to persuade others to embrace a common goal or desirable outcome. They explained how they had to communicate purpose and build support for a unified direction, often in the context of an internship experience or their leadership of a student organization. They recognized that everyone had to commit to a common cause. They understood that to get everyone to take the same journey, they had to be able to communicate *why* others should want to join in, what it would mean to them, how they would benefit, and whom they would serve.

Creating a common vision is about developing a *shared* sense of destiny. It's about enabling others to see how their own interests and aspirations are appreciated and aligned with—and will be incorporated into—the vision. It's about enabling others to see themselves in the future that you are envisioning and to want to be included in the vision development process. A shared vision enables all the people connected with the work to see more clearly what's ahead of them and what the future will look like when they have added their piece—and, in this way, it motivates everyone to commit their individual energies to its realization.

Visions seen only by the leader are insufficient to generate organized movement. You must also get others to see a way forward, one that is filled with exciting possibilities that lie ahead. You must breathe life into visions by crafting a compelling mental image; listening to the hopes and dreams of others so that they clearly understand how their values and interests will be served; showing how they can make a difference; stressing the uniqueness of the vision; and being upbeat and expressive to attract followers through your energy, optimism, and sincerity.

Craft a Compelling Mental Image

To get followers on board with a vision, leaders must speak about the future, long before the journey forward even begins, in such a way as to convey a mental picture of what things will be like when everyone arrives at the destination.

Visions are images in the mind: they are impressions and representations. A beacon of light cutting through the fog is an image that you can picture in your mind. You make this image real to others by expressing it in concrete and tangible terms. For example, think about the city of Paris, France. What things first come to mind? Probably the Eiffel Tower, the Arc de Triomphe, the Seine, Notre Dame, good food, wine, romance—all of which are images of real places, experiences, and emotions. No one recalls the kilometers, population, or gross domestic product of Paris. The same would be true for your colleagues, team, or organization. The reason for this is that human memory is stored in images and sensory impressions, not in numbers. People recall images of reality, not abstractions from reality.

Images are windows looking out on the world of tomorrow. When leaders talk about going places that people have never been, they start by imagining what this would look like. This process is not so different from planning a vacation. You think about the travel involved, the amenities associated with the place where you are staying, the weather and how that influences the clothes you will pack and the activities you hope to experience and enjoy, the people who live in the place you are visiting, the people who may accompany you on the trip, and so on. In a similar fashion, leaders paint a picture of the future and make manifest the purpose so that others can see it, hear it, taste it, touch it, and feel it.

Painting a picture of the future requires making full use of the power of language in communicating a shared objective and giving life to visions. Using metaphors and other figures of speech provides vividness and tangibility to abstract ideas. Express your hopes for the future by using descriptive language, giving examples, and relating anecdotes. In making concrete the intangible vision, you must ignite people's passion, developing a shared sense of destiny. What's key is getting others to imagine in their mind's eye the image of what could be, how it could be, and why it must be.

Listen Deeply

Listening is actually more important than talking in getting others on board. No matter how grand the dream, if others don't see in it the possibility of realizing their own hopes and desires, they won't follow. That is where listening comes in. Leadership requires attentively listening to constituents—and understanding people at a much deeper level than you may normally find comfortable. It requires exploring their strongest yearnings and deepest fears and being profoundly aware of their joys and sorrows. By getting to know your constituents, listening to them, and soliciting their advice, you become better able to give voice to their feelings and aspirations—not just your own.

Listening is part and parcel of your realization and understanding that leadership is a relationship. People want to be listened to, and they are genuinely motivated when they feel that you understand, appreciate, and plan to incorporate their hopes and dreams. Make the time to hear what people have to say by getting out of your cubicle, moving away from your desk or machine, and wandering into other people's workplaces. Share coffee, breakfast, lunch, an afternoon break, a virtual check-in, or some unstructured occasion with others and find out what's going on with them, what's possibly frustrating them, and what they care about.

Few people can easily articulate what they want or even clearly know what they need, which is even more reason for you to listen deeply to them. Listening is not just about the words; it's about paying attention to what's unspoken, noticing what makes people smile or grimace, observing how they are spending their time, reading between the lines, and so on. High-level listening skills are essential for lawyers. They reformulate and reposition their client's claims and grievances, and they transform those into strategies for success in a transaction or litigation. Without close, thoughtful listening the lawyer is unable to perform those key functions for clients. Listening for the purpose of building a relationship is different than listening with an intent to reply, rather than reflect and understand. Many potential agreements are missed because someone was more focused on making their point than understanding what the other party was trying to say. Listening also opens you up to learning, which again is too often neglected in law school education—thinking that you have to know the answer to every question and always be right.

One second-year law student told us about an important moment as he was apprehensively considering joining a large national law firm upon graduation shortly after the coronavirus pandemic hit. The partners made every effort to assure him that the firm would endure, that the lawyers and staff would be rewarded for their hard work, and that the firm's leaders remained strong and united in inspiring their team to continue doing great work for the firm's clients. "This is what I needed to hear," the student told us, "because while I'm not afraid of putting in the hours, I wanted to feel that the firm had a long-term perspective and had the best interests of people at heart." It was by listening to their new firm prospects that the partners got him on board with their shared vision of the future.

Show How Followers Can Make a Difference

Leaders can attract followers by showing how their vision can make a difference.

Everyone wants a tomorrow that is better than today, and while people do not all want the same thing, they do all want an improvement. Leaders must be able to discern what that improvement would look like for the people with whom they interact and work.

There is a deep yearning inside people to make a difference. They want to know that they're doing something meaningful on this planet—that there's a purpose to their existence. Work can provide that purpose: increasingly the workplace is where people pursue meaning and identity. The best teams and workplaces are able to bring out and make use of this human longing by communicating the meaning and significance of what's being done so that people understand their own important role in creating it. When you can clearly communicate a shared vision of an organization, you ennoble those who work on its behalf. Studies involving respondents from forty different countries (encompassing sixteen different languages) found that connecting employees with purpose increased their levels of engagement and productivity.[6] Stressing the "why" to people—as in "Why are we doing this, and why does it matter?"—activates the brain's reward system, increasing not only how favorably people feel about what they are doing, but also how much effort they put into it.[7] Furthermore, law students' job searches confirm this desire for meaningful work. After graduation, law students look for a firm or company that has values they share and can embrace, including a philosophy that newcomers to that organization are more than cannon fodder, doing the grunt work that no one else wants to do. Associates want to feel that they play a crucial role regardless of job title or specific task responsibilities.[8] One contributing factor for associate turnover in law firms is that they don't feel that their work is valued, especially concerning working relationships with clients.

Meaningful engagement with the work of the firm and a sense that the firm's values mesh with associates' values increase the sense of being valued and appreciated.

While you can't impose your vision of the future on others, you can liberate the visions that are already stirring inside of people. When you communicate a shared vision, you are awakening and arousing the belief that people can achieve something grand and unique. What truly pulls people forward, especially in more challenging and volatile times, is the exciting possibility that what they are doing can make a profound difference in the lives of their families, friends, colleagues, clients, patients, congregations, and communities.

Tout the Unique Aspects of the Vision

You are unlikely to successfully enlist others in a project, campaign, or cause by announcing, "I'd like you to join me in doing the ordinary." There is an innate desire within most people to accomplish something that no one else has yet achieved, so touting the unique aspects of your vision will attract followers. There's no advantage in being on a team or working for a company or law firm that does precisely the same thing as the one across town. If you want people to sign up with you, they have to understand how whatever you are proposing is distinctive. Uniqueness fosters pride and boosts the self-respect and self-esteem of everyone associated with the organization—and the prouder that people are of the work that they are doing and the organization for which they work, the more engaged they're likely to be. The fairly recent explosion of start-up companies bears out this desire for uniqueness: the business world is rife with such companies that offer not only unique products, but also unique visions—and young people, attracted by the nature of these businesses, have been flocking to them.[9]

Exhibit Energy and Positivity

In getting everyone on board, leaders need to heed the research, which shows that people want to follow those who are enthusiastic, exude energy, and have a positive attitude.[10] Upbeat people attract others and convey the feeling that the journey will be an invigorating adventure and that the leader is in it for the long haul. People want to follow those with a can-do attitude, rather than those who are cynics and give ten reasons why something is impossible or those who make others feel bad about themselves. When negative remarks become the norm, people's brains lose mental efficiency,[11] which is all the more reason that you need to focus on the bright side. A positive approach to life broadens people's ideas about future possibilities, and these exciting options build on each other.[12] In affirming environments, people are more open to seeing possibilities and more willing to experiment. Positivity increases the ability to cope with adversity and strengthens resiliency during high-stress times.

In explanations for why they are magnetically attracted to particular leaders, people often describe those individuals as charismatic. But *charisma* has become such an overused and misused term that it's almost useless as a descriptor of leaders.[13] To better understand this elusive quality, social scientists observed the behavior of individuals deemed charismatic. What they determined was that people who are perceived to be charismatic are simply more animated than others. They smile more, speak faster, pronounce words more clearly, and move their heads and bodies more often.[14] The most successful talks on TED.com, for example, were attributed to presenters who used nearly twice as many hand gestures as their less frequently viewed peers.[15] This finding was even replicated in studies that used simple animated stick figures as the speakers. The speakers judged to be most energetic and enthusiastic employed many more hand movements overall, and their frequency of physical movements was predictive of those who received the most applause from their audience.[16] Much of the same has been shown to be true of courtroom attorneys.[17]

Accordingly, *charisma* can best be understood as a willingness to be expressive. The more expressive you are, the more likely those around you will be infected by your enthusiasm. Successful trial lawyers understand that being expressive and enthusiastic encourages jurors to feel positive about them, and therefore their clients, which is important irrespective of the legal merits of the case or proceeding. Think about how engaging people are when they start talking about their personal-best leadership experiences or about their ideal futures, or even their upcoming holidays and vacations. When relating hopes, dreams, and successes, people are almost always emotionally expressive: they lean forward in their chairs, they move their arms about, their eyes light up, their voices ring with excitement, and they smile. By adding such expressivity and emotion to your words and behavior, you will increase the likelihood that people will remember what you say and act on it. Consider how you will share the enthusiasm that you have with others, rather than locking it away and assuming that expressiveness is somehow unprofessional or not lawyer-like.

Of course, none of these suggestions about being positive and more expressive will be of any value whatsoever if you don't believe in what you're saying. You can't just put on an act or performance; your enthusiasm must be sincere and authentic. If the vision is someone else's and you don't own it, you will have a difficult time enlisting other people in it. If you have trouble imagining yourself being part of the future described in the vision, you certainly will be unable to convince others that they should sign up for making it a reality; and if you're not truly excited about the possibilities, you can't expect others to be. Most of the meaning from a lawyer's professional life is derived from their service to clients' and causes.

From Inspire a Shared Vision to Challenge the Process

Many companies are emerging from the realities of the coronavirus pandemic with a shared vision about the need for and efficacy of remote work. And company leaders are instituting changes in response to this shared vision. Indeed, the workplace is evolving from WFH (work from home) to WFA (work from anywhere), and this shift presents both challenges and opportunities to creating collaboration and high performance in hybrid and remote teams.[18]

This kind of change is being led by law firm leaders, too. Although many law firms have transitioned their employees to working from home during the pandemic; although many have questioned the long-term workability of remote lawyering. Husch Blackwell, though, has already committed to keeping one team of lawyers on permanent remote status. As a clear example of challenging the process, the managing partner of the virtual office (called "The Link") said, "We don't see this as work-from-home. We see this as work-from-anywhere."[19]

The path forward to the future requires doing things differently from how they are currently being done. The truth is that you can't get to a *better* tomorrow by simply doing the same things in the same way that you are doing them today. Change and leadership are synonymous, as illustrated by the examples of the transition from Inspire a Shared Vision to Challenge the Process, the focus of the next chapter.

FOLLOWING THROUGH

- Leaders Inspire a Shared Vision by enlisting followers in trying to achieve a dream of the future that includes serving more than themselves.
- Inspiring a shared vision includes envisioning the future and getting others on board.
- Leaders who envision the future are always forward thinking, but the process to get to that end includes not only looking forward, but also looking behind and incorporating the present.
- Leaders need buy-in from followers to take a vision from a singular idea to a shared aspiration.
- Leaders enlist others by crafting a compelling mental image, listening deeply, showing how followers can make a difference, touting the unique aspects of the vision, and exhibiting energy and positivity.

REFLECTIONS

1. What is your vision about the law and its role in society? On a scale from one (low) to ten (high), how excited and passionate are you about this vision? Without being judgmental, is your vision narrow or broad? In what ways does your vision align with those of your intended audience and clients you wish to serve?

2. What are the differences between being inspired by the client's goals and being a representative of the client's wishes? How will you handle a situation in which some aspect of your client's behavior repulses you?

3. What do you know about the hopes, dreams, and aspirations of those with whom you are working? What steps can you take to find out more and determine how well they are aligned with your own?

4. Consider the possibility of starting your own law practice or business. How do you go about envisioning the firm, its anticipated clients, the types of legal work it will offer to clients, and the unique aspects of the venture?

FIVE

Challenge the Process

Learning only happens outside of your comfort zone, by doing things that you don't already know how to do.

THE LEAD-IN

- Seizing the Opportunity to Improve
  - Be Proactive
  - Pinpoint Motivations
  - Use Outsight to Achieve Innovation
- Experimenting and Taking Risks
  - Achieve Small Wins
  - Ensure Psychological Safety
  - Learn from Mistakes
  - Embrace a Growth Mindset
  - Exhibit Psychological Hardiness
- From Challenge the Process to Enable Others to Act
- Following Through
- Reflections

Leaders Challenge the Process.

Lawyers make their living by challenging processes, rules, and others' actions. They advocate for clients, and often for themselves, by taking on the government, corporate interests, employers, and others in positions of power and influence. Lawyers frequently challenge the status quo for the benefit of their clients. Lawyers who are in leadership roles must, like leaders in other contexts, challenge the processes and influences that confront their law firms, nonprofit organizations, and government offices or agencies. Of course, leaders challenge not simply for the sake of stirring things up, making waves, or rocking the boat, but for the sake of something better—for example, a better legal rule or policy or a fairer outcome to affected parties. They are at the front lines of seeking change and improvement and securing justice.

Challenging the process includes *seizing the opportunity to improve* and *experimenting and taking risks.* Leadership is not about maintaining the existing conditions or doing what everyone else is doing. Leadership happens when you actively look outside of job descriptions and venture beyond current limits, standards, and norms to find innovative ways to improve.

This demands a willingness to experiment and fosters risk taking, where the outcomes are focused as much on learning as they are on results. "Nothing ventured, nothing gained" is the leaders' mantra because the only people who don't make mistakes are those who don't do anything new or different. When managers and coworkers are asked to designate their most effective leaders, the responses are closely related to how frequently these people engage in the leadership practice of Challenge the Process.

Seizing the Opportunity to Improve

Nothing stifles creativity and innovation more than accepting the axiom "If it ain't broke, don't fix it." Something always needs fixing. An opportunity for improvement exists in every organization, every law firm, every community, every school, and every home.

Taking on a new job or assignment is an ideal opportunity to ask probing questions and challenge the way things have always been done. Those are the times when you should ask, "*Why* do we do this?" But don't just ask this when you're new to a job or assignment; make this one of your routine questions. Treat every day as if it were your first day. Ask yourself, "If I were just starting, what would I do differently?"

These are tough questions that do not have easy answers. Just ask the lawyers leading law firms, corporate counsel offices, and district attorneys' offices when the 2008 recession impacted the legal community (and many others) with depressed revenues, layoffs, downsizing, and strong new competition from non-law firm competitors. Clients pulled back legal business, and firms jettisoned recently hired lawyers. Increased commodification of legal services, sweeping changes in technology, poor management decisions, and other disruptive forces at work in the legal services fields defined the period.[1] Those economic, social, and professional factors created a situation akin to a new job or assignment—and required great leadership and management actions and initiatives by lawyers leading those impacted organizations. Some failed, but many found ways as a result of their leadership to seize the opportunity to adjust and improve, thus stabilizing their organizations and positioning themselves for success. Similar phenomena were experienced during the coronavirus pandemic and accompanying economic and societal turmoil.

Be Proactive

While external factors contribute to change—often in unanticipated ways—this does not mean that you should wait for something to happen that upsets the proverbial apple cart; you must be proactively seeking opportunities to improve. Proactivity consistently produces better results than reactivity or inactivity.[2] In shadowing senior executives, researchers discovered that the most successful ones were not waiting for information to come to them but rather were out and about gathering knowledge so that they could understand what to do next.[3] Furthermore, research indicates that people who rank high in proactivity are considered to be the most effective leaders. For example, in assessing their peers, students gave high marks for proactivity to those who were more often engaged in extracurricular and civic activities targeted toward bringing about positive change—and rated them as better leaders.[4]

Proactivity involves making something happen when you notice or find out about something that isn't working—creating a possible solution for the problem, gaining buy-in from constituents, and implementing the desired outcome. Ask your colleagues what really bugs them and what gets in the way of them doing the best job possible. Take time to periodically wander around your workplace or neighborhood and look for things that don't seem right. As they say in basketball, none of the shots you *don't* take ever go in the hoop. You've got to make something happen—to shoot the ball—in order to score some points.

The work of one junior associate with a national law firm exemplifies proactivity. She saw ways that the firm could improve when it came to developing young talent. She drafted a seventy-some-page handbook for junior attorneys to follow in their early, often difficult, days at the firm. The practical guide bridged the gap between graduating from law school and assimilating into law firm practice; and, importantly, it became a model for communication between partners and the firm's newest attorneys on how to integrate their skills and perspectives into the law firm. Her initiative in creating the handbook also led to better work assignments for her on law firm deals as other lawyers realized how her resourcefulness helped the firm with new talent.

Although proactivity is a critical factor in finding challenges, in the end it's not so important whether you find the challenges or they find you. What's important is whether you are proactive in dealing with challenges. When opportunity knocks, will you be willing to open the door?

Pinpoint Motivations

Part of the answer to that question is knowing what motivates *you* to do your best, day in and day out. Meaning and purpose give people the motivation not only to deal with the challenges and uncertainties of life but also to actively seek change and overcome the general tendency toward homeostasis. The research evidence is well established that if people are going to do their best, the task or project in which they are engaged must be intrinsically motivating.[5] When it comes to excellence, it's definitely *not* "what gets rewarded gets done"—it's "what *is* rewarding gets done."

Our experience with law students is that they are, by and large, a highly motivated group. Surveys show that "solving complex problems," "making a difference in my community," and "helping others who don't understand the complexities of law" are frequent reasons why people decided to go to law school and become lawyers.[6] They like challenges and are willing to put in the work necessary to meet them, both for themselves and for their clients.

The desire for challenges actually looms large in all groups of people. Researchers have conducted intensive studies to explore the nature of activities that contain rewards within themselves.[7] Findings show that people enjoy their chosen activity because of the pleasure they derive both from the experience and from using their skills; extrinsic rewards such as power, prestige, and glamour were ranked least important as motivators. Researchers have concluded that for a task to be rewarding in and of itself, "it seems that its most basic requirement is to provide a clear set of challenges."[8] People who justify their employment solely on economic grounds will seldom contribute more than the minimum.

Of course, routines are often the enemies of challenge—and change. So are established procedures and demands—all those memoranda, telephone calls, reports, meetings, plans, documents, emails, and the like. You can get so busy in the day-to-day details of your work that you become ensnared in an activity trap, where you are very busy but not making much progress toward anything meaningful. Also, given the process in litigation where cases, especially large cases, can take years to resolve, associates often do not get to experience the beginning-to-completion of a matter and can lose out on feeling any sense of accomplishment and purpose.

Use Outsight to Achieve Innovation

If you are going to detect opportunities for challenge (and change!)—before those opportunities wither, become demands, or create huge problems—you must use your *outsight.* Outsight is the sibling of insight, and it means being able to see beyond yourself and your individual perspective, to perceive external realities more clearly. Without outsight, innovation cannot happen; and insight without outsight is like seeing clearly with blinders on—you just won't get a complete picture.

Studies into how the brain processes information suggest that in order to see things differently and more creatively, you have to bombard your brain with things that it has never encountered. Neuroscientists explain that novelty is vital because the brain, which evolved for efficiency, routinely takes perceptual shortcuts to save energy. Only by forcing yourself to break free of habitual thinking patterns can you get your brain to recategorize information.[9] Consider the practice of "associating," which involves making connections across "seemingly unrelated questions, problems, or ideas."[10] Consider how you might stir imagination by starting a discussion with your law firm colleagues about how Disney would handle your client relationships or how your recruitment and onboarding programs would be developed by Southwest Airlines. While a serious law student may think this would be a whimsical approach in their firm, not so if done with the purpose of generating ideas about imagining what change could look like.

Relatedly, a key factor in finding meaningful challenges is the ability to look around and see your environment in new ways—ways that expose openings for innovation. Inspiration can come from just about anywhere: clients, court rulings, contractors, clerks, research and development labs, support staff, disruptive technologies, seminars, competitors, and so on. The point is that there is no shortage of sources for possible ideas. You must find ways to keep in touch with trends in your discipline and professional and industry marketplaces; with the viewpoints and perspectives of people from a variety of backgrounds and functions; and with ongoing social, political, technological, economic, and artistic changes. Do more than just meet the minimum, annual "continuing legal education" requirement for your jurisdiction; rather, take on the process of continuous improvement and development that marks membership in a "learned profession." Be sensitive to even the fuzziest sign or weakest signal that there's something possibly new, novel, unusual, unfamiliar, and even strange on the horizon.

In the law business, skills at innovation and an "innovator's mindset" have allowed lawyers to seize opportunities to improve. These skills and mindset have permitted law firms to improve client relations, enhance attorney performance, create programs to increase diversity and inclusion at the firms, and institute other positive changes in how law is practiced. Faced with a highly uncertain economic terrain coming out of the 2008 recession, law firms looked to innovation and creative thinking in spurring changes in their use of technology, adding value to their clients' business, and building the firm's strengths in the face of disruptive change.

Similarly, the COVID pandemic raised interesting, and difficult, questions about the future of appropriate locations for legal work (at law firm offices or remote) for law firm leaders.

Outsight is essential. As the managing partner of one national law firm explained, "While we don't know exactly what the legal profession will look like in five years, there's a growing sense that it won't look like it does today."[11]

Experimenting and Taking Risks

In order for innovation processes to be successful, leaders must be comfortable with experimentation, which by definition involves risk taking. Learning only happens outside of your comfort zone, by doing things that you don't already know how to do (or do as well as you could, yet). Risk is the chance or probability of something bad happening; you will be harmed or adversely affected if you take an action. So doing something new, because it has an uncertain outcome, brings along with it some degree of risk. Still, as it is said, "nothing ventured, nothing gained," and so leaders approach challenging the process with an experimentation mindset.

Achieve Small Wins

Innovation is often thought about as boldness, but boldness is not necessarily about go-for-broke, giant-leap projects. More often than not, it is about starting small and gaining momentum. Change conceived of too boldly or broadly can be so overwhelming that you can't even figure out where or how to get started. It can defeat the capacity to even imagine what might be done and actually have the effect of dampening motivation to do anything. Small, visible steps are much more likely to lead to early victories than big-bang efforts.

Consider the example of Ruth Bader Ginsburg, who throughout her career as a lawyer, law professor, and jurist continued to take risks, particularly on behalf of women in law, employment, and society, in pursuit of her ideals of equality and fair treatment. By breaking down each of the barriers in front of her, she worked her way, small win by small win, to her exalted position on the US Supreme Court, where she could really make a difference for her lofty goals.[12] Similarly, banking and tax attorney Clarence Jones left his lucrative career to join the legal team for Dr. Martin Luther King Jr. By representing King in various legal challenges and embracing King's inspiring messages, Jones dedicated his legal career to many small but transformative wins for those seeking equality of treatment in the American legal system. Like many lawyers involved in public interest lawyering, Jones was able to use his technical legal knowledge and skills to achieve social change.[13]

Research confirms this concept of small wins leading to big changes. The long-standing understanding within scientific and academic communities is that major breakthroughs are the result of the work of scores of researchers, as countless contributions finally begin to add up to a solution. Researchers have shown that the sum total of all the "little" improvements in technology, regardless of the industry, contribute more to a substantial increase in organizational productivity than all the great inventors and their inventions do.[14]

This is also the case for individual change, as quite often a small and unobtrusive nudge in the right direction of small actions can lead to long-term shifts.[15] To get people to *want* to change the way they're currently headed, you need to nurture an experimental attitude and begin with a one-step-at-a-time approach, where each success builds people's commitment to pursuing a course of action. When you break big problems and projects into small, doable steps, it becomes easier to get people to say yes.

This incremental change process has been called "small wins."[16] Small wins form a consistent pattern of accomplishment that attracts people who want to be allied with a successful venture, which builds their confidence and reinforces their natural desire to feel successful. Since additional resources tend to flow to winners, a small win means that slightly larger steps or wins can be attempted next. A series of small wins contributes to constructing a stable foundation on which bigger risks can be taken, with each win providing information that facilitates learning and adaptation. This simple strategy of winning step-by-step succeeds more often than massive overhauls and gigantic projects. It's not just that it's easier; it is also because personal and group commitment is built in the process. Consider this in the context of planting trees. Planting one tree won't stop global warming, but planting one million trees one at a time can make a significant difference. Planting that first tree gets things started. The visible success shows others that they, too, can plant a tree and make a difference. So too, lawyers who have built their own law firms from scratch did so one client or case at a time until they achieved a sustainable and profitable business.

Small, incremental, and consistent steps forward have a significant impact on both people's motivation and their self-confidence.[17] When people don't feel overwhelmed by a task, their energy goes into getting the job done instead of wondering, "How will we ever solve that problem?" Finding all the small ways that people can succeed at doing things differently makes people want to be, and stay, involved.

Ensure Psychological Safety

Of course, when you experiment, not everything works out as intended. Mistakes and false starts are a natural and necessary part of the process of innovation and leadership. This means that as a leader you have to make it "safe" for your followers to not get everything 100 percent correct the first time. Without feeling sufficiently safe, people will be unwilling, even unable, to experiment and take risks.

The idea of "psychological safety" is not a personality factor but rather a workplace characteristic—a hallmark of effective leadership and a highly functional workplace. Psychological safety exists in an environment where mutual trust and respect nurtures candor and a sense of obligation to communicate when there are disagreements, as well as opportunities.[18] It exists where people believe that if they make a mistake, or ask for help, their colleagues will not think less of them, pick them apart, ridicule or punish them.

Fear inhibits venturing outside of one's comfort zone and impedes information sharing, asking for help, and experimenting. Due to fear, people remain silent even when they believe they have something to say that has the potential to add value. People do not do their best when they are afraid: research in neuroscience shows that fear consumes physiological resources, impairing analytic thinking, creative insight, and problem solving.[19] This situation has been likened to the difference between playing not to lose (avoiding losses) and playing to win (seeking gains).[20] Playing not to lose is a mindset that focuses, consciously or subconsciously, on protecting against the downside (i.e., embarrassment, ridicule, security) and thus necessarily involves fear. Playing to win, alternatively, is focused on the upside (i.e., seeking opportunity); although it involves taking risks, the environment is encouraging rather than fear inducing.

There is substantial empirical evidence that psychological safety matters both personally and organizationally, affecting everything from employee error reporting to return on investment.[21] A multiple-year study of over 180 teams at Google found that psychological safety was the critical factor explaining why some teams outperformed others.[22] Similarly, a study involving more than twenty thousand people around the world indicated that when employees felt safe, there was a 347 percent increase in the probability of highly engaged employees, a 154 percent increase in great work, and a 33 percent decrease in moderate to severe burnout.[23]

Psychological safety for lawyers in law practice is particularly challenging since there is often a prevailing ethos of perfectionism, lawyer autonomy over their work, and a reluctance to admit that a party in a case or a legal ruling has you stumped.[24] Fear of retribution or embarrassment inhibits many young lawyers who become fearful of admitting their limitations to peers and supervising lawyers, and this in turn blocks their creativity and fosters mediocrity and complacency by those associates. The best law firm leaders are cultivating psychological safety among their young talent with the goal of greater workplace satisfaction, higher associate retention, and an all-around better work environment.

Given the importance of psychological safety, it is critical for leaders to employ strategies for implementing it in the workplace. One strategy for creating psychological safety is to ask questions that invite participation, and especially of specific people who might not otherwise speak up (perhaps due to structural or cultural reasons). In asking questions, you create a space for other people to contribute their thinking. This conveys your interest in their perspective and respect for their opinions. Show a genuine interest in what others are saying by asking them to tell you more about their thinking and experiences: "Can you say more about that?" or "Can you give an example?" Show appreciation rather than judgment for people taking risks; for example, say, "Thank you for speaking up about this matter or option." Another strategy is to ask questions in a way that addresses what might be motivating people's reluctant silence and possible defensiveness. For example, don't ask, "What mistakes did people notice when we did XYZ?" Instead, consider reframing the question: "Did we do everything as well as we could have when we did XYZ?" Test for consensus rather than assuming that silence means agreement: "Who has a different perspective?" or "What might we not be taking into account?"

Finally, you can promote a "humble mindset" among your colleagues, and within team meetings, by focusing on what can be learned rather than simply what didn't work and who might be to blame.[25] This means being willing to acknowledge your own fallibility and shortcomings. Assuming a modest level of goodwill in your organization, according to researchers, "[m]ost of the time your colleagues will respond well to genuine expressions of vulnerability and interest."[26]

Learn from Mistakes

There's no denying that change and leadership involve taking risks—and that when you engage in something new and different, you will make mistakes. Everyone does. That's what experimentation is all about. There are lots of trials and errors when testing new concepts, new methods, and new practices. Keep in mind, though, that few mistakes are fatal—and success typically comes from quickly learning from experience and fixing mistakes rather than being able to get things right at the start.

Telling yourself to "get it right the first time" is a ridiculous standard to set because you won't. What's truly paralyzing about the too-often-voiced notion that "failure is not an option" is that it substantially increases the pressure to never experiment, veer outside one's comfort zone, or do anything risky. The fears and anxieties produced by this perspective are magnitudes greater than those experienced when your attitude is that the only way to succeed is to try. The real issue is "how fast you can learn?" How quickly can you learn from your mistakes and your failures before you get it right? Taking a page from the military's AAR (After Action Review) and health care's MMRs (mortality and morbidity reviews), consider how you and your colleagues, even while in law school, can conduct a rigorous, systematic, collaborative, and transparent review of what happened (in the class, in the organization, in jury selection, in evidence preparation, in closing remarks, etc.) for the purpose of learning, to examine areas of improvement.

The personal-best leadership case studies are testimony to how mistakes, setbacks, and even failures have played a role in leaders' eventual successes.[27] Without them, there would have been little to no learning, and leaders would have been unable to realize their aspirations or achieve momentous breakthroughs. Many echoed the thought that the overall quality of work improves when people have a chance to be tested, and possibly even fail. Regardless of the field or profession, studies consistently show that there is no success without the possibility of failure.[28] This is reflected in the words of American author, entrepreneur, and humorist Mark Twain: "Good decisions come from experience. Experience comes from making bad decisions." The objective is never about making a mistake; the focus is on learning, and if you never do anything different than you've always done something, then learning (as evidenced by growth and development) simply doesn't happen.

Embrace a Growth Mindset

Unless you are willing to try something that you have never tried before, you won't ever know what you are capable of doing. Let's say you are doing something right now that you know how to do. Then someone comes along and suggests that there's a better way. Your initial reaction might be, "Well, that's okay, but the way I'm now doing it works good enough, and I'm comfortable doing it this way." You could continue with the status quo, but you need to realize that this is not how learning, or progress, happens. You can only learn and move forward when you experiment and experience doing differently what you already know how to do well. Therefore, the best mindset for a leader is a growth mindset: "I don't know how to do this, but I would like to be able to."

A growth mindset is the belief that your basic qualities can be improved and strengthened through your efforts—in contrast to a fixed mindset, which presumes that your qualities are inherent and carved in stone. With a growth mindset, you believe that you (and other people) can learn to be better leaders, while holding a fixed mindset means that you think that no amount of training or experience is going to make anyone better than they already are.[29]

Those with a growth mindset embrace learning opportunities. Clinical education courses in law school offer students the opportunity to learn essential lawyering skills and attitudes "on the job." Skills development programs offered by bar associations and organizations, where young lawyers can experiment with behaviors under the guidance of skilled and experienced lawyers, are equally valuable. These programs provide opportunities for young lawyers to both attempt the tasks that lawyers perform—preparing motions for summary judgment or voir dire examination of a witness, for example—and try out the comportment of being a representative of and advocate for clients.

Research has shown that individuals with a growth mindset are more tenacious and perform better when working on simulated business problems than those with a fixed mindset.[30] Other studies have shown that people with a growth mindset are more willing than those with a fixed mindset to embrace challenges, persist when facing obstacles, and sustain efforts even when confronted with resistance. These studies show that those with a growth mindset have a greater propensity to support experimentation and, unlike people with a fixed mindset, are open to feedback about their actions.[31]

Mindsets, and not skill sets, make the critical difference in deciding to take on challenging situations.

Exhibit Psychological Hardiness

Uncertainty and risk come along with any effort to make matters better and improve on the status quo. What's critical is how you view change. In particular, psychologists have reported that people who experience a high degree of stress and yet cope with it positively have a distinctive attitude toward stress, which they call "psychological hardiness."[32] Psychological hardiness contributes to resilience, the ability to process stress in such a way as to bounce back (or forward) quickly from the adversity.

In groups as diverse as lawyers, corporate managers, entrepreneurs, students, nurses, working professionals, artists, and combat soldiers, those high in psychological hardiness are much more likely to withstand serious challenges and bounce forward from failure than those low in psychological hardiness.[33] It isn't the stress of uncertainty and challenge that makes people ill—rather, it is how they respond to stressful events.

Healthy responsiveness to stress is critically important for lawyers because they often function in a high-pressure environment with long hours, schedules managed by others (such as court administrators and judges), and great uncertainty. Many professional surveys and studies have documented the strong degree of work-related pressures on many lawyers and how this frequently contributes unfavorably to their well-being.[34]

The three key elements of being psychologically hardy are *commitment, control,* and *challenge.* First, to turn adversity into advantage, you need to commit yourself to whatever is happening. You have to get involved and engaged and be curious. You can't sit back and wait for something to happen. When you commit, you find in whatever you are doing something that seems interesting, meaningful, or worthwhile. Second, you have to take control of your own life. You need to attempt to influence what is going on. While all of your attempts may not be successful, you can't sink into powerlessness or passivity or feel like a victim. Nor can you engage in denial or feel disengaged, bored, and empty. Third, to be psychologically hardy, you need to view challenge as an opportunity to learn from both negative and positive experiences. You can't play it safe. Personal improvement and fulfillment emanate from the continual process of getting engaged in the uncertainties of life.

During the coronavirus pandemic lockdown, it was evident that those who handled the crisis the best were psychologically hardy. They were examples of how resilient individuals respond to adversity—able to maintain hope and find meaning and a larger purpose in the various individual changes required despite the unfortunate pain, loss, and suffering. They made a personal commitment to do something, even something very small, to take control of what they could: they volunteered to help others, shifted their small businesses to serve a need for food or equipment, picked up groceries for the most vulnerable, or found ways to express appreciation to caregivers and first responders.[35]

From Challenge the Process to Enable Others to Act

Many start-up companies are great examples of the transition from challenging the process to enabling others to act. For example, Airbnb began when its founders needed money and so rented out air mattresses on their floor. The idea was an outlier and took several years to really get off the ground. In its early years, the founders "launched an ambitious project to get its hosts to love the company. They visited all of their hosts in New York to personally stay with them, write reviews, and professionally photograph their places."[36] Eventually, the company has enabled many people to earn extra money as hosts and take greater charge of their lives.

The legal profession, too, offers many similar examples of the transition from challenging the process to enabling others to act. For example, although it is rare for associates to argue before the Supreme Court, an openly gay associate at Hogan Lovells in Washington argued a case before the Court in 2019. Neal Katyal, a firm partner and a leading Supreme Court advocate, served as "second chair" on the argument and said that he "saw this as part of his own commitment to trying to change the low numbers of women and minorities who argue at the Supreme Court."[37]

Seizing opportunities for improvement. Experimenting and taking risks. Creating a series of small wins that generate momentum. Of course, you can't do any of this all by yourself, which means you need to Enable Others to Act, the focus of the next chapter.

FOLLOWING THROUGH

- Leadership is not about maintaining the status quo; it is about challenging processes, rules, and others' actions.
- Challenge the Process includes seizing the opportunity to improve, a willingness to experiment, and taking risks.
- Leaders don't simply wait for external factors to drive change; they proactively seek out what needs to be changed.
- Leaders are motivated to improve by whatever is meaningful and rewarding to them.
- An innovative mindset drives leaders.
- Small wins lead to big changes.
- Mistakes are part and parcel of experimenting and taking risks, so leaders must ensure the psychological safety of their constituents.
- Leadership means learning from mistakes, having a growth mindset, and exhibiting psychological hardiness.

REFLECTIONS

1. If you could start law school, an internship, or your first job over again, with the benefit of hindsight, what would you do the same or differently? How can you take advantage of these insights—not just for yourself, but also for others who will follow in your footsteps?

___

___

___

___

___

___

___

___

___

___

2. What do you admire about how other organizations, inside or outside of the legal field, behave and how they handle adversity? What can you learn from their experiences to create similar processes in your school or work setting?

3. Think of a memorable mistake that you have made because you took a risk. In what way did that situation turn into a learning experience? How would your life have been impacted had you never experimented and taken that risk?

4. What part can you play in providing psychological safety for your colleagues and your clients? Turning the tables a bit, what supportive assurances would you want to hear from your classmates (or fellow interns or associates in your firm) about their "having your back"?

SIX

Enable Others to Act

While seemingly paradoxical, the most effective leaders are those who give their power away to others.

THE LEAD-IN

- Building Trust and Fostering Collaboration
  - Collaboration Requires Trust
  - Demonstrate Trustworthiness
  - Collaborate for the Greater Good
  - Leverage Reciprocity
  - Enhance Connections
- Strengthening Others
  - Grant Choice and Discretion
  - Promote Accountability
  - Bolster Self-Confidence
  - Provide Skills and Knowledge, Training and Mentoring
- From Enable Others to Act to Encourage the Heart
- Following Through
- Reflections

Leaders Enable Others to Act.

Leadership is not a solo endeavor. One important clue to determining if someone is a leader, is looking around and seeing if anyone if paying attention to them, and following their lead (advice). Personal-best leadership experiences were never achieved by leaders themselves.

Teamwork is as critical in law as it is in sports, and lawyer leaders are the "captains" of the team. Their job is to enable others to act—by harnessing their colleagues' talents and resources while fostering collaboration and encouraging discovery—for the good of the team:

> In sports, teamwork and collaboration are essential to the success of each athlete and every team. Depending on whom you talk to, the practice of law may not be a contact sport. What is clear [though] is that clients are keeping score on how well their lawyers and their law firms work and play together. Moreover, judging from the perspectives of legal practitioners from small, medium-sized, and large national law firms, they all agree that teamwork and collaboration are critical elements to achieving better outcomes for their clients and ensuring the financial wellness of their firms.[1]

Many similarities are also apparent from looking at orchestra conductors. Most musicians are at least as, if not more, talented with their unique musical instruments; in fact, the conductor is unable to play all of the instruments and will never play a single note. The orchestra members look to the conductor to lead, through a clear vision, with infectious energy and passion, and to ensure that their musicians feel significant and appreciated. The conductor, like the most effective lawyers, creates harmony by getting everyone to play together, working through what otherwise might be dissonance as a result of anyone being out of sync by performing independently.

Enabling Others to Act includes *building trust and fostering collaboration* and *strengthening others*. Leadership is not a solo pursuit. It's a team effort. Leaders create an environment in which the people on their team, in their department, or in their program can do their work collaboratively. They know that for others to act their best, they need to build trust, facilitate relationships, and strengthen people's competence and confidence. Empirical data has shown that leadership effectiveness ratings increase in direct proportion to how often managers and coworkers report observing leaders engaging in the leadership practice of Enable Others to Act.

Building Trust and Fostering Collaboration

Trust is *the* central issue in human relationships. Leaders need to trust their followers, and followers need to trust their leaders and each other. Without such trust, leaders will be unable to foster collaboration with and among their followers, and collaboration is necessary to enable others to successfully implement a shared vision. In other words, without trust, you cannot lead.

And when it comes to trust, the responsibility for anteing up first rests with the leader. When the leaders say "trust me," but their actions don't demonstrate that they trust others or they don't take the time to listen and show that they are willing to be persuaded, then trust doesn't blossom or flourish. Trust begets trust. The truth is that trust comes first; following and collaboration come second. The feeling of "us" is built into the word trust.

Collaboration Requires Trust

Without trust, collaboration will not happen. People unable to trust the words and work of others end up doing all of the work themselves, or they supervise work so closely that they become overcontrolling micromanagers. These actions damage trust because members of the team feel they are not valued, and developing or enhancing their skills and career path is unimportant. As a consequence of not trusting others, such leaders are seen as untrustworthy themselves—and so others don't want to collaborate with them. Psychologists find that peers are more likely to listen to and get along with individuals who are capable of trusting people than those who view the world with suspicion and distrust.[2]

Studies in which people are told they can trust their peers and manager consistently show that their discussions and decisions are significantly more positive than are those from group members primed to expect that their colleagues cannot be trusted. Members of the high-trust groups are more open about their feelings, experience greater clarity about the group's problems and goals, and search for more alternative courses of action. They report having more influence on outcomes, satisfaction with the interactions, motivation to implement decisions, and closeness as a team than those in the low-trust group.[3]

Although these studies involved simulations, the participants behaved and responded the way they did as a consequence of simply being *told* that they could or could not trust one another. Their actions demonstrated that trust or distrust can emanate from a mere suggestion.

Believing that one can trust others, and be trusted in return, is a significant predictor of how people will behave. Consider the experience of a third-year student with a highly engaging and rewarding legal internship at a Silicon Valley start-up. The deputy general counsel was responsible for most of the day-to-day operations in the legal department, and he created a culture of collaboration among the attorneys and the interns. He arranged regular meetings where lawyers and interns would check in with one another, update their current projects, determine whether they had capacity for additional projects, and share insights into how matters were handled successfully. The purpose of the meetings was not just to discover if everyone was working hard but to create a collaborative, efficient, and professionally engaging workplace. As a result, everyone in the workplace (office) will feel trusted and able to learn from one another.

Building trust through reciprocal relationships is often challenging for lawyers. One reason is that lawyers generally rank fairly low on the charts for social ability and high on the charts for skepticism.[4] Another is because law practice is often adversarial, and so lawyers are not always open to others' views, especially those of their opponents. Notwithstanding these constraints, lawyers with a leadership mindset must work on building trust in order to collaborate, not just because it is financially advantageous (for example, it reduces the costs of dispute resolution), but also because it is beneficial to clients and the "right" thing to do.

Demonstrate Trustworthiness

Trustworthy is what people say about someone who can be trusted, and trustworthiness is demonstrated in a number of ways. For example, trustworthiness is evident when you pay attention to what others are saying, consider alternative perspectives, draw on people's abilities, afford opportunities to make choices, and provide influence over group decisions. Nurturing openness and involvement, conveying empathy and compassion, and helping others address their concerns and solve their problems shows trust. Such actions confirm people's belief that they can rely on you to do what's in everyone's best interests.

In fact, showing concern for others is one of the clearest and most unambiguous signals of your trustworthiness. For instance, you might volunteer to collaborate with people who are having difficulties completing an assignment, or arrive early to greet everyone and inquire about how they are doing, or take the time to coach people who are taking on new jobs and responsibilities. When others know that you will put their interests ahead of your own and they see this in your actions, they won't hesitate to trust you.[5] When people believe that you have their interests at heart—that you care about them—they're more likely to feel that they can talk freely with you about their aspirations, as well as their challenges.

A particularly salient way to show concern for others is to actively listen to them. The more people feel that you listen to them and understand their feelings and perspectives, the more favorably they will feel about their relationship with you and the more likely they will be to trust you and be open to your influence. Studies find a strong empirical relationship between how people feel about their workplace and the extent to which their leader actively listens to diverse points of view.[6] Typically, in a high stress work environment, such as a law firm, there is a tendency for people to listen for the least amount of information they need to complete a task, so that they can quickly move on to the next assignment. Practicing active listening affords a deeper level of understanding, tapping into not just what the other party is saying, but attending to a host of nonverbal cues—for example, the tone, volume, and pacing of their speaking and their body language (facial expressions, gestures, eye contact, etc.).[7]

Some lawyers are simply not good listeners. Active listening, for example, is not asking your team members for input and then immediately responding back to them that the idea they put forward is unlikely to work or not relevant, or simply that you have a better idea. When your legal education is based on criticizing ideas and coming up with counterarguments, these may be knee-jerk tendencies. When leaders and lawyers have this mindset and respond like this to their clients and associates, then people won't believe that they really want or care about their input, and they disengage. The situation becomes even more counterproductive when the leader assumes that a lack of input implies either agreement or consent.

Active listening involves more than simply paying attention. The best listeners do much more than remain silent while the other person is talking.[8] They are focused on the other person and not on their own thoughts. Active listening is a conversation, where both parties are more interested in trying to understand the other than thinking about what they have to say in reply.

Active listening means: asking questions that stimulate discovery and insight; being engaged in a way that makes the conversation a positive experience, causing the person to whom you are listening to feel supported and valued; showing appreciation for others' unique viewpoints to demonstrate respect for them and their ideas; and being sensitive to what others are going through, which creates bonds that make it easier for people to accept your guidance and advice. Great listeners also tend to offer suggestions and have been described as "trampolines" in that speakers feel that they can bounce ideas off of them.[9]

It's important to remember that both parties in a conversation have filters through which all communication flows. Listening skills are particularly important for lawyers in their many roles—as counselor, negotiator, advocate, and especially leader—because of their responsibilities to clients, so being constantly in touch with personal filters is essential to their work.[10] Being aware of that filter is critical to accurately communicating—especially with individuals and team members who have different backgrounds and experiences. You will need to work through your own filters (and implicit biases) and also appreciate the cultural identity lens of the other people involved when gathering input (verbal and nonverbal) about their interests and needs.

Collaborate for the Greater Good

Positive interdependence is the overriding mindset that facilitates trust and collaboration. It is the understanding that people have to rely on one another for their mutual success. With positive interdependence, everyone knows that it is the team's outcome that gets rewarded and not merely each person's efforts. While each individual within a group has a distinct role, people on world-class teams know that if they only do their separate parts well, they are unlikely to achieve the group's goal. Positive interdependence is the sense that "we're all in this together."

Lawyers frequently work in teams, so being a "team player" and understanding the leadership dynamic in building, serving on, and leading a team is a critical competence for lawyers. Fictional depictions of lawyers see them working in solo law practice settings, such as the iconic lawyer Atticus Finch in *To Kill a Mockingbird* or Perry Mason on the television show of the same name; and, to some degree, this may have been accurate at one time. But today only about 10 percent of the United States' 1.2 million lawyers practice alone, with another 31.8 percent practicing in firms of two to one hundred lawyers.[11] Another 30 percent of American lawyers practice in government law offices and corporate law departments.[12] Teams, committees, practice groups, and other groups of lawyers make decisions about the firm or law department, work with teams to service their clients, serve on bar association and trade organization groups (like the American Law Institute), and work on plaintiffs' or defendants' litigation teams in multidistrict litigation. Leading these groups and teams requires legal competence, but, more importantly, it requires collaborative skills.

Consider what was learned from a series of studies in which people were rewarded either for being the highest-performing team as a whole or for being on a team in which the rewards went to the highest-performing individual on each team. Though the latter (competitive) teams finished their tasks faster than the former (cooperative) teams, they were much less accurate, often simply because members withheld critical information from each other.[13] To boost the accuracy of these competitive teams, researchers had them complete a second task, where this time around rewards would go to the entire team for high performance. Unfortunately, neither accuracy nor speed improved. People struggled to transition from competition to cooperation: once they had experienced their colleagues as competitors, they were no longer able to believe that they could trust their colleagues.[14] Completing even a single task under a structure that rewarded competition was enough to create win–lose mindsets, and these persisted even after the structure was removed.

Thus, the leader's responsibility is to make sure that the long-term benefits of working together are greater than the short-term benefits of working alone or competing with others on the team. In other words, you must ensure that people understand that by working together they will be able to accomplish something that no one can accomplish on their own.

Organizational environments dominated by rainmakers and a culture of "eat what you kill" fosters conflicts and disharmony, as also evident with hyper-competitive students who want to finish at the top of their class and tend to avoid participating in study groups or share resources.

Leverage Reciprocity

When people collaborate for the greater good, norms of reciprocity permeate those relationships. In other words, there is a mutual, fairly equal give-and-take. If people know, for example, that you'll reciprocate, they realize that the best way to deal with you is to cooperate themselves and thus become recipients of your cooperation in return. Reciprocity leads to predictability and stability in relationships—in other words, trust. It's less stressful to work with others when you understand how they will behave in response, which keeps both relationships and negotiations from breaking down.[15]

The power of reciprocity in cooperative relationships is dramatically demonstrated in a well-known series of studies involving the Prisoner's Dilemma. As often dramatized on TV and in movies featuring police interrogations, two alleged lawbreakers are separated and confronted with a series of questions to which they must individually decide how to respond based on what they believe their colleague will say or do. There are two basic strategies: cooperate (don't say anything—i.e., cooperate with each other) or compete (blame the other party). And there are four possible outcomes based on the choices that they make: win–lose, lose–win, lose–lose, and win–win.

The maximum individual payoff comes when one person selects a noncooperative strategy and the other individual chooses to cooperate (i.e., to keep their mouth shut!). In this "I win and you lose" approach, one gains at the other's expense. While this might seem to be the most successful strategy—at least for the noncooperative player—studies show that it rarely proves to be successful in the long run, mainly because the other player won't continue to cooperate in the face of the first player's noncooperative strategy. This typically leads to both parties deciding not to cooperate (ratting out the other), attempting to maximize their respective individual payoffs, which means that both lose in the end. However, when both parties choose to cooperate, both win, though in the short run the personal payoff for a cooperative move (win–win) is less than what it might be for a competitive one (win–lose).[16]

Dilemmas successfully solved by this reciprocity strategy are by no means restricted to the Prisoner's Dilemma. You face similar dilemmas every day, both personally and professionally. For example, if your spouse or partner is particularly busy and it's their turn to wash the dishes but you decide to do them instead, will they do the same for you next week when you are facing grueling deadlines? What are the long-term gains of inviting a colleague to coauthor a law review article with you that you could just as easily submit as a solo author? Reciprocity turns out to be the most successful approach for even such daily decisions because it demonstrates both your willingness to be cooperative and an unwillingness to be taken advantage of. As a long-term strategy, reciprocity minimizes the risk of escalation: if people know that you'll respond in kind, why would they start trouble? Whether the rewards of cooperation are tangible or intangible, when people understand that they will be better off by cooperating, they're inclined to recognize the legitimacy of others' interests in an effort to promote their own welfare.[17]

Enhance Connections

In addition to reciprocity, another important factor in facilitating relationships and building trust is making sure that people feel connected to one another—and that these connections will endure. When people expect their interactions with one another to continue into the future—for example, they expect to run into one another at some event, continue to serve together on a project team for several years, or participate together on a subsequent task force—they are much more likely to cooperate in the here and now.

When you know that you have to deal with someone again, the consequences of today's actions on tomorrow's dealings are that much more pronounced. One of the enduring arguments made in lawyer civility training is that the lawyer you treated so poorly today may be on the hiring committee of a law firm you want to join or, worse yet, may receive a judicial appointment to a court you must appear in. In the end, enduring relationships, more than one-time or short-term ones, provide incentives to find ways to work together cooperatively to ensure mutual success in the future. Consider ways that you can network with your classmates (alumni and others associated with the law school) and opportunities to sustain those relationships over time. The relationships—friendships and clerking experiences, for example—formed in law school can often endure throughout your careers. In this regard, however, it is important to remember the wise adage that "what goes around comes around."

Strengthening Others

While seemingly paradoxical, the most effective leaders are those who give their power away to others. That is, they don't make themselves strong by hoarding resources and keeping others weak, ill informed, and ill equipped, but they make those around them feel strong and capable. They listen to and credit others' ideas. They make sure that people do not feel left out of the loop when it comes to important decisions. They help colleagues feel ownership and a sense of responsibility for achievements. They enhance the competence and self-confidence of those they interact with. Law students uniformly tell us that the best thing about first-year study groups is that members challenge each other's research, thinking, and conclusions—but actively support and encourage one another in the process.

Traditional thinking promotes the archaic idea that power is a fixed sum; and, correspondingly, if you give away any of your power to others, you will have less power and be less powerful. Not surprisingly, people with this view hold tightly to the power that they perceive is theirs and are extremely reluctant to share it. This notion is wrongheaded and inconsistent with all of the evidence on high-performing organizations. When you give some responsibility to others, they become invested and passionate about the assignment. Feeling powerful—literally, feeling "able," which comes from a deep sense of being in control of life—they are better able to persist in their efforts to achieve.

When you make other people feel powerful, in tangible and/or intangible ways, you are demonstrating profound trust in and respect for their abilities; this strengthens people's resolve not to let your trust and faith in them dissipate. Gallup surveys, involving millions of people around the world, decidedly show a close link between how powerful and engaged people feel at their workplace and their productivity, commitment, and retention.[18] Clearly, by strengthening individuals, leaders empower the entire organization.

Grant Choice and Discretion

The ability to make choices and exercise discretion is a key factor in making people feel that they are powerful. Freedom is the ability to make choices. *Trapped* is the word that people generally use when they believe that they do not have any latitude about how they can behave. When people feel stuck, they often act as rats caught in a maze. With no alternatives, they typically stop moving and eventually shut down. Having a sense of genuine autonomy makes people powerful and increases their willingness to more fully exercise their capabilities.

Researchers have found that the perception of increased choice activates reward-related circuits in the brain, which makes people feel more at ease, enhancing their willingness to experiment and venture outside of their comfort zones.[19]

High-performing organizations result from their employees' willingness to work beyond their job descriptions, and this happens when they have the latitude and discretion to make choices about both the work they do and how they do it. No one wakes up in the morning and gets excited about going to class (or work) so that they can be incompetent and disruptive. People want to be responsible, productive, and self-directed; and they want to take initiative. Constantly being told what to do by someone and how to do it by some rulebook stymies these inclinations.

Furthermore, when people have to stop what they are doing and ask the higher-ups what to do—even if they think they know what needs to be done and feel they can do it—the entire operation slows down. The only way to create an efficient and effective organization is by finding opportunities for people to use their best judgment in applying their knowledge and skills. Doing so is an explicit exercise in trust. There were abundant examples of how this worked during the coronavirus pandemic when, out of necessity, decision-making responsibilities were effectively pushed down to lower levels in the organization than ever before. Delegation generally demonstrates confidence and trust in another's capability, and providing stretch assignments also helps people develop and grow.

The experience of one third-year law student well illustrates the benefits of choice and discretion. He reported that in an internship with NASA's legal department, his supervising attorneys gave him broad discretion in creating "best practices" guidebooks, contract drafting handbooks, and communication guidelines for both the legal team's internal use and the office's correspondence with clients. "Through these actions, I was more heavily invested in creating deliverables that I could be proud of and that others would find beneficial." Trusting others paid greater dividends than simply making the student feel valued—the benefits redounded to the entire organization.

Promote Accountability

With greater freedom of choice, the more personal responsibility people accept. Strengthening others necessarily entails people experiencing a greater sense of accountability. Accountability is a critical element in every collaborative effort. When people take personal responsibility and are held accountable for their own actions, their colleagues are more inclined to work with them. Specifically, the more that people believe that everyone is taking responsibility for their part of the project—and has the competence to do it—the more trusting and the more cooperative they will be. People will be more confident in doing their part when they believe that others will do theirs.

Furthermore, personal accountability is enhanced when the situation is structured so that people have to work collaboratively with one another. People are motivated to do well when they know that their peers are expecting them to be prepared and to do their job. The feeling of not wanting to let the rest of the group down strengthens each individual's resolve to do their best.

The notion of accountability to others is a critical part of the formation of young attorneys' professional identity. It begins in law school with increasingly important assignments; moot court partner pairings; and "live-client" clinic course work for clients, and internships with law firms and judges. These provide students with the basis for understanding and appreciating their roles in the practice of law, which require punctuality in submission of court proceedings and transaction documents, the utmost attention to the needs of the client, "zealous" but ethical advocacy for the client's needs, and continuing attention to maintaining professional competence. These duties all begin with the lawyers' ability to hold themselves accountable.

The importance of accountability continues as law students segue into practice. Tellingly, the most frequent complaint about lawyers' client relations (right along with concerns about attorney fees and billing) is their failure to communicate effectively with clients (such as slow or no return calls) and failing to keep their clients informed about the legal matter in question.[20] In addition, lawyer malpractice claims are largely caused by rancorous attorney–client relationships and poor communications between the attorney and client.[21] Lack of accountability for these areas has reputational and financial consequences for attorneys and their firms.

Bolster Self-Confidence

But even if individuals are given the latitude to be accountable with choice and discretion to do something, it doesn't mean that they *will* do it. They may be reluctant to exercise their judgment because they lack the confidence to perform critical tasks in specific situations, fear making mistakes, or lack relevant information about the job.

Without sufficient self-confidence, people will not have the commitment required for taking on tough challenges. It's been said about would-be leaders that "it's hard to lead a cavalry charge if you think you look funny on a horse," and this humorous observation is supported by research. Lack of confidence manifests itself in feelings of helplessness, powerlessness, and often crippling self-doubt. In building your self-confidence and doing the same for those around you, you are bolstering what psychologists call *self-efficacy*—the inner strength necessary to forge ahead in uncharted terrain, face opposition, and make tough choices.[22] Self-efficacy is not a warmed-over version of the power of positive thinking. True strength comes from the self-confidence of knowing that someone expects you to succeed.

Research documents how self-confidence affects people's performance. In one study, participants were told that decision making was a skill developed through practice: the more they worked at it, the more capable they became. The researchers told another group of participants that decision making reflected one's basic intellectual aptitude: the higher their underlying cognitive capacities, the better their decision-making ability would be. Both groups worked through a series of problems in a simulated organization. Participants who believed that decision making was an acquirable skill continued to set challenging goals for themselves, used effective problem-solving strategies, and fostered organizational productivity. Their counterparts who believed that decision-making ability was inherent (that is, you either have it or you don't) lost confidence in themselves as they encountered difficulties. They lowered their aspirations for the task, their problem solving deteriorated, and organizational productivity declined.[23] Having confidence and believing in your ability to handle the job, no matter how difficult, is essential for achieving positive end results.

Provide Skills and Knowledge, Training, and Mentoring

As necessary as choice and discretion, accountability, and self-confidence are, they are insufficient by themselves to strengthen others. While you can communicate your confidence in others, people cannot do what they do not know how to do. This is where training/development and mentoring/coaching come in.

Without the knowledge, skills, information, and resources to do a job expertly, people cannot, in fact, do that job proficiently. Providing increasing levels of responsibility and discretion requires an accompanying increase in training and development experiences, as well as the chance to learn on the job. In order for people to feel highly capable, they must continuously improve and develop their skills and abilities.

Mentoring is another path toward educational improvement. Mentors enable people to be their best by asking probing questions, providing constructive feedback, and modeling positive behaviors.[24] A three-year study of the impact of training revealed that high-improvement learners were four times more likely to indicate that they had mentoring conversations than individuals who showed little or no improvement.[25] In other words, improvement isn't merely about educational experiences; it's also the mentoring associated with those opportunities that matters. Unfortunately, research indicates that more than three out five people promoted into frontline leadership roles report that they have never had a mentor.[26]

Being a mentor is not so much a job or position as it is a process—one that relies especially on an interpersonal relationship. The relationship doesn't need to be official or even formally acknowledged. You can be a mentor to anyone as long as you have a sincere interest in helping enhance and enrich the other person's competence and confidence. Being a few semesters ahead in school, or a few years ahead in your legal career, often places you in a position to be more relevant, accessible, and available to your junior colleagues. You don't have to wait for any formal role to exercise leadership, and while in law school, second- and third-year students (and new associates in practice) can provide mentorship as an informal type of leadership.

Law school students indicate that being mentored by an experienced judge or lawyer is one of the most important objectives of any clerkship or internship—even more significant than financial remuneration or academic credit. Another highly coveted position for law students is to serve as a professor's research assistant. Effective law school mentoring programs facilitate learning relationships so that, as a student, you can acquire the skills, values, and professional judgment from experienced lawyers and judges. Although law schools have been building greater experiential learning opportunities, like simulation and legal clinic courses, into the curriculum, even more hands-on experiences are needed, which can be provided by practicing lawyers. Most, despite limited time, are usually quite welcoming of students as mentees, as they recall their own early years of working with a mentor, so they are eager to "pay it forward." Also, keep in mind that it is unlikely that a single person can provide all the advice and counsel you might need. Think about contacting several people, each of whom might provide wise counsel in separate arenas.

The importance of mentoring programs doesn't imply a failing of legal education. Although law students often evoke the quip of George Bernard Shaw that "those who can, do; those who can't, teach," the truth is that law schools have found that mentoring programs don't replace but rather reinforce and strengthen classroom work. And mentoring programs are equally important for lawyers, experienced and new alike.[27]

Similarly, law firms are increasingly creating mentoring programs for new lawyers to improve the likelihood of both success and retention. These are targeted generally for cohorts of young lawyers, and, in particular, women, people of color, and LGBTQ individuals, who are most at risk of early departures from the firm. Often these firms will ask associates who are progressing well in the firm to be paired with a new lawyer (or sometimes, the firm will permit new lawyers to request a particular partner or senior associate to serve as their mentor) to help new lawyers navigate the complexities of law firm practices and social structures. Smart applicants for law firm positions will request information on mentoring opportunities and practices in the firm prior to agreeing to join the firm. Coaching programs may supplement mentoring activities. In these relationships, usually between one attorney and a coach from either inside or outside the organization, the behaviors and perspective that advance (or constrain) progress, opportunities for professional growth and advancement, and the skills and attitudes needed for success and fulfillment are explored.[28]

From Enable Others to Act to Encourage the Heart

Many companies understand that although a job well done is a reward in itself, another important, and very motivating, reward is external affirmation. For example, Motley Fool has "made every day Employee Recognition Day."[29] The company has "a peer-to-peer recognition tool [that] allows employees to give each other shout-outs that can later be converted into prizes."[30]

Law firms, too, recognize the importance of external recognition. "[P]ersonalized, instant recognition from... managers" is often more important to employees than money.[31] At Beveridge & Diamond, PC, managers and attorneys "personally and publicly congratulate an employee on a job well done. Doing so in the form of an email blast to the whole firm is doubly rewarding."[32]

Leaders strengthen others by making it possible for them to exercise choice and discretion, develop in others the competence and confidence to act and to excel, and foster the accountability that compels action. Exemplary leaders use their power and influence to build trust, foster collaboration, and strengthen others because they know that the best performance emanates from capable and confident people. It is also true, however, that without feeling appreciated and valued for their efforts, people will become discouraged. Therefore, leaders must be diligent to Encourage the Heart, which is the focus of the next chapter.

FOLLOWING THROUGH

- Leadership is a team effort, so leaders must Enable Others to Act.
- Building trust, fostering collaboration, and strengthening others enable people and groups to function effectively.
- Trust engenders collaboration; collaboration will not happen without trust.
- Actively listening is an important way to demonstrate trustworthiness.
- A leader's job is to motivate others to collaborate for the greater good, encouraging norms of reciprocity and fostering durable connections.
- Leaders who strengthen others bolster their own strength.
- Choice and discretion; accountability; self-confidence; and skills, knowledge, and mentoring are all elements that make people—and, in turn, their organizations—more powerful.

REFLECTIONS

1. Think of an instance when one of your classmates or colleagues did or didn't prove to be trustworthy. How did this experience shape and define your relationship going forward?

2. Recall an experience when you have been in a group of peers (for example, on a sports team, law student organization, or part of a group of law firm interns). Were you collaborative, competitive, or possibly adversarial with one another? What factors contributed to your behavior?

3. If you are in a study group and some members are not doing their part in terms of preparing outlines for their sections of the reading, what are some positive methods of dealing with this issue to promote cooperation and collaboration?

4. How are you reaching out to find mentors? What qualities are you looking for? Identify five people whom you would trust as a personal/professional advisor—why did you select them? How would you approach them about becoming a mentor?

SEVEN

Encourage the Heart

Authenticity goes up when you get personally involved.

THE LEAD-IN

- Expecting the Best and Getting Close to People
    - Treat People as Winners
    - Establish Clear Standards
    - Seek Feedback
    - Get Out and About
    - Personalize Recognition
- Creating a Spirit of Community
    - Provide Opportunities for Social Support
    - Make Achievements Public
    - Establish a Fun Environment
    - Prioritize Personal Involvement
- Encourage the Heart: A Comprehensive Finale to The Five Practices of Exemplary Leadership®
- Following Through
- Reflections

Leaders Encourage the Heart.

The positive comments from the chief counsel were quite impactful on a second-year law student interning in a federal government agency. That office leader made a point to set aside at least ten minutes in weekly team meetings to discuss the accomplishments of the individual lawyers, as well as the support staff. The public acknowledgment of these contributions to the agency's mission, the student reported, enabled "the lawyers and clerks to develop a sense of appreciation for one another, as well as the drive to continue succeeding, and motivated everyone in the agency to perform at the top of their game."

Encourage the Heart includes *expecting the best and getting close to people* and *creating a spirit of community*. People need external inspiration and affirmation. Exemplary leaders are always there to help others find the courage they need to do things that they have never done before and to recognize individual contributions and celebrate team accomplishments. In these ways, leaders figuratively give heart to others. Managers and coworkers alike report that the most effective leaders are the people who most frequently engage in the leadership practice of Encourage the Heart.

Expecting the Best and Getting Close to People

Leaders must have high expectations, both of the people with whom they work and of themselves, because these expectations become the lens from which people view reality or the frames into which people fit reality. And to generate and communicate those expectations and form the bonds that motivate people to continue to meet those expectations, leaders must be out and about, getting close to others. This mindset can be paradoxical for some lawyers because their work encourages them to be skeptical of their perceptions of people and legal situations; they must anticipate risk and envision the multitude of ways things can go wrong. Lawyer leaders must be able to properly holster those traits and engage with their followers and constituents in a forward-looking and leading way.

Expectations shape how people behave, and there is ample empirical evidence that people act in ways that are consistent with the expectations that other people have of them.[1] People are much more likely to see what they expect to see, even when their perspectives differ from what actually may be occurring. If leaders expect people to be successful, they will treat them as if they are successful, and in this fashion leaders' expectations trickle down to their followers. If you expect others to fail, they probably will. If you expect them to succeed, they probably will. Expectations also influence your own behavior as a leader. The high expectations that leaders have of others are based in large part on their expectations of themselves. This is one reason why it is so critical for leaders to Model the Way. Your own record of achievement and dedication and your daily demonstrations of what and how things need to be accomplished give credibility to the expectations that you have of others.

Expecting the best of others manifests the greatest impact when leaders are out and about, getting close to others. Without getting close to the people around you, how will you know them well enough to know what can be expected of them—and to effectively communicate those expectations? Without getting close to others, how will you give personalized feedback to bolster and sustain the behaviors that meet expectations?

Expecting the best and getting close to people aren't hard to do, and you don't need to be seated on a hierarchical perch to do them. They cost you next to nothing and yet pay daily dividends. You can't ask for a better investment than that.

Treat People as Winners

Begin with the expectation that the people with whom you work are already winners. It's not that they will be winners someday—they are winners right now! If you believe that people are winners, you will treat them that way.

Moreover, if you want people to be winners, you have to behave in ways that communicate to them that they are winners. It's not just about your words; it's also about your tone of voice, posture, gestures, and facial expressions. No yelling, frowning, deceiving, heckling, or belittling. Instead, be friendly, positive, supportive, and reassuring. Admittedly, this can be challenging under high pressure and stressful situations, which only underscores its importance.

To instill a winning attitude in people, treat them in a way that bolsters their self-confidence. For example, offer positive reinforcement, share lots of information, listen deeply to their input, give increasingly challenging assignments, and lend them your support and assistance. Research and everyday experience confirm that people with high self-esteem "feel unique, competent, secure, empowered, and connected to the people around them."[2] People are strongly influenced by leaders who believe in them and continually reinforce that belief through their actions and words. Feeling appreciated increases a person's sense of self-worth, which, in turn, precipitates success at work and at home.

Positive expectations create positive images in the mind, which is where positive futures for self and others are first constructed. Unless you and others can see yourselves as being successful, it is tough to produce the behavior that leads to success. For example, people who had never participated in bowling were randomly assigned to different groups and instructed in effective techniques. Following these lessons, the bowlers were videotaped practicing. The groups were then shown selective portions of the videotapes: one group of the videotaped bowlers saw only the positive things they did; the other group saw only the negative. Those who saw only their positive moves improved significantly more than any of the bowlers in the other group, and they were the most interested in continuing with the sport in the future.[3]

In a series of studies, psychologists showed that by starting with the statement, "I'm giving you these comments because I have very high expectations, and I know that you can reach them," the feedback they provided proved to be forty percent more effective in subsequently changing targeted behaviors.[4] You can easily imagine what happens to participation in a classroom when every statement by students is criticized and ridiculed by the instructor.

Fortunately, legal education has moved away from the model provided by the fictional (but, according to good hearsay, based on a Harvard Law School professor of many years) Professor Kingsfield in the novel about law school, *The Paper Chase*. Today, students benefit from considerable support from their schools in attempting to understand and adapt to the demands of law school and future entry into the legal profession.

The cycle of expectations and winning is a virtuous circle. When you believe in people's abilities, your favorable expectations cause you to be more positive in your interactions with those people; and those encouraging behaviors produce more winning results, reinforcing your belief that people can do it. What's really powerful about this virtuous circle is that as people see that they are capable of extraordinary performance, they develop that expectation of themselves, and another virtuous circle begins.

Establish Clear Standards

Positive expectations are necessary to generate high performance, but that level of performance isn't sustainable unless people are clear about the ground rules and expected outcomes. Without knowing the standards, tasks often just feel like busywork.

Clear standards give work a context, something that people believe they can work on together and be recognized for accomplishing. Standards help people keep their eyes on the target, focusing their attention and helping them ignore distractions.

Performance standards in law firms, especially large national firms, increasingly look to competencies that lawyers should be demonstrating in their work.[5] Firms identify the most important "core competencies," or "success factors," and then construct a system for evaluating the extent to which their lawyers are (or are not) meeting expectations. Commonly, these firms identify skills and traits such as legal excellence, client orientation, leadership, and commitment to development of business.[6] On the other end of the spectrum, many smaller law firms do not have any systematic method of measuring associate performance; and, as a result, a critically important element of feedback is not available.

Seek Feedback

People need to know if they're measuring up to the standards or just marking time. People's motivation to increase their productivity on a task *only* goes up when they have a challenging standard *and* receive feedback on their performance.[7]

Law students and young lawyers will learn from their mistakes, but they learn more from positive interactions with senior lawyers as well as judges, opposing counsel, and others. While in law school, and as a new attorney, you will seek information on how well, for example, you conducted cross-examination of an expert witness or completed a draft of an SEC filing. Honest assurances about the quality of your work, or constructive criticism of your work product, are critical in the development of your professional identity.

Unfortunately, feedback is not always forthcoming. Many senior lawyers or supervising attorneys were brought up in the "suck it up and just get your work done" era of law firm organization.[8] Law students' most frequent complaint about their clerkship experiences at firms and corporate counsel offices is that they receive little or no feedback on projects that they have worked very hard to get right. It is "like the project fell into a black hole," many students exclaimed.

In a simulation of creative problem solving, participants were praised, criticized, or not given any feedback on their performance compared with how well hundreds of others had done. Those who heard nothing suffered as great a blow to their self-confidence as those who were criticized.[9] Clearly, no news has the same impact as bad news. As one young lawyer wisely observed, "the fear of making teams complacent often leads senior lawyers to skip recognizing individual accomplishments, but in reality, the lack of feedback is highly counterproductive and diminishes morale."

Standards without feedback, and feedback without standards, have been shown to have little effect on motivation; however, together, they keep people on track. With clear standards *and* detailed feedback, people can self-correct, and more easily comprehend their place in the bigger picture. You already know how unnerving it is to go for months in a law school class without any feedback or sense of how well you are absorbing and comprehending the materials. While it is true that people might not always like the feedback (or as students, the grade) they receive, being able to improve doesn't happen very easily without some sense of how they are doing now. With feedback, you can decide whether you are on the right track going forward and determine what help you need to be most productive.

Get Out and About

In order to provide timely and relevant feedback, leaders are out and about. They don't spend all their time in a cubicle, remain stuck behind a desk, glued to the screen, or fastened to some equipment. Leaders have to be mobile and visible. You have to get close to people, and you have to be curious about them and what is going on. This can be a challenge for lawyers as they typically prefer more monastic or autonomous working situations.

Being out and about allows you to get to know others on a personal level and thus be more effective in how to most effectively provide feedback and work together collaboratively. Since proximity is the single best predictor of whether two people will talk to one another, you have to get close to people if you're going to communicate and know what is going on with them. When you are working with colleagues in different offices, or in virtual workplaces, you have to make conscious efforts to spend time with people because they are not informally available to interact with.

You demonstrate that you care about others when you are *paying attention* to what they are doing as well as to how they are feeling. When you are clear about the standards expected and believe that people will perform like winners, then you're going to notice lots of examples of them both doing things right and doing the right things. When you pay attention to what's going on around you, especially with regard to how people are doing and feeling, you develop a sixth sense of what people need to know about how they are doing, and are able to acknowledge and demonstrate empathy for their feelings.

Another benefit of being out and about is that it increases your own visibility. As you are getting to know other people, they are also getting to know you. Paying attention and actively appreciating others increases their trust in you. If people know that you genuinely care about them, they're likely to reciprocate and care about you. Furthermore, you can't improve as a leader if you're unable or unwilling to find out more about how your actions are affecting the behavior and performance of those around you—and you can't find out if you aren't out and about and visible. Leaders who most frequently seek feedback, listen, and attend to it are significantly more likely to act fairly toward employees and be seen by their employees as acting fairly.[10]

You might be thinking that being out and about pushes against the oft-repeated refrains that leaders "shouldn't get too close to their people" and they "can't be friends with people at work." Well, set these myths aside! Over a five-year period, researchers observed groups of friends and groups of acquaintances (people who knew each other only slightly) performing motor-skill and decision-making tasks. The results were unequivocal. The groups composed of friends completed, on average, more than three times as many projects and were over 20 percent more effective in decision-making assignments than groups consisting merely of acquaintances.[11] Feeling a connection with others motivates people to work harder for the simple reason that people don't like to disappoint or let down individuals whom they consider to be friends. People stick around longer in jobs when they feel that they have colleagues who know them and have their best interests at heart. People who report that they have a "best friend at work" are significantly more engaged, get more done in less time, have a safer workplace with fewer accidents, share ideas, feel informed, are innovative, and indicate having more fun on the job.[12]

There is an important caveat, however, in these findings. You and your friends have to be firmly committed to the group's goals. If not, then groups of friends may not do better. This is precisely why it is essential that leaders be clear about standards and create a condition of shared vision and values.

Personalize Recognition

People feel frustrated, and seldom work to their capacity, when their efforts and achievements are taken for granted. One benefit from getting close to the people around you is that it allows you to *personalize* rather than generalize both your expectations and appreciations. Of course, you have to do more than provide drive-by praise—you have to do more than simply walk around your organization or community saying, "Thank you, whoever you are, whatever you are doing." Realize that a one-size-fits-all approach to recognition feels disingenuous, forced, and thoughtless; and no matter how well intentioned, over time these routines can increase cynicism. Because the most meaningful recognition experiences are personal, this requires that you to get to know your colleagues well enough to tailor the recognition to their needs, values, and aspirations. By personalizing recognition, you send the message that you took the time to notice an achievement; sought out the responsible individual;

and delivered the appreciation in a timely, individualized manner. This kind of personal "touch" by a colleague or supervising attorney is particularly important to law students and young lawyers who have excelled throughout much of their pre-law school experiences and often link their success to the recognition and appreciation of others.

Don't make the mistake of assuming that people respond only to formal or monetary rewards because often it's the simple, personal gestures that are the most powerful rewards. "A sincere word of thanks from the right person at the right time," researchers have noted, "can mean more to an employee than a raise, a formal award, or a whole wall of certificates and plaques."[13] In fact, personal congratulations rank at the top of the most powerful nonfinancial motivators identified by employees.[14] (And an added bonus is that research has found that people who practice gratitude, as compared to those who do not, are healthier, more alert, more energetic and resilient, better able to cope with stress, and more successful.[15])

Creating a Spirit of Community

Human beings are social animals, hardwired to connect with others.[16] When social connections are strong and numerous, there's more trust, reciprocity, information flow, collective action, and happiness—and, by the way, greater wealth.[17] As we've maintained, leadership is all about relationships. Thus, a leader's job is to cultivate this spirit of community. Some of the most strategic methods for creating a spirit of community are providing opportunities for social support, making achievements public, establishing a fun environment, and prioritizing personal involvement.

Provide Opportunities for Social Support

Supportive relationships at work, characterized by a genuine belief in and advocacy for the interests of others, play a critical role in maintaining personal and organizational vitality. People just feel better about the work that they're doing when they enjoy the people with whom they're working. When people feel a strong sense of affiliation and attachment to those they are working with, they are much more likely to experience greater personal well-being, commitment to the organization, and perform at higher levels.[18]

Research has consistently shown that performance increases in a socially supportive team atmosphere. In a study of twenty-five thousand call center agents, people were divided into two groups, with one group taking staggered breaks alone and the other group taking breaks with their coworkers. In this latter group, those who had fifteen minutes to socialize and chat with colleagues, had a twenty percent increase in performance over their peers who took breaks alone.[19] Furthermore, in top-performing teams, people give each other nearly six positive comments for every criticism. In medium-performing teams, this ratio diminishes to about two positive comments for every negative one. The ratio falls even more dramatically for the poorest-performing teams; in those teams, members give nearly three negative comments for every positive one![20]

Likewise, motivation increases in an atmosphere reinforcing that "we are all in this together" because this makes the work environment a place where people want to be, work hard, and stay. An extensive ten-year study revealed that social support networks were essential for sustaining the motivation to serve. Service-performance shortfalls in organizations were highly correlated with the absence of social support and teamwork.[21] Furthermore, service burnout decreases when coworkers support each other and share in mutual achievements because working with others is not only enjoyable but also rejuvenating and inspirational.

The case for social support is further boosted by the fact that an exchange of information is more likely to be facilitated, whether in formal or informal interactions, when people like one another—and, of course, an exchange of information will bolster organizational success. Even in the age of social media, people are just more likely to share things when they're in a gathering with other people than when they're sitting alone at their workstations or on their mobile phones. When lacking social support, individuals regularly ignore cooperative opportunities, distrusting other people and their motives.

Social support is beneficial not only for organizations' bottom line but also people's personal bottom line. Longitudinal studies, in both the United States and Europe, have found that people who make use of social support have higher incomes compared to those people who have not tapped into a social network. This was true both two and nine years after the study's baseline period.[22] This makes sense because people who feel distant and detached are unlikely to get much of anything significant done at all—and they will be compensated accordingly. It is worth speculating that this relationship between social support and financial success is a likely factor in the results of research, involving more than three million people around the world, showing that social isolation is far worse for people's health than obesity, smoking, and alcoholism.[23]

Make Achievements Public

All over the world—in every country, in every culture, and in every organization and community—people stop working on certain days during the year and take the time to celebrate. Impromptu ceremonies are often convened to rejoice in a courtroom victory, making partner, the publication of a new marketing effort, the launch of a new service, the signing of a new contract, the opening of a new facility, the receipt of some civic or professional award, and the like. Banquets are organized to acknowledge individuals and groups who have accomplished the extraordinary. Colleagues get together with one another at the conclusion of working on an exhausting task force and give each other high fives for a job well done.

Why do people take time away from work to gather together? Sure, everyone needs a break from the pace and intensity of their jobs, but celebrating is not a frivolous excuse to goof off. Celebrations are among the most significant ways people have to proclaim their respect and gratitude, renew their sense of community, and remind themselves of their shared values and traditions. Celebrations serve as important a purpose in the long-term health of organizations and communities as does the performance of daily tasks.

Performance improves when leaders bring people together to rejoice in their achievements. Recognition on an individual level increases the recipient's sense of worth, which improves performance—but public celebrations have this effect *and more*. Every time you can bring people together is a chance to renew commitment. Exemplary leaders in these gatherings and occasions seldom let pass the opportunity to make sure that everyone knows why they're all there and how they have been and are going to continue acting in service of that purpose.

Whether the occasion is to honor an individual, group, or organizational achievement, celebrations offer leaders the perfect opening to explicitly communicate and reinforce the actions and behaviors that are important in realizing shared values and shared goals.

By making achievements public, leaders build a culture in which people know that their contributions are not simply recognized but appreciated and valued. And by making achievements public, leaders not only build people's self-esteem but also enable others to vicariously experience a sense of accomplishment that allows everyone to feel part of one team. They provide a ready-made opportunity to reiterate shared values and common goals.

An important outcome of celebrations is reminding people that they are connected with others. Bringing people together in an atmosphere of trust, collaboration, and gratitude reinforces the fact that it takes a group of people, working together with a common purpose, to achieve the extraordinary. Such celebrations strengthen people's resolve to continue in times of turmoil and stress. In addition, celebrations are an opportunity to expose people to others in the organization with whom they do not usually interact. When celebrations cut across functional and hierarchical boundaries, people get a chance to exchange ideas with, and be stimulated by, people outside their own areas. While in law school these often take place informally, and students are typically grateful and acknowledge the leadership provided by those who organize them.

Because celebrating is not customary in many law firms, those that do happen take on special significance. Although celebrations should be enjoyable, entertainment should not be their primary purpose. Rather, their primary purpose is to create meaning. Celebrations must be honest expressions of commitment to fundamental values and appreciation for the hard work and dedication of the people who lived the values and achieved the standards. Elaborate productions that lack sincerity are more entertainment than encouragement. Authenticity makes celebrations not only fun but purposeful.

Celebrations significantly affect how people feel about their organization and their leaders. At these occasions, it's vitally important when you are the leader to be clear about the behaviors that you want to reinforce. People are going to leave the event remembering and repeating what you say about what is being recognized and why.

Establish a Fun Environment

Leaders are on the lookout for every possible opportunity to inculcate fun into the work environment because fun isn't a luxury at work.[24] Every personal-best leadership experience was a combination of hard work and fun. In fact, most people agreed that without the enjoyment and the pleasure they experienced interacting with others on the team, they would have been unable to sustain the level of intensity and hard work required to achieve their personal best.

Neuroscientists argue that "laughter is not primarily about humor, but about social relationships. In fact, the health benefits of laughter may result from the social support it stimulates."[25]

Shifts in the psychological contract between employers and employees, workforce demographics, and the work itself are necessitating that people experience their organizations as places where they can do more than just work.[26] A fun work environment "intentionally encourages, initiates, and supports a variety of enjoyable and pleasurable activities that positively impact the attitude and productivity of individuals and groups."[27] Having fun sustains productivity, creating what researchers refer to as "subjective well-being" and contributing positively to affective, cognitive, and behavioral functioning of employees. In addition, studies demonstrate that having fun enhances people's problem-solving skills because fun makes them more creative and productive—which, in turn, fosters lower turnover, higher morale, and a stronger bottom line.[28]

In fact, fun and organizational success are deeply intertwined. The Great Place to Work Institute annually asks tens of thousands of employees to rate their work experience based on a number of statements reflecting workplace factors, including "This is a fun place to work." On *Fortune*'s 100 Best Companies to Work For list, which the Great Place to Work Institute produces, employees in the best organizations responded overwhelmingly--an average of eighty-one percent--that they are working in a "fun" environment.[29] Law firms compete for "best place to work" recognition. They often tout their commitment to pro bono lawyering, wellness programs, mentorships and support for associates which reflects both the competitiveness of keeping top notch talent satisfied and their efforts to enhance the work environment.

Prioritize Personal Involvement

When it comes to the leadership practice of Encourage the Heart, in addition to providing opportunities for social support, making achievements public, and establishing a fun environment, leaders have to be personally involved in order to create a spirit of community.

Often being personally involved simply means just making sure that you take the time and effort to "hang out" with your colleagues. One of the best ways to show people that you genuinely care and that you appreciate their efforts is to be with them. Another way is to constantly be on the lookout for opportunities to "catch people doing things right," and this isn't done very well by staying behind a desk, counter, computer screen, or steering wheel. You need to see and know firsthand what's being done right—not only so that you can let individuals and teams know to "keep up the good work," but also so that you can tell others about the behaviors and actions that make a difference.

Telling stories about how people demonstrate their commitment to values is a compelling way to show your personal involvement, and it is one of the quickest and most effective ways to communicate how people are supposed to act and make decisions.[30] By sharing up-close-and-personal accounts of what it actually means in a real-time context to put shared values into practice, you create role models within your organization or community that everyone can relate to. And in this way, you make shared values come alive.

Storytelling accomplishes the objectives of teaching, mobilizing, and motivating better than bullet points in a slide presentation or tweets on a mobile device, and firsthand examples are more powerful and memorable than third-party examples (it's that striking difference between "I saw for myself" and "someone told me about"). Listening to and understanding the stories that you tell inform people more about the values and actions you most pay attention to than company policy declarations or the employee manual. Stories communicate what really goes on within the organization. Well-told stories reach inside people, giving them an emotionally compelling way of learning what is really important about the experience.

Authenticity goes up when you get personally involved. You send a positive signal that you want others to be successful when you directly and visibly show them that you care and cheer them along. Moreover, you're more likely to see others take these same actions if you engage in them yourself.

Encourage the Heart: A Comprehensive Finale to The Five Practices of Exemplary Leadership®

Encourage the Heart is an appropriate final step for The Five Practices of Exemplary Leadership because it focuses on the followers and makes them feel good about being constituents of the leader—and as all effective leaders know, successful leadership doesn't happen without followers and the strength of the relationship with them.

But Encourage the Heart is an appropriate final step for The Five Practices for another reason, too. Although each of the leadership practices are separate and distinct, there is overlap among them because they build on each other and often require many of the same leadership skills and attitudes. Those skills and the elements of the prior leadership practices in particular spill over into Encourage the Heart.

To Model the Way, leaders' high expectations of self are the basis for high expectations of others, as is true to Encourage the Heart. Furthermore, both practices feature setting an example, affirming shared values, and storytelling as leadership behaviors engaging followers.

To Inspire a Shared Vision, leaders must get out of their cubicles and listen to their followers, just as leaders must do to treat people as winners and express their gratitude to Encourage the Heart. In addition to Inspire a Shared Vision, leaders must exhibit energy and positivity, characteristics that certainly come into play when leaders make achievements public and establish a fun environment to Encourage the Heart.

To Challenge the Process, leaders must ensure psychological safety. This also features in the process of followers taking risks as they rise to meet expectations when leaders Encourage the Heart. Encourage the Heart also comes into play in keeping people motivated through the small wins process that is central to Challenge the Process.

To Enable Others to Act, trust and collaboration play key roles. To Encourage the Heart, leaders must get out and about to enhance followers' trust; collaboration, connections, and reciprocity all play a role in creating a spirit of community and providing opportunities for social support. Furthermore, the choice and discretion, accountability, and self-confidence necessary to Enable Others to Act lay a foundation for the expectations necessary to Encourage the Heart.

In sum, lawyer leaders must engage in all five leadership practices not only individually but also in an intertwined manner. Together, The Five Practices of Exemplary Leadership create exemplary leaders.

FOLLOWING THROUGH

- Effective leaders show that they care by providing external inspiration and affirmation.
- By expecting the best and getting close to people and creating a spirit of community, leaders Encourage the Heart.

- If you treat people as winners, establish clear standards, and provide feedback, people will behave like winners.
- Encouragement is a personal form of feedback and strengthens trust within relationships.
- People who like the people where they work will stay at those jobs longer and be more successful employees. To create an enjoyable work environment, leaders must provide opportunities for social support, make achievements public, inject fun into the mix, and prioritize personal involvement.

REFLECTIONS

1. Do you consider the people with whom you work most often to be winners or losers? Does your categorization affect the way you behave with them? Have you found your first impression to be misleading, and have you been wrong about someone? Reflecting on some of those experiences, what caused you to change your mind about someone?

2. Are you getting the feedback necessary to know both how you are doing and what you need to be doing better? What steps can you take to solicit feedback? How can you prevent yourself from being defensive when that information is different from what you were expecting?

3. What's the most meaningful recognition that you have ever received? What characteristics of that situation made it memorable?

4. What makes your classroom, school, or workplace "fun"? What factors keep you and those around you from experiencing joy with one another and with the work you are doing?

Part III

This third part addresses the context for lawyers to exercise leadership—for example, thinking about leading in client relationships, in internal relationships (such as within the law firm or corporate legal office), and in public roles. The six chapters in this part examine key issues regarding professional identity, ethics, decision making, emotional intelligence, diversity, and handling conflict and adversity. The chapters give you the opportunity to think more deeply about how The Five Practices operating model can help you become a better lawyer and better leader.

EIGHT

Professional Identity: Becoming a Lawyer, Becoming a Leader

Can a good lawyer be a good person? Legal educators, lawyers, and professional ethicists often reverse this question and ask, 'Can a good person be a good lawyer?'

THE LEAD-IN

- Professional Competence as Lawyers (and Leaders)
    - Lawyer Effectiveness Skills
    - Timetable for Acquiring Lawyer Effectiveness Characteristics
- Professional Identity and Values
    - Legal Education and Professional Identity
    - Identification of Personal Values
- Challenges of Integrating Personal and Professional Values
    - Values, Inherent Aspects of Law Practice, and Psychological Issues
    - Moral Ambiguity
    - Complexity of Roles
    - Legal Ambiguity
    - Mentoring/Support Issues
    - Ethical Challenges in Real Life and Pop Culture
- Professional Identity as a Leader
    - Leadership: A Deliberate Choice
    - Self-Evaluation and Personal-Best Leadership Experiences
    - Leadership Role Models
- Following Through
- Reflections

How do law students (and lawyers) become lawyers who lead? In part II, we addressed the question of when and how you can become a capable and effective leader by developing The Five Practices of Exemplary Leadership. In this chapter, we examine how individuals become lawyers and—concomitantly—become lawyers who lead.

Certainly, you gain the title of *lawyer* by passing a bar examination, but the catalyst for becoming an effective, ethical lawyer is the transformational process that you experience in law school as you learn new skills and abilities and hone existing ones, as well as integrate your personal value system with professional values.

The process of forming a professional identity as a lawyer is essentially the same as the process of forming a professional identity as a leader. The two processes are not successive—they overlap. When you become a lawyer, you *can* become a lawyer who leads.

Professional Competence as Lawyers (and Leaders)

The study of why people decide to become lawyers not only provides an opportunity for insightful reflection by every law school student, but is also important to legal educators. Of course, law schools are financially dependent on a continuing stream of people seeking to become lawyers, but even more significantly legal educators have a responsibility to teach, train, and prepare their students for a lifetime of effective and ethical client service, as well as for the advancement of the legal profession itself.

Most people attracted to law school score well on standardized cognitive skills examinations (like the LSAT entrance exam) and have demonstrated academic success in their undergraduate studies. Admission to law school is highly dependent on both—a relatively strong score on a cognitive skills test and an undergraduate degree. However, neither of these factors has been shown to predict success as a lawyer, and some people have even questioned whether they significantly correlate with anything beyond grades in the first year of law school.[1]

What about other skills, knowledge, and abilities that have been shown to predict both retention and success as a lawyer? Law students enter law school with some of the competencies and attributes that are associated with the probability of a successful law career, but even those have to be developed, honed, and tailored to the work of lawyers and the context of the law.

There are additional considerations, perspectives, and capabilities that shape the trajectory of a successful legal career, and you need to learn about and embrace these during your law school educational experience. You can learn how to play golf (or play chess or create ceramics or act or write poetry) when you are in your forties, but you'll be much better off if you began to learn, and practice, when you were in your teens and twenties—and the same can be said for those engaged in the profession of law.

Lawyer Effectiveness Skills

Studies of the developmental process of new entrants to peer-reviewed professions (such as law, medicine, and engineering) show that all professional school students face similar challenges. First, they must learn the cognitive skills and abilities of that profession (that is, knowledge about and ways of thinking). Second, they must develop the hands-on and real-world skills for being an effective professional in that field.[2] And, third, they must internalize the norms and values of the profession. These three are foundational to successful entry into a professional field, requiring students' commitment to mastery as well as the preparatory professional school's commitment to providing learning and development opportunities (such as classroom activities, internships, mentoring, and coaching to assist students in acquiring these educational outcomes). This is the process by which professional schools, including law schools, transform their students into highly competent practitioners.

In the recent decade, many law schools have instituted courses and programs designed to assist their students, commonly in the first year of law studies, in acquiring a clear understanding of what it means to think, act, and feel like a lawyer.[3] To reach this point of personal identity as a law professional, students must understand and fully accept: (1) their deep responsibility for clients', employers', and the legal profession's needs and requirements; (2) the development of sound professional judgment; (3) a commitment to their own well-being; and (4) ownership of their professional development throughout their careers. We contend that developing an understanding of and competency in leadership are invaluable as part of the process of acquiring your identity as a lawyer who makes a difference.

How complicated is the effective, ethical practice of law? Surveys involving experienced lawyers, who were asked, "What is important for lawyers to be able to do?" revealed dozens of skills and behaviors that lawyers need to be effective as lawyers.[4] The list includes *technical* (or content) skills, like the ability to do legal analysis and reasoning, fact-finding, legal researching, speaking, and writing, and constitute a *baseline* for the practice of law. However, by a factor of nearly three-to-one, the list is dominated by critical interpersonal and organizational skills, most of which are associated with effective leadership. For example, influencing others, active listening, high levels of emotional intelligence and resilience, sustaining a passion and commitment to one's work, empathy, and continual self-development.

Such surveys of practicing lawyers and of law firm clients, asking about what lawyers need to be able to do, underscore the challenges to law students and young lawyers.[5] Lawyers must be able to focus on and understand clients' business and legal needs, engage in sophisticated and creative problem solving, approach their work with an entrepreneurial mindset, manage projects, and be highly collaborative on teams and work groups. This extensive, and daunting, list of "necessary skills" to meet client and firm expectations should not be considered as a superhero "leaping buildings in a single bound" role for budding lawyers. Rather, these critical lawyering skills, like the skills and behaviors of effective leaders, can be taught and learned by everyone who wishes to be at the top of their game, as a lawyer and as a leader.

Timetable for Acquiring Lawyer Effectiveness Characteristics

The long list of skills identified to be an effective lawyer—most of which parallel the characteristics associated with effective leaders—is intimidating and especially so to a law student or even to a new lawyer. Like many students, you might ask, "Do I need to be able to do all of these immediately after passing the bar examination?" The answer is no. Some of them are acquired (to some small or great extent, varying from individual to individual) prior to professional school, such as analytical and writing ability, integrity and honesty, and a personal commitment to community service. Many are introduced and initially developed during professional school, such as persuasiveness and negotiations. Still others are more fully developed after becoming a lawyer, such as networking, business development, and mentoring. The important point right now is to determine how you can be developing these skills in the formative stages of your life and career. The challenge is especially acute in the domain of leadership because the law school curriculum overwhelmingly emphasizes content skills (through classes and coursework) such as learning contract law doctrine and case analysis.

Irrespective of whether these effectiveness factors are developed before, during, or after law school, lawyers must enhance and strengthen their abilities to demonstrate and use them. This is achieved through a process of personal and professional growth that is based on a conscious effort to become an exceptional lawyer—and it is achieved in the same way, as discussed in the preceding part of the book, for those students and aspiring lawyers who want to become exceptional leaders.

Professional Identity and Values

Using these professional effectiveness characteristics as a jumping-off point, how do law schools, and, indeed, legal employers during the early years of new lawyers' "post-bar" development, assist individuals in the formation of their identities as lawyers and members of a profession? Following the publication of several influential reports on the state of legal education, the development of professional identity has become a required part of the foundational or core curriculum of law schools. The answer to the questions of "what is professional identity" and "how is it formed and shaped in law students and young lawyers" is found in the integration of personal values with professional values.[6]

Legal Education and Professional Identity

The aim of law school has always been to enable students to "become lawyers." The educational process employed has important implications, not only for the people who want to become a lawyer. It's also important in terms of the law schools' admission of people likely to be successful in law school and pass a bar examination and the schools' ability to effectively prepare people for careers in law and as members of a "service" profession.

An important and very influential contributor to this discussion has been a Carnegie Foundation report.[7] Entitled "Educating Lawyers: Preparation for the Profession of Law," it identified three so-called apprenticeships necessary for the study of law: (1) substantive knowledge and analytical skills, (2) practice skills, and (3) ethical professional identity. These, it was argued, are the central mission of legal education as it seeks to prepare its graduates for work in the legal profession.

The report's contention was that students form their identity as a lawyer by integrating their personal values with their perceived values of the profession, and that legal educators can support the formation of professional identity by giving students opportunities to engage in representations of professional ideals (for example, in clinic law courses or programs), to connect in a meaningful way with engaging models of ethical commitment within the profession, and to reflect on their own emerging professional identity in relation to those ideals and models.[8] Subsequent research studies have confirmed the importance of students having these experiences and being engaged in activities that prepare them for service to clients and the legal profession. All of them agree that professional formation for law students should include "(1) ongoing solicitation of feedback and self-reflection, and (2) an internally developed standard of excellence at [necessary] lawyering skills."[9]

Identification of Personal Values

The formation of professional values requires a clear sense of the personal identity of the "lawyer in formation"—their values, priorities, goals, and insecurities. The identification and establishment of personal values continues to be a subject of great interest to educators, behavioral scientists, and human resources professionals. Research has generally found that the acquisition and formation of personal values come from people's life experiences, especially in their early, formative years via modeling by influential people such as parents and other family members; teachers and coaches; societal influencers such as religious, political, and cultural role models (sometimes strong, positive ones—but sometimes not so much); and friends and colleagues.[10] By the time of puberty, many of those values, perspectives, and traits have settled firmly into people's psychological beliefs, attitudes, and values.

Fortunately, people are not irretrievably locked into those perspectives. Through educational and other life experiences, new attitudes and behaviors can be learned. Law school provides a rigorous, and, for most students, novel educational experiences—invoking a challenging set of opportunities that is often described by graduates as "transformational."

Challenges of Integrating Personal and Professional Values

The conflicts between professional demands (to clients, courts, and opposing counsel, for example) and personal values are rampant in law practice, irrespective of the setting in which the lawyer acts as a lawyer. Law students and young lawyers will often find their personal values challenged as they are tested by the morals and ethics of their peers and teachers, as well as the clients and organizations they represent.

In particular, law students wonder how well their personal value structure and orientation will align with their future professional roles, affecting their decision making in practice, their exercise of professional judgment, and their conception of the lawyer they want to be. The integration of personal values and perspectives with the values and expectations of lawyers is challenging to many. Law students commonly spend hours with their classmates discussing and debating difficult questions such as the following:

- "Will I be able to zealously represent a person accused of rape (or child molestation or war crimes)?"
- "How will I respond to a litigation client when this person insists that I overlook a damaging, but relevant, document in a discovery request?"
- "How candid must I be with a judge when she questions me about contrary case authority? Do I conveniently ignore it, shade my description of its relevance, or something else entirely?"

These questions, and many others, will arise not only in your law school classes but in your daily legal practice. The more you have embraced the professional ethics associated with being a lawyer, and feel grounded in your professional identify as a lawyer and representative of the legal profession, the better you will clearly see the path forward through the many thorny and complex issues that you will be confronted with.

Values, Inherent Aspects of Law Practice, and Psychological Issues

The concerns of law students about their ability to square their personal value system with the anticipated ethical decisions and behaviors in their roles as lawyers have been empirically linked with enhanced depression, anxiety, and unhappiness with their decision to become lawyers.[11] These conditions and disorders are exacerbated in young lawyers because now they must actually juggle the multiple, often conflicting, ethical and practice demands of lawyering. These psychological problems are created by inherent aspects of the practice of law, particularly those areas that law students read about and experience during law school: the moral ambiguity found in many professional situations, the complexity of roles that lawyers are expected to play in their work, the legal ambiguity in practice situations, and the lack of effective mentoring and guidance by ethically centered lawyers.[12]

Moral Ambiguity

Law students' concerns about their anticipated roles as lawyers revolve around the existential question: "Can a good lawyer be a good person?" Legal educators, lawyers, and professional ethicists often reverse this question and ask, "Can a good person be a good lawyer?"

The question arises from students' perception of the tensions between being a public professional (or a "lawyer statesman") versus being an amoral technician of the law.[13] You may at times fear, as depicted by Rudy Baylor, the young attorney in John Grisham's novel in *The Rainmaker*,[14] that your legal career will start down a path of cynicism, detached from the joys of work, and that you will constantly wrestle with differential morality in terms of your roles. Many students wonder about and are consumed by a nagging dread of operating in a value-conflicted occupational setting after law school.

This concern is warranted. Many legal positions or lawyer roles, such as work in a government setting or in "cause lawyers" situations, involve dealing with how to integrate personal values into work.[15] Consider how Dr. Anthony Fauci, director of the US National Institute of Allergy and Infectious Diseases, described his experience on his first day as chief medical advisor to President Biden as "liberating" after serving in the same role in the previous administration. He explained that he no longer had to be worried about his public comments and getting pushback from his own team about them.[16] This expressed value—autonomy—is an aspect of law practice that attracts many individuals to consider law as a career, but it doesn't come easily in the first few years of legal practice. Private law firm practice settings, which for law school graduates constitute the vast majority of occupational positions, are viewed as less accommodating of personal values than other positions because those lawyers take their cases and their clients as they find them—they often don't have the luxury of selectivity in obtaining clients. Lawyers need to be able to find comfort in work that permits an integration of personal values and professional necessities.

Complexity of Roles

A common concern of law students is how to get their heads around understanding and accepting the many roles that they will be expected to undertake when they finish school and begin work as a lawyer. Sometimes in the same week, if not the same day, a lawyer in private practice is expected to counsel clients; zealously represent them in legal proceedings, negotiations, and transactions; educate them on legal norms relevant to their business or personal life;

recommend business actions that will help them avoid future legal problems and be more successful; and serve as a check on any "darker impulses." For the average twenty-four-to twenty-seven-year-old, armed with four years of college and three years of law school and possibly little work experience, that is a formidable list of activities at which to become proficient. The questions are not necessarily easier at thirty or even forty years of age.

The complexity and uncertainty of these essential abilities often result in bouts of fear of failure, of malpractice, and of peer embarrassment in lawyers. Or it leads to a sense of apathy because lawyers develop the attitude that if they don't care very much, then setbacks and screw-ups are easier to put into some mental framework of accepting, forgetting, and moving on.

Legal Ambiguity

Another psychological barrier to feeling a strong sense of professional competence and well-being is the ambiguity inherent in many law situations. This ambiguity leads to young lawyers' omnipresent belief that "I don't know what I don't know," and how that is going to result in embarrassment and professional errors.

The first introduction to this ever-present mental challenge occurs right at the beginning of law school when students are introduced to the common law tradition, involving, as it does, reliance on precedent and the indeterminacy of judicial decision making in cases. These materials in the first year of law school—as well as jokes about "whether you win or lose the case depends on what the judge had for lunch"—lead to feelings that there is just no way to accurately predict if your arguments to the court are enough to win the case, coupled with work in which there is most often a "loser." Experts in law studies and psychology have concluded that the traditional method of educating students about the complexity of outcomes in litigation leads to significant levels of stress, which, in turn, contributes to high levels of psychological distress, substance abuse, depression, and suicide.[17] There is also evidence that the traditional Socratic method of educating law students, especially in the first year, has a high negative impact on levels of distress and alienation in law school by women and marginalized groups, another cost of adhering to this controversial pedagogical method.[18]

Mentoring/Support Issues

Still another contributing source of psychological distress is the relative lack of mentoring and professional support for law students, as well as for young lawyers. Certainly, the increase in clinical and experiential law courses has improved student perceptions about "what the job requires and how I will perform as a lawyer" and has served to demystify some ambiguous and stressful areas of lawyers' work, but mentors are still needed to help acclimate students to the real-world challenges of law practice.

Traditionally, senior lawyers are expected to provide support to younger lawyers. However, in a survey of 1,200 lawyers (78.6 percent of whom were law firm associates), more than half (57 percent) reported poor support and weak or nonexistent formal mentoring in their firms, and only fifty percent reported that partners at their firms "genuinely cared about associate lawyer development."[19] Yet the research shows that mentoring of associates, especially informal mentoring, makes a difference in their success.[20] While many associates reported that formal mentoring programs have less impactful effects, fifty-seven percent of the lawyers who made partner reported having multiple informal mentors, while only twenty-six percent of those not making partner reported mentoring by colleagues. While the organized bar provides some mentoring opportunities (through, for example, "Young Lawyer" educational programs that pair experienced volunteer lawyers with young lawyers), these opportunities cannot reach all of the new lawyers who need and would welcome mentoring and guidance as they learn about how to be a good lawyer.

Consider taking the initiative yourself to cultivate a set of advisors, or mentors, you can approach for perspective when school and work gets challenging, even frustrating. A diverse set of perspectives can help you work through difficult issues and demands in practice (and even while in law school). They may also remind you about the high aspirations associated with the law and its role in society and reignite your internal passion and sense of purpose. Keep in mind as well that there are likely multiple people who can support you, and each might be sought out for a specific rather than general reason.

Ethical Challenges in Real Life and Pop Culture

Conflicts in integrating personal and professional values are not only evident in real life, but also are highlighted in films and novels. In real life, the theme of personal conflicts between a lawyer's personal values and the demands of the position or the practice of law was brazenly illustrated by former President Trump's efforts to get the Department of Justice to subvert and overturn the 2020 election. Many depictions of lawyers in films and novels reflect the challenge of moral ambiguity and the conflict between individual integrity and the demands of the job.

Rudy Baylor, in *The Rainmaker*, is enticed by an unscrupulous adversary (a prominent trial lawyer) to skirt ethical norms and behavior, and he laments the challenge for young lawyers to avoid becoming another "bottom-dwelling shark."

Unfortunately, these frequent treatments of conflicts in values in often daily newspaper and social media headlines and in popular culture provide neither a useful nor a dependable guide to law students and young lawyers on how to align their personal values with the tasks they are asked to perform and the expectations of their clients, judges, and other lawyers.

Adopting the perspective provided by The Five Practices of Exemplary Leadership® operating system provides vital guide rails to the challenges of successfully navigating the practice of law, especially clarifying your values and aligning actions with them. The next chapter also looks more directly at various perspectives on being an ethical lawyer leader.

Professional Identity as a Leader

An important way for law students and lawyers to navigate the challenges in forming their professional identities, irrespective of the direction they wish to take in their careers, is to develop and strengthen their leadership competencies and attitudes. The process of becoming a lawyer shares many attributes and similarities with the formative process of becoming a leader—indeed, they are inextricably linked.

How do you come to think of yourself as a leader? How do you proceed in your personal and professional development to serve others as a leader? Answering such questions begins with the understanding that leadership is a deliberate choice. Self-education follows from that understanding: self-evaluation, which includes studying your own experiences as a leader and engaging in periodic self-reflection of your values—what's important to you—and reviewing their alignment with your decisions and revising as necessary; and evaluation of the behaviors of effective lawyer leader role models. Such self-education is key to developing into a lawyer who successfully leads others.

Leadership: A Deliberate Choice

Previously, we explained that developing yourself as a leader and your leadership capabilities is not an accidental process or outcome. You must want to lead; there are no (or few) "accidental" leaders. Of course, some people are thrust into a leadership role or situation by circumstances that are unforeseen, but, even then, becoming a leader and engaging in essential leadership practices and behaviors must be intentional if you expect a high probability of successful outcomes.

The pursuit of leadership is sometimes a matter of necessity within the lawyer's organization. Most organizations, even—dare we say it?—private law practices, are faced with the need for fundamental (and, sometimes, existential) change every four or five years.[21] The need to continuously improve and keep up with changes (be they technological, economic, political, judicial, local, or global, and so on) requires leadership across the organization, whether in a law firm, corporate or governmental counsel office, or judicial chambers. The most successful firms, regardless of their business, are characterized by high levels of leadership behavior across the many ways that one might slice up an organization.[22]

Often, the pursuit of leadership is a matter of personal goals. However, serving as a leader always reflects a desire not only to exercise influence in the pursuit of purposes greater than self-interests but also to feel a sense of satisfaction in the achievements of others. Both of these desires must be prominent regardless of whether others ask you to take on a challenge or situations occur where uncertainty, turmoil, and the need for fundamental changes push you to step forward and lead.

Self-Evaluation and Personal-Best Leadership Experiences

Self-evaluation is an important ability for forming a professional identity as a leader. Leadership of self is a fundamentally important law school lesson, as it is in the practice of law. After all, the very first person you have to lead is yourself! One of the most attractive attributes of practicing law is being a highly educated professional with a high degree of autonomy.

However, you are in a profession that is demanding in terms of high expectations for professional performance and integrity and where failure or inattention to duties can be costly in terms of professional malpractice and disciplinary actions.

Law school graduates still have much to learn in order to successfully practice law. In particular, an ability to lead oneself toward appropriate conduct is critical to a young lawyer's success. Thoughtful consideration of one's own "life story" is a highly useful way to pay special attention to the important attributes of a lawyer's professional life. Appreciating the lessons (and blunders) resulting from one's experiences and embracing a meaningful understanding of personal strengths and weaknesses in leading others shape how a person learns to be an authentic leader.[23] Similarly, understanding the importance in professional life of the five key components of "emotional intelligence"—self-awareness, self-regulation, motivation, empathy, and social skills—can literally only come from a genuine and thorough "study of self."[24]

Reflecting on your personal-best leadership experience is a particularly powerful way to gain insights about yourself as a leader and the behaviors that matter. Describing a situation where you were at your personal best as a leader is an effective method for realizing that you are already a leader and capable of making a difference. The follow-up is taking the time to discern from this experience and determine what you need to learn so that you can be an even better leader and be even more comfortable engaging in the leadership behaviors that matter, building on your strengths and taking actions to improve on areas of weakness.

The process of self-examination, leading to a great understanding of leadership capabilities, is often an important outcome of completing a leadership course in law school.[25] Although such courses are a meaningful way to hone leadership skills, many students don't appreciate this benefit. Unfortunately, the majority of students who don't take a leadership course in law school choose not to do so because of a very short-sighted view that the information covered will not be on the bar exam. Furthermore, they believe that they can learn leadership on the job. In these regards, they are misinformed—and usually just plain wrong.

Leadership Role Models

Moving beyond self-evaluation and your own personal-best leadership experience is examining the personal-best leadership experiences of others. This analysis can only strengthen and deepen your understanding about leadership as a process, one that you can adapt and apply in various contexts.

Role models play an important part in the formation of leadership attitudes for law students. Many lawyers understand the necessity of change and recognize the importance of being able to effectively lead others through change because of past leadership examples from school, social groups, internships, and previous jobs. They've witnessed good leadership examples and poor ones, and they have been able to gain and incorporate lessons from both. If you keep your eyes open, the same can be said about your time in law school. What are the behaviors of your best teachers, and how do they make you feel (e.g., respected, motivated)? In contrast, how do your least favorite teachers lead in the classroom? Look around at your classmates who have accepted leadership of or been selected to chair various law school organizations and activities. Again, what behaviors differentiate the best leaders from the rest?

Analyzing the behaviors of those whom you admire as leaders is an important avenue for learning about how to lead—by emulating what these leaders do well and by avoiding those behaviors that result in mediocrity and disincentive. Pay attention when you have the opportunity to view, interact with, and work with lawyers (or judges) who manage or supervise lawyers and student clerks and interns. The observations and lessons that students bring to the classroom from these experiences are that effective lawyer leaders, regardless of the type of legal entity, manage themselves and their time well; convey a sense of mission and enterprise to everyone (including secretaries, paralegals, and law clerks); are truthful and respectful; and have ennobling ideals. This blend of competence as a lawyer and heartfelt commitment to service is inspiring to law students, and to law firm associates beginning their careers as lawyers.

One third-year law student related his experience as a law firm clerk for two managing lawyers. One was highly competent and patient, giving clear instructions and frequently explaining to everyone how important their work was for the cases and transactions that the office was handling. The other was petty and sometimes mean to subordinates and often covered up his own shortcomings by blaming others. The student reported that he learned from both of these lawyers, but the lessons learned from the latter, were both cautionary and, to some degree, damaging to the student.

It is true enough that sometimes a law student or new law firm associate can learn useful practice skills from an assigned supervisor who is an ineffective or even a negative manager/leader (role model). However, law students who witness ineffective and negative leadership in their formative stage often form a negative opinion of the practice of law and of the legal profession. If this is your experience, then you need to balance the equation by finding experiences to be with positive, inspiring lawyers who model effective leadership. Furthermore, though you may work for a poor leader, you don't have to be mentored by one.

Learning that leadership matters in attorney–client and workplace relationships is a crucial realization as you transition from student to young lawyer and even from novice to accomplished lawyer. By observing role models in action, students have discovered that leadership skills and attributes coalesce into highly effective lawyering skills and attributes.

FOLLOWING THROUGH

- Developing skills for the effective, ethical practice of leadership mirrors the process of developing skills for the effective, ethical practice of law.
- It is essential for law students to reflect on who they are and what they care about, as well as the values and beliefs that drive their actions, in order to keenly understand the professional world they will be entering, and the challenges inherent in their decision to become a lawyer.
- Law students, while looking forward to a professional life of considerable responsibility, autonomy, and self-direction, will be confronted with the demands of service to others and quickly achieving a high level of practice skills and legal knowledge. Law practice is, in many respects, a retail business with various client demands and needs. Students often ponder and wrestle with the question: "How can I keep focused on my personal values while facing competing and often inconsistent demands?"
- Students must clarify their personal values and aspirations and thoughtfully examine the skills and attitudes needed for success as a lawyer, figuring out how to align those two perspectives in their personal and professional lives. Leadership development provides an effective way of beginning that analysis and preparing for a lifetime quest of integrating these twin demands.
- Law practice and the legal profession require practitioners who appreciate the connection between leadership and the practice of law and successfully model the way to incorporate the two.
- Students need to identify and connect with mentors, even in the absence of a formal mentoring program in law school or in law practice. The research is clear that having mentoring relationships during formative career stages materially increases the likelihood of success in the practice of law.
- One important area in which lawyers become role models is how they view ethical issues and handle the inevitable choices that must be made in the practice of law. Learning to lead one's self is the best method of handling those issues, while as a law student and continuing to discern throughout one's career.

REFLECTIONS

1. Think about your personal characteristics. What do your stand for? Identify three to five of your top attributes; qualities that you believe distinguish you (such as intelligence, kindness, decisiveness, etc.) Where's the evidence that you are living up to these characteristics?

2. What is important to you in your life—as a person, a citizen, and an aspiring attorney? How are these domains similar? Where do they conflict, and what are you prepared to do about any disconnects?

3. When it comes to the law and/or leadership, who are your role models? On what basis did you select these individuals? What characteristics do they have in common, and what does that suggest in regard to your own behaviors and actions?

4. Who is a lawyer leader who you find is a positive role model? Is this person's professional identity as a lawyer or as a leader more prominent, or are the two identities approximately equal? Do you feel that this is a good distribution? Explain.

NINE

Becoming an Ethical Lawyer and Leader

Lawyer leaders share an important responsibility to act ethically in their service to and relationships with their followers.

THE LEAD-IN

- Values, Ethics, and Morals in Law and Leadership
- Ethical, Service-Oriented Lawyer Leadership
    - Service
    - Ethics
    - Ethical Service across Roles
- Ethical Leadership and Clients
    - Trust, Reputation, and Confidence
    - Informal Leadership Role
    - The Lawyer as Counselor
- Formal versus Informal Leadership
    - Leadership and Lack of Formal Authority to Lead
    - Law School Student Organizations
    - Leadership Established by Position of Authority
- Leadership Education in the Legal Profession
    - Law Practice Pressures and Tensions
    - Broader Obligations of Lawyering
- Following Through
- Reflections

The work of lawyers requires a clear ethical focus. Law is a values-driven profession in which its practitioners receive great benefits in both status and compensation and are held to high societal expectations and ethical requirements. Being guardians of the law, lawyers are among the most powerful societal class in America, and they are generally expected to meet personal and professional standards that are higher than those expected of other professionals and their fellow citizens. Little of life in America proceeds without the involvement of lawyers (with "the law" often being implicit), so lawyers' commitment to ethical behavior is critically important to both social and political order, as well as to sustain the exalted status of the legal profession.

Lawyers cannot be ambivalent about what they believe is right and wrong, nor can they question whether they *should* do "the right thing." Similarly, there is a moral compass that leaders must use to lead the way in their relationships with their followers. It derives, as we've noted several times, from the personal values of leaders and their commitment to the service of others rather than to themselves.

Leaders model the way and set an example for others to embrace and follow, and this influence is most powerful when people observe their leaders acting in ways that are consistent with their beliefs, and especially with shared values. The work of leaders, then—from articulating the values of the organization and inspiring action by their constituents and clients, to reinforcing the team's goals—is a manifestation of the leader's personal values. They shape the sense of what is needed and, when aligned with those of others around them, are motivational in enlisting others in a common vision and establishing guide rails for acting and moving forward.

Clearly, ethics play an outsized role in both law and leadership. And although not all lawyers take on formal leadership roles, leadership is an element of most (perhaps all) lawyers' roles, so an examination of ethical service in lawyer leadership is important. There is a close fit in how lawyers' duties to their clients, to society, and to the legal profession align with their duties to followers and others in their service as leaders. The front line of interaction between leaders and their followers, and between lawyers and their clients, is the influence that leaders and lawyers apply to their relationships. To be most effective, both lawyers and leaders must employ ethical persuasion, which moves others toward shared goals. The needs of the legal profession—and, by extension, the broader duties of lawyers to the legal system, its institutions, and the public—require effective, ethical leadership. It is fair to say, therefore, that in order to mold ethical leaders, law schools must improve their leadership and development education—it is indeed their ethical responsibility to the profession to do so.

Values, Ethics, and Morals in Law and Leadership

Discussions about the obligations of lawyers and of leaders often revolve around beliefs and conclusions about the significant roles that ethics and morals play on the values and behaviors of the leader or lawyer. Values are learned and are viewed as mental constructs or "states of affairs" that are considered by the individual to be important to them.[1] People frame their own values in terms of modes of behavior (being honest, or being intelligent) and in terms of desired states of being (like living a comfortable life, or having a reputation for honesty).

Your values are your own, although they are often shaped through the process of socialization by your parents, family, friends, and teachers. Your values may or may not involve ethics or morals. Ethics is a branch of philosophy that uses reason to arrive at principles or rules to govern the conduct of yourself and others. Morality, which is often conflated with ethics, is really focused on how various rules of conduct are applied or followed in actual behavior. They are the "shoulds" and "oughts" of peoples' lives.[2] Ethical and moral reasoning should not be confused with codes of ethical conduct, such as the Model Rules of Professional Conduct governing lawyers' behaviors, although many of the proscriptions and advisory guides in a code of "ethics" may be based in ethical or moral norms.

These concepts of individual values, and moral and ethical reasoning, are critically important for lawyers and leaders. The formation of a personal identity as a lawyer requires students to develop a "fiduciary mindset" embracing the ethics of duty to serve clients, the ethics of aspiring to meet the core values and principles of the legal profession, a values commitment to develop independent professional judgment to help clients through decisions for their benefit, and to provide public services to improve the justice system and advance the rule of law.[3]

Your efforts to reason through to correct decisions or outcomes will result in more ethically and morally sound choices than otherwise. Everyone has implicit biases or prejudices that affect their decision making, generally without any real appreciation or realization that they have them.[4] Ethical decision making and judgment are also negatively affected by the tendency to favor people who are like yourself and when being insensitive to recognizing a conflict of interest.

Ethical, Service-Oriented Lawyer Leadership

The combination of service and ethics defines lawyer leaders. Like lawyers who serve their clients, lawyer leaders serve their followers by enabling them to clarify their goals, clearly articulating strategies to achieve these objectives, and providing the moral support and resources necessary for people to persevere in order to achieve success—and they do it by building on a foundation of ethics.

Service

Studies have found that what generally attracts people to law school is their desire to serve others. The *After the JD* longitudinal study confirmed that lawyers report high satisfaction with their careers because the legal profession permits them to provide value to society.[5]

For lawyers who serve others through leadership roles, the satisfaction levels can be substantial. The ability to help others achieve their aspirations is motivational and rewards leaders as their followers' experience success. Recent law school graduates find themselves surprised by how frequently they are asked to provide legal advice (often without compensation!), and to offer their perspective and judgment in pro bono work with nonprofit and community organizations. Society generally considers these both informally and formally to be part of lawyers' duties is to the public; that is, more than simply a good thing to be doing but also the "right" thing to do. The Preamble to the Model Rules of Professional Conduct encourages lawyers "to improve the law and the legal profession, and to exemplify the legal profession's ideals of public service."[6]

Ethics

As a profession, lawyers agree to conform their actions to a code of professional responsibility and to be held accountable for their actions through disciplinary rules and canons of professional conduct. As a law student you are introduced to the ethics of the profession in the required course in professional responsibility; and, in most jurisdictions, would-be lawyers must pass a professional responsibility examination before they can even sit for the bar exam. In addition, lawyers must annually satisfy ethics education requirements.

Just as ethics matter in the professional life of lawyers, they are also a foundational aspect of leadership and linked with the credibility of those lawyers who lead others in their roles as lawyers. There is no examination of professional responsibility for lawyer leaders. So what guides them in the performance of their leadership roles? There is a fundamental quality to leadership that is rooted in ethical behavior and moral influences for lawyers who lead themselves and others. In particular, successful lawyer leaders are those who take the ethos of their ethical standards to the leadership roles that they assume and who use their skills as advocates and counselors to influence for a greater good those whom they lead.

Ethical Service across Roles

Lawyer leaders, regardless of their roles, share an important responsibility to act ethically in their service to and relationships with their followers. Lawyers practice law in many settings and situations and across myriad relationships that require leadership. For example, lawyers exercise leadership in their roles as managing partners of law firms, general counsel of companies, and heads of legal departments. They demonstrate leadership in their relationships advising clients on legal, business, or personal matters; establishing strategy in litigation or transactions; or engaging with co-counsel, opposing counsel, or judicial officers in various matters. These situations and relationships, and others like them, require the same essential skills and attributes—importantly, ethical behavior—that leaders in public and private organizations use and apply when persuading their constituencies to work toward a common objective.

Ethical Leadership and Clients

Advising and counseling clients is a form of ethical leadership that requires both strong ethical foundations and strong leadership skills. The duty to act ethically flows directly from the moral and practical relationship between lawyers (leaders) and clients (followers). Moral and ethical norms have a central importance to services as a leader. Leaders are judged by the framework of values that is the basis of their relationship with their followers—establishing levels of trust between leader and follower.[7]

Trust, Reputation, and Confidence

Ethical leadership entails being trustworthy. Good people deserve good leadership, and trust is the foundation for any meaningful relationship. Without trust, you cannot lead. Without trust, you cannot get people to believe in you or even in one another. You build trust on the basis of vulnerability, that is, a willingness to go first and put yourself at some risk before you can be certain that you will not be taken advantage of in some way by the other party. You inspire trust from others to the extent that you are seen as honest and committed to the best interests of the individual (or team or organization) with which you are working. While not everyone will be 100 percent honest every time, the truth is that people don't commit to (versus comply with) the requests of someone they believe to be lying or deceitful. People's levels of motivation decrease, often dramatically, when they perceive a leader as dishonest or as someone who has not kept commitments and promises—that is, as being hypocritical and/or unethical.[8]

Trustworthiness implicates reputation, which, in turn, affects the relationship between leaders and their followers. The duty of lawyers to act ethically flows not only from serving as advisors and counselors to their clients, but also from ethical norms imposed by legal sources (e.g., licensing authorities like state supreme courts) and peer advisory groups (e.g., bar associations). These normative prescriptions can, if contravened by a lawyer's conduct with respect to a client, result in disciplinary action. More fundamentally, failing to act with honesty and integrity will damage a lawyer's reputation. Robert S. Bennett, the Washington, DC, lawyer who represented several US presidents and other top government officials, advised that "[t]he single most important quality a lawyer must have is a reputation for honesty and integrity" because "judges and lawyers know who can be trusted and who can't be trusted."[9]

Trustworthiness also implicates confidence, that is, the confidence of clients that they can trust their attorney and their attorney's competence and judgment. Lawyer–client relationships demand more than your technical and lawyering skills, even if they are considerable, and the reputation you may have deservedly earned for those skills. The client expects you to know what you are talking about when giving advice and counsel; although clients are seldom knowledgeable enough about the law to dispute your arguments, most essential is that they believe that you can be trusted, are acting with integrity, and have their best interests at heart.

This premise has been referred to as *the first law of leadership*—"If you don't believe in the messenger, you won't believe the message."[10] Juries and judges also tend to adhere to this same premise.

Academic counselors wisely inform law students that their grades and academic proficiency can be important in getting their first job. Thereafter, however, no one really cares about how well you performed in school; rather, it is about how well you develop a composite of technical skills and build a reputation for having integrity, exhibiting good judgment, conferring sound counsel, and demonstrating unflagging commitment to the cause of the client—in other words, being an ethical leader.

Informal Leadership Role

Only in exceptional circumstances do lawyers have hierarchical or authoritative control over their clients. Instead, lawyers lead their clients though their service to the clients; and working together, they achieve what is appropriate, desired, and realizable.

Lawyers have a responsibility to help clients think through their best interests, assisting them in arriving at the best decision—from the clients' perspective—and then honoring and supporting that decision. It is important to note that a client's perspective may, at times, differ from your own perspective. For example, you may believe that it is possible to win the case in court, but the client would rather plead to a lesser charge and be released from jail. The choice, of course, is the client's.

This complex dynamic between lawyers and clients has confused some observers, as they fail to comprehend the role of leadership that the lawyer plays in guiding and informing the client through the process of achieving the client's goals and honoring the client's decisions.

Think of it this way: You would not be counseling your client very well by exclaiming, "Just follow me!!" Instead, you will be a better counselor by saying something more along the lines of, "Let me help you."

This multifaceted relationship between the lawyer's official role in legal proceedings and the notion that lawyers cannot "lead" their clients has been rightfully described as a paradox (i.e., two choices that are contradictory but interdependent).[11] Although the core roles that lawyers play as advocates for clients and those when they are leading change are seemingly in opposition, there are constructive approaches to reconcile and accommodate these oppositional influences in the work that lawyers do. Many successful lawyer leaders have built useful bridges between their work as leaders and their work as advocates.

The Lawyer as Counselor

When looking for a bridge between the lawyer advocate and the lawyer leader, it is useful to consider the attributes of a "skilled counselor." These attributes include both service-oriented and ethics-oriented leadership components.

The *Model Rules of Professional Conduct* describe the instrumental role that attorneys provide in counseling and advising their clients. Rule 2.1 ("Advisor") requires lawyers, in representing a client, to "exercise independent professional judgment and render candid advice," including references to "relevant moral and ethical considerations."[12] These professional standards require that lawyers act in a manner that is morally appropriate and conforms to ethical norms. Further, attorneys are required to advise their clients about appropriate and inappropriate conduct. This policy of Rule 2.1 is not intended to turn lawyers into moral philosophers or preachers about some undefined set of ethical considerations. Rather, it is intended to inform lawyers that they should be guided by what is right, avoid clearly prohibited actions and improper advice, improve the country's legal institutions, and make a more just society.

A skilled counselor, in the context of the legal profession, can be described as a lawyer who has developed and evolved into a client's most valuable resource in managing risk, appreciating legal restrictions and consequences, and making sound personal and business decisions. Obviously, such lawyers have excellent leadership skills. They constantly strive to both listen well and understand what the clients' goals and wishes are. Doing so permits them to identify opportunities for settling cases that result in a "win–win" for all parties. They are able to empathize with their clients' economic plight or legal problem without judging them. They have impeccable integrity and view themselves as fiduciaries to their clients and their clients' concerns. Judge Benjamin Cardozo described the high duty that fiduciaries, such as lawyers, owe to others as "something stricter than the morals of the market place. Not honesty alone, but the punctilio of an honor the most sensitive, is then the standard of behavior.... [T]he level of conduct for fiduciaries [has] been kept at a level higher than that trodden by the crowd."[13]

In addition, a skilled counselor has the ability to put the client's interest in the context of the lawyer's complex role as counselor, advocate, and public citizen. These lawyers are able to subordinate their own ego for the benefit of their clients. They are clear-eyed about what they are dealing with and exercise sound professional judgment. Their experience and their personal traits permit them to look at the big picture in formulating advice for their clients. They have the ability to conceptualize what the client wants, integrated with what the client needs, and provide advice accordingly.

Formal versus Informal Leadership

In examining lawyers' relationships to their clients and others, you must consider the distinction between lawyers performing duties in situations where they have formal, direct authority (that is, they have legal or factual authority to take action for others) and those where they do not have formal authority but rather influence the decisions that are made by others.[14] The difference in leadership roles between those situations in which the individual has clear authority and those situations where formal authority is lacking is an especially important distinction for lawyers. The absence of authority changes the dynamics and may require the leader to use a different calculation of skills (in particular, different ethical persuasive skills), attitudes, and behaviors in achieving desired outcomes.

However, it is important to recognize that there is not one leadership theory or approach for people who have legitimate authority or a position of power over others and another leadership framework for those who don't have such authority or power but still need to move others toward mutual objectives. Lawyers who lead others because they have direct authority—such as in heading up the corporate legal department, leading a group of military lawyers in litigation, or serving as CEO of a nonprofit organization—can easily employ The Five Practices of Exemplary Leadership® (detailed in part II). Lawyers who have no formal, directing authority—such as when engaging with clients, mentoring young associates in the firm, or serving as an officer of the state bar association—can still use many of those same leadership practices, although they adjust as needed to account for the informality of their leadership role in their relationship with colleagues.[15]

Leadership and Lack of Formal Authority to Lead

Some of attorneys' most important roles, for example, counseling clients, are ones where they lack any formal authority or a position of power and must, instead, rely on persuasion and influence to properly and ethically lead. A client is not the lawyer's follower; the attorney has a fiduciary relationship with the client, but this doesn't necessarily confer a legitimate right to require the client to defer to or follow the lawyer's counsel.

For example, when clients advise their lawyers that they plan to violate the law, their attorneys can only offer perspective and counsel on the implications of this future course of action, lacking any formal authority to direct the clients' behavior and choices. The rules of professional conduct, however, do prescribe that the lawyer withdraw from representing such clients if, after advising these people, the individuals proceed with the unlawful conduct. (By the way, attorneys are not responsible for their clients taking actions that are detrimental to their case but not illegal.)

Law School Student Organizations

A rich ground for understanding the differences between formal and informal authority to lead is the realm of student organizations in law school and how their leaders influence their peers in making good decisions. Dozens of students have told us about the challenges of leading student organizations and of inspiring and motivating their followers (fellow students).

No doubt, at one time or another, you and/or your friends have frustrated student leaders by playing "pizza grab-and-go." Leaders of student organizations (even faculty administrators) frequently use free pizza (or its equivalence) as the lure to attract students to lunchtime sessions with invited speakers. Often, however, student leaders are disappointed to note that many students show up at the beginning of the presentation, grab a few slices of pizza, and leave to enjoy their lunch elsewhere. More disheartening is that sometimes the pizza-purloining students are actually members of the student organization that sponsored the speaker!

The point is about more than pizza and involves an ethics lesson in appropriate behavior by organizational members and by the leaders. Student leaders typically lack direct authority over the invited students and even the members of their organization. They want to have a good turnout (audience) for their invited speakers but can't develop a plan to entice students to attend other than free food. The "right thing" for the student members is to either skip the event or, if they attend, to enjoy the educational experience augmented by pizza. The group leaders need to persuade their members that the act of participation is connected to their duties as students and group members and would be a decision to act in a morally appropriate manner.

One of our students faced a somewhat similar situation when serving as chair of a volunteer committee of trainee solicitors (lawyers) from across Manchester, England.[16] The national Trainee Solicitors Group arranged a conference to take place in his city for all of the trainees in the United Kingdom, and he wanted his committee to make the event successful in terms of attendance numbers, although the event was formally outside of the usual committee's responsibilities.

He got his colleagues together and publicly declared that he was willing to do all that he could to ensure that there would be at least three hundred delegates at the event. (With three weeks to go, the enrollment was only at seventy-five.) After sharing his own feelings—"I spoke passionately about how good it would feel to be there at a packed event and to look around thinking that we had achieved that"—he invited others on the committee to similarly commit to this attendance goal. Since this event was neither part of the committee's goals nor the reason members had volunteered for the committee, he wouldn't have been surprised had the majority said no. To his "pure joy" sixteen out of the twenty members said yes, they were willing to do all they could to make the event a success. And the fact that there were some "doubters" actually energized everyone involved, he noted, and "the committee members were more passionate than I had ever seen them before." In the end, after a solid, combined effort from all quarters, they succeeded in getting over three hundred attendees to the event.

His passion not only fueled his own drive but also was contagious in getting others to work as hard as they could to realize a future possibility. His commitment to a highly successful event, together with being a role model for his colleagues, not only accomplished the group's goal but also strengthened the bonds of all members to succeed together, teaching both the practical and the aspirational aspects of doing the right thing.

Leadership Established by Position of Authority

Lawyers do, at times, provide leadership in situations where they exert or possess varying degrees of formal authority. For example, lawyers have formal leadership authority when they work in administrative and management roles for their law organizations (e.g., managing partner, general counsel); when they lead other organizations (public or private), perhaps in an advisory role or on a volunteer basis; and when they are judges instructing defendants (or jurors or courtroom counsel) about what they can or cannot do.

The rules governing the ethical behavior of lawyers not only apply to these formal leadership situations, but also recognize the significant formal leadership role that lawyers play in society. Lawyers are viewed as "public citizens" who are "officers of the court" and possess "special responsibility for the quality of justice" and "a vital role in the preservation of society."[17] The governing rules of conduct articulate a broad set of professional duties to preserve a "government under law."[18] Essentially, therefore, all lawyers (whether in government, a law firm, etc.) serve in positions of formal authority in terms of society and thus have fiduciary duties to exercise their authority and power ethically in the service of justice and the rule of law.

It is noteworthy that lawyers in positions with formal authority manifest their leadership through persuasion and influence just as lawyers with clients do, but the persuasion and influence of formal lawyer leaders have more unquestioned power. For example, lawyers in government service practice law in a mostly hierarchical setting, with lines of legitimate authority and responsibility, such that they can, and must at times, use their rank to issue commands and orders that others have little choice but to follow. Still, if they are good listeners, respected, demonstrate good judgment, and use their powers of persuasion rather than privilege, others will follow irrespective of their rank or authority.

Leadership Education in the Legal Profession

Law students are often introduced on their very first day of law school to the idea that they are joining "a learned profession" and that this connotes something unique and distinctive, elevated beyond simply a job or occupation. However, too often the follow-up to this rhetoric is lacking, even missing entirely, as evidenced by the scant effort that law schools make to educate their students on what it means to be a member of a profession.

So, what does it mean to be a member of a profession—specifically, the legal profession? Are there unique differences implicating exclusive duties and responsibilities for participation in the legal profession, such as licensing or regulatory considerations, that demand ethical behavior and standards beyond those expected from other professions and professionals? In particular, are there unique differences implying exclusive duties for lawyer leaders? And how do lawyers integrate their duties as lawyers and their duties as leaders? An avenue for navigating the tensions between serving as a lawyer and serving as a leader is leadership education and development.

Law Practice Pressures and Tensions

In the contemporary practice of law, there are considerable tensions between serving clients' interests, serving the legal institutions, such as courts and government organizations, and serving the public good—all of which are duties of lawyers.

Law students are often taught that the client's interests are the lawyer's priority, to the exclusion of other considerations. In corporate law practices, lawyers may be torn between multiple pressures in situations where economic considerations force them to promote strategies and tactics in litigation, negotiations, and transactions that they may find distasteful. Lawyers often opt for the easy route of saying, "I am morally opposed to this behavior, but I have to engage in it to keep the client, sustain my monthly billable hours, and the like." This refrain often becomes a slippery slope. Lawyers, like everyone else, should keep in mind that they must model ethical behavior to earn and sustain people's trust and respect.

Law students often return to campus from clerking or internship engagements in which they routinely observed experienced lawyers modeling inappropriate behavior. This troubles them, especially because they lack the ability to put such behavior into an acceptable context and, moreover, often found themselves compelled to take the same actions. A key lesson here is that there is no "playbook" for appropriate professional conduct (although the rules of professional responsibility provide a foundation), and every law student and young lawyer needs to build their own, constructed from their personal values and beliefs and their recognition that they are part of a profession.

Law schools need to focus more on leadership education and development in order to address these pressures and tensions. For example, in representing clients in matters involving government agency regulation of the clients' conduct or activities, lawyers often take defensive positions to minimize the clients' exposure to risk and liability. What may be lacking or missing are the occasions when lawyers counsel their clients on the importance of compliance with the law and with agency policies and not just the method of eluding detection or sanctions—that is, an emphasis on doing what is right rather than avoiding being caught or punished for doing what is wrong. Leadership courses can educate law students about finding opportunities to emphasize doing what is right.

Broader Obligations of Lawyering

While the rules of professional conduct suggest that the lawyer's obligation is to satisfy the client's rights, interests, and desires, the canons also recognize the broader obligations of lawyering. The primary obligation of lawyers, according to Roger Cramton, a highly respected expert on legal ethics, is to "the procedures and institutions of the law," which reflect the lawyer's duty to advance the rule of law and improve the legal institutions that lawyers are expected to lead.[19] Clearly, lawyers' behaviors are largely contextual when they serve as litigators, negotiators, and counselors, for example; but in all of those contexts, they have deep duties to their clients as well as duties as officers of the court and as public citizens.

Unfortunately, law schools have failed to educate students more deeply on the broader array of duties that they owe after admission to the bar, having relegated the composition of ethical duties to a single course and failing to deeply engage students in the ethical and moral dimensions of law practice. Supreme Court Justice Ruth Bader Ginsburg was fond of a story about a first-year law student who expressed concern about the ethical implications of a class discussion. The professor was describing a lawyer's tactic that left the student "bothered and bewildered," so the student asked, "What about ethics?" "Ethics," the professor coolly explained, "is taught in the second year."[20]

It is not that law schools never discuss ethics. Professors may challenge their students by presenting both actual and hypothetical situations that test their ability to lead themselves and others in an ethical manner while dealing with the demands of the work that lawyers do in various contexts. And students learn that the rules of professional conduct do not require lawyers to abandon their morals when they work with clients or when they enter the courthouse doors.

There are avenues for withdrawing from representation if continuing raises ethical concerns and problems. Of course, lawyers do have opportunities to discuss, and perhaps influence, their clients regarding both moral and practical implications of the strategies and tactics associated with litigation, negotiation, and transactions.

Nonetheless, the key focus of law students and young lawyers should be on the broad set of duties that they owe not just to clients but also to the legal system and its institutions and to the public. Lawyers are not just technicians of the law and legal system—they are guardians and protectors of the values and ethics of these institutions, the systems of laws, and the virtues associated with the rule of law. Law schools have a responsibility to indoctrinate students into this set of duties in order to properly educate future lawyer leaders.

FOLLOWING THROUGH

- Lawyers enter the legal profession because they have a desire to serve others.
- As guardians of the law, lawyers must adhere to high personal and professional standards and commit to ethical behavior.
- Ethical persuasion is the foundation of ethical, service-oriented lawyer leadership, and a skill that can be learned.
- Lawyers practice in various settings and situations, only some of which entail official leadership positions. In a typical lawyer–client relationship, lawyers don't act as formal leaders but rather lead their clients via their role as counselor to make wise, legal, and appropriate decisions.
- Regardless of whether the leadership role is formal or not, the same basic skills and abilities are necessary—as is a foundation of ethical behavior.
- A more concerted effort toward leadership education and development in law schools would help their graduates not only handle the constant stream of tensions and pressures that test their ethics, but also prepare for their broader obligations as officers of the court and public citizens.

REFLECTIONS

1. What does it mean to be ethical? How do you determine if an action is ethical, fair, or just? In what ways did the course in professional responsibility satisfactorily (or not) answer your questions about appropriate ethical comportment in the practice of law?

2. When, if ever, do the ends justify the means? What philosophical or ethical principle would you use to determine such a situation as an attorney? How about as an individual (e.g., partner, employee, coworker, parent, friend, etc.)?

3. What does it mean for a lawyer to behave as a counselor? How do lawyers and leaders persuade people to do things that they are not already doing? When does persuasion become pressure and/or manipulation?

4. What has your experience participating in student organizations while in school taught you about leadership, but also about being a good team player?

TEN

Making Decisions, Leading Innovation

Good decisions are reflections of good judgment, which is literally the 'calling card' of the most successful lawyers and one of their most valuable abilities.

THE LEAD-IN

- Scope of Decision Making
- Decision Making: Judgment and Experience
    - Judgment Honed by Experience
    - Judgment, Experience, and Values
    - Process of Making Good Judgment Calls
    - Judgment: A Learned Skill
- Mechanics of Making Sound Decisions
    - Classifying the Decision
    - Delineating the Problem
    - Getting It Right
    - Planning for Action
    - Gauging Effectiveness
    - Stepping Outside of the Process
- Challenge of Indecision
    - Causes of Indecision
    - Solutions to Indecision
- Effective Change and Leadership
    - Components of Change
    - Need for Change

  - Incremental versus Disruptive Change
- Change and Innovation
  - Innovative Decision Making versus Traditional Problem Solving
  - Components of Innovation
  - Roadblocks to Innovation
  - Innovation and the Need for Leadership
- Following Through
- Reflections

Lawyers constantly make decisions. Lawyers make decisions in the practice of law, in the management of their firms, and in their personal lives. Decisions made in the practice of law frequently have great consequences for the lawyers themselves, for their clients, and for their professional organizations. Every decision means changes, and change is the province of leadership. Attorneys who are effective decision makers—based on the speed at which decisions are reached, the soundness of the decisions, and the ability to convince all of the parties involved that the decisions are the right ones to make—are valued highly. The decision to lead change, to become an agent of change, is a critically important decision for lawyer leaders in their organizations, starting with the decision about whether and what changes are necessary or desirable.

On the one hand, many decisions that lawyers make are routine, even mundane at times. On the other hand, lawyers often have to make significant, even life-or-death, decisions for their clients, firms, and other legal entities. During the past decade, the business of law has experienced dramatic challenges and market disruptions, and there is little reason to believe that these will dissipate or disappear anytime soon. They may, in fact, accelerate in scale and scope in the future, placing increasing importance on leadership. The decisions that lawyer leaders need to make in the face of these extraordinary trends require a talent for innovation in adapting to and leading change.

Scope of Decision Making

The scope of lawyers' decision making is broad and closely connected to the roles that they fill in their organizations (for example, corporate counsel or district attorney), the clients whom they serve, and their relationship to those clients.

The ability to ensure that good decisions are made is what lawyers, in large part, are paid to do as one of the fundamental or core services that they provide to their clients. Decision making, of course, varies by clients and by situations. Cases involving clients who are facing substantial prison sentences or the death penalty introduce a different level of stress and consequences for making effective decisions than do choices, for example, on handling incorporation for a new start-up business or handling a complex real estate transition. Still, the individual and organizational consequences for a patent application error, a missed antitrust issue, an incomplete entertainment contract, and the like can be quite severe and consequential. Irrespective of the complexity of the task with which lawyers are presented and the severity of the consequences for their decisions, the process for making effective decisions has more similarity than differences.

Any discussion of lawyer decision making would not be complete without a reminder that there are certain decisions that lawyers make and there are particular decisions that their clients make. This is an important distinction (or set of questions) that consumes important time and materials in the professional responsibility class required for all law school students to complete. Some decisions in the practice of law are made only by the client, and the attorney must accept that the decision was made solely by the client with or without the advice of counsel—for example, if it is up to the client to accept or reject a plea deal, or to go to trial in a civil case that could cost the client a great deal in litigation and business expenses.

Conversely, there are decisions that are made solely by the lawyer. For example, a trial lawyer doesn't ask a client if the client's case should be filed in federal court or in state court if there is no federal jurisdiction or if the proper motion is for judgment on the pleadings. The lawyer may advise the client on the decision that the lawyer reaches, but it is a judgment call shaped by the lawyer's experience and strategizing and by the particularities of the case. Finally, there is a set of issues about which clients make decisions with the assistance of the lawyer—for example, where a decision must be made on a transaction, such as forming a business relationship or arranging a corporate acquisition, which call for the client's business skills and the lawyer's legal judgment. Perhaps, technically, these are "client decisions," but the reality is that the lawyer serves the client's needs by shaping an understanding of the nature and complexity of the case or issue and guiding the client toward an appropriate decision that they both implement and accept. This is often referred to as "servant leadership" of the client.[1]

Although lawyers make many client-related decisions, it is obvious that lawyers make many decisions that have nothing, or very little, to do with their clients. Law firms' decisions, for example, about hiring and firing matters, purchasing assets to support the law practice or business, and joining the local or national bar association are all decisions that lawyers frequently make that have no real connection to a client's needs or the lawyer's role in advising the client. Lawyers, in situations like these, function much like decision makers would in any business setting.

A third decision-making arena takes place when a lawyer is in public service (for example, a member of Congress or legal advisor to the governor). Decisions in these settings are often shaped by the lawyer's perception of the best interests of the public (citizens) and/or the governmental entity. These decisions are as influential as other decisions made for, or together with, individual clients.

In all of these settings and situations, decision making is complex because typically one decision leads to another decision and so on. For leaders, there is no dearth of decision-making experiences, and each decision is as important as the next. There is an expression that "one bad decision leads to another," and this can, unfortunately, hold true in the scope of a lawyer's duties. Much like the experience of a sailor or engineer, a small error at the beginning of a voyage or a small error in the design of software will have huge consequences farther down the line. These experiences—where sound or poor decisions at the beginning of a litigated case or a business deal affect the success of the legal matter—are common among lawyers and suggest the accuracy of the old saying, "hindsight is 20/20." But they also serve to create a bank of experiences that lawyers can draw on and often to share with junior associates to lead more successful ventures in the future.

Decision Making: Judgment and Experience

Given that these settings where lawyers make decisions and the scope of decision making expected of lawyers is broad, how do lawyers excel at making decisions for themselves and for others? What are the characteristics of good decision making, and how can they be learned?

Lawyers develop and hone their capacity to arrive at effective decisions over time; through education and intelligence, as well as the drive and motivation to succeed (win), and, in particular, judgment shaped by their on-the-job experiences.

Judgment Honed by Experience

Good decisions by lawyers and by leaders alike are reflections of good judgment, which is literally the "calling card" of the most successful lawyers and one of their most valuable abilities. Lawyers make judgment calls all the time. Whether or not to accept a particular client or agree to take on a case, whom to hire and to retain, and what advice to give a client about accepting a plea arrangement offered by the district attorney—these are all examples of the decisions commonly made by lawyers that are strongly shaped on the basis of their judgment.

Law students and new lawyers often ask how good judgment is acquired by exceptional lawyers, and the straightforward answer is that it is gained through experience. Illustrating the point, presidential advisor and lawyer Ted Sorenson recounted this story about how lawyers acquire judgment:

> A new associate happens to be seated at lunch next to a senior partner and the younger person says to the veteran, "Tell me, why is it you have this big reputation for judgment?" "Well," the partner replies, "there are people who seem to respect my judgment." "If you don't mind my asking another question, why do they respect your judgment?" "Well, I guess I've made the right decision enough times," the partner says. "If you don't mind me bothering you, what was the basis on which you made the right decision?" "Oh," the partner replies, "that comes from experience." "One last question: What's the experience based on?" "Wrong decisions," the partner replies.[2]

Judgment, Experience, and Values

Experience will shape how leaders choose to apply their judgment to incorporate their values into their decisions. When lawyers are exercising leadership and/or in leadership roles, their decisions are not made in a bubble; rather, those decisions are evaluated by their followers. For example, a decision to take on a controversial client (perhaps representation of an alleged child molester or a controversial organization such as the National Rifle Association or Planned Parenthood) may have implications on how others view you, or the firm, in one direction or another. Of course, representing a client you don't agree with might say a lot about your commitment to the legal process, and doesn't mean you necessarily support gun ownership or abortion.

This is not to suggest that you should only take on cases, clients, and projects that are popular but rather that the decisions lawyers make, large and small, send significant signals about their values and beliefs. Considering leadership as "values in action" means that every decision you make needs to be conscientiously aligned with who you are and what you care about; to do otherwise will damage your credibility.

It is important to note that you will be judged not only by the decisions that you make, but also by the decisions that you deliberately don't make (as opposed to indecision, as noted below). These non-decisions will also clearly be decisions, albeit often invisible but nonetheless important in terms of getting a clear glimpse of your values.

Process of Making Good Judgment Calls

A great deal of making good judgment calls is a matter of a process that both leaders and lawyers follow in response to a particular situation. Most of these situations involve people (who to hire and why, for example), strategy (whether to add a new law office on the other coast, for example), or a crisis (response to a crisis). It is difficult to imagine a situation in which the exercise of good judgment is not critically important.

The first part of the process for making a good judgment call involves preparation, taking the necessary time and research to size up the particular problem, situation, or person and understand the context in which the decision must be made. For example, is it a routine decision or an existential one? The second part of the process is making the call (thereby avoiding the pitfall of indecision), and the process concludes with executing or implementing the decision.

Deciding is important, but ensuring that it is put into action is the critical part of the process.

One of the most important attributes of lawyers who consistently exhibit good judgment is that they determine and then focus squarely on what is most important. They are not snookered or sidetracked. Their decisions go to the heart of the matter under consideration. This is similar to what constitutes great decision making by executives: "[T]hey concentrate on what is important. They want to know what the decision is all about and what the underlying realities are which it has to satisfy."[3]

Judgment: A Learned Skill

Judgment is typically not something anyone is born with. Rather it is an acquired skill and therefore one that you can learn and develop.

Learning from your own experiences, especially stumbles and setbacks, is, as previously noted, the primary way to hone your judgment. Experience, gained from both good and bad decisions, really does provide a foundation for the development of sound professional judgment. Not making the same mistake twice is evidence of learning and, as such, adds to your growing repertoire of experience related to judgment.

John Dewy, the American philosopher and educational reformer, noted that people don't necessarily learn from experience, they learn by reflecting on experience. Doing the same thing over and over again and expecting different results can be a sign of insanity. Reflecting on your experience is necessary for learning, and doing something differently the next time around, however slightly, is about leadership. Reflection is foundational to self-awareness, and understanding yourself better. Mistakes and failures are the stepping stones to getting better, improving your judgment, and acquiring wisdom. The only people who don't make mistakes are those who don't do anything. Reflection provides insights into *why* some decision or action did or did not work out, and rather than feeling upset or embarrassed, generates ideas about what to do the next time around. Reflection both provides and builds perspective, and enables you to see what is happening in the moment in a larger context.

Another route to enhancing your judgment is through interaction with law firm mentors (possibly acquired through internships and clinic settings) and practicing attorneys. While in law school you should be asking those with more years of practice than you have about how they approached difficult questions or problems—whether in client representation or in matters of the operation of the firm. Be sure to find out about the thinking process behind how they arrived at their decisions. Studying how successful lawyers and leaders have made tough calls and decisions is an invaluable way to develop your own judgmental ability. One benefit to the case study approach in American law schools is that it permits deeper understanding of the reasons that lawyers and judges made decisions in cases.

Mechanics of Making Sound Decisions

As we have discovered in our Leadership for Lawyers classes, and in discussions with practicing lawyers and business executives, many people in managerial roles and positions have not sufficiently thought about the processes they use in making decisions. When asked about how they make decisions or why they made a particular decision, people often simply remark, "It seemed like the correct thing to do." This response fails to appreciate the effectiveness of the process they used (at best, it acknowledges only that the decision's outcome "worked out okay"—not even that it was optimal). Another frequent response provided is, "I went with my gut," which means that the individual decided without a conscious understanding of the factors underlying that intuition. Neither of these responses result in much insight into the process of learning; the response might just as well have been "I got lucky," and that's not a ringing endorsement about one's capability in making good decisions and soundly exercising judgment. Clients don't hire lawyers because they "are the luckiest people they know" but because of their reputation for exercising good judgment and obtaining great outcomes.

Having clarity about the process of making good decisions is important to the practice of law, which is based on precedents. It is also critical to the practice of leadership, ensuring the consistency and trustworthiness necessary for building and sustaining authentic relationships.

And just like becoming an exemplary leader, effective decision making is a learned skill, not something that either you have or you don't. The skills associated with being a good decision maker can be learned and strengthened by understanding the elements associated with a sound decision-making process. That process involves a set of steps that can be used to make most decisions, beginning with an understanding of what type of decision is needed.

Classifying the Decision

At the onset consider whether the decision you are being asked to make is mostly routine or substantive. Effective decision makers will approach these two types of decisions differently, even though they will employ a very similar decision-making process.

Some decisions involve relatively routine choices and judgments. For example, what's for dinner or whether you want to buy the premium-priced pineapple rings in the grocery store versus going with the less expensive generic brand. While there may be qualitative and even quantitative differences in these choices, their consequences or outcomes are relatively inconsequential—and especially so in the long run. Choices here seldom set precedent.

Other decisions have more substantive consequences, and the outcome of a case, a project, or a business initiative may hinge on the basis of one correct or incorrect decision. Some Silicon Valley, Wall Street, and Pennsylvania Avenue lawyers describe the high stakes associated with certain cases, and the client's financial capability to support litigation, as "bet-the-company" decisions. In these instances, the decision may have existential consequences for the client. Other types of decisions might have strategic consequences for the counsel. For example, "Should our firm open a new office, with all the expense associated with that, in Chicago (or some other location)?" or "Should the firm enlarge its practice fields to develop an intellectual property litigation department?"

Delineating the Problem

Once the decision has been classified, you need to consider the nature of the problem, which requires a decision. For example, does the problem involve a series of events—and, if so, is it necessary to formulate a policy or precedent that can be applied in future instances—or is this a one-off situation? Another consideration is whether the issue or problem indicates a need to fix a singular element or overhaul a potentially massive infrastructure, or something in between the two. A further consideration is determining for this problem who needs to be involved, whether from the perspective of bringing the requisite expertise and experience and/or from the vantage point of executing the decision. Bringing a range of diverse voices to the table ensures that the necessary competencies are involved, and it also goes a long way to increase confidence that key perspectives were not missed, especially from those whom your decision is attempting to address, as well as from those subsequently responsible for execution.

Getting It Right

Often, the delineation of the problem to be solved will help establish parameters or boundaries for the type of answer that is necessary to resolve the matter at issue. At this point, an effective decision maker will ponder and focus on what is the *right* action or decision and not what is just *acceptable* or passable. Sound decision making requires a desire to "get it right." While law students and budding lawyers may be admonished to "not let perfect get in the way of good" and "don't overthink it," it is essential for your reputation as an attorney and leader that you form an appreciation for the correctness of the decision that must be made. Your credibility and reputation are on the line.

A desire to get it right can present a personal challenge for law students and young lawyers who report feeling almost paralyzed by fear of making a wrong (or poor) decision, even in the face of a professor's or mentor's assurances that "you're not expected to be perfect." Working through these challenges requires an ability to understand your limits and strengths and being comfortable with doing the very best work you can do, irrespective of how it may turn out. Self-awareness and the ability to reflect on your strengths and limits allows a sense of grace, knowing that inevitably some mistakes are going to be made and preparing yourself to accept that fact and the associated consequences.

Planning for Action

Another step in the process is to build into the decision the actual action necessary to resolve the matter. You know how frustrating, unmotivating, and wasteful it is to be engaged in a situation where a decision is made, only to find out that nothing subsequently happened or changed. For example, too often elected officials will pass legislation and then not provide the necessary funding and resources to implement the decision.

Gauging Effectiveness

The final step is to gauge the validity and effectiveness of the decision against the actual course of events that played out. Ask yourself, "Did the decision make a difference? Did it accomplish its goals?" Take some time to reflect on the entire process and consider what you did that is worth repeating, and what you realize you would do differently in the future. Such reflection builds judgment.

Stepping Outside of the Process

The introduction of a deliberate process into making decisions, which some consider to be largely an intuitive action, can seem daunting and cumbersome. Yet, what the research finds, and what we've found from our own discussions with successful lawyers, is that attending to an intentional decision-making process is fundamental to leadership success. The best decisions, while sometimes made under pressure, are not generally made when people are feeling stressed.

Making decisions from a clear head, based on principles, calmly and not impulsively in reaction to pressure is very important. Still, it is true that effective decision making is not a simple list, a one-size-fits all approach, or a specific step-by-step experience. You will need a blend of decision-making skills, being part tactician, part therapist, part strategist, and part content expert. You will be required to provide clear-eyed analysis; and, on occasion, you will want the guts of a riverboat gambler.

Challenge of Indecision

Some of the descriptions of the proper steps to arrive at a sound decision may sound unrealistic because they suggest that decision makers have all the time in the world to get to their decision when, in the real world, decisions often have to be considered, rendered, and evaluated in a rather short time span—sometimes on the spot and under multiple pressures. One of the major problems that organizations face in moving through the effective decision-making process is dealing with the issue of "indecision"—the failure to make timely and sound decisions because of various real, imaginary, and self-imposed constraints on the decision makers. The inability to make a prompt decision is particularly troubling to young lawyers who often lack the self-confidence to make a difficult decision due to their lack of experience.

Causes of Indecision

Decision makers in law firms (and exemplary leaders) are busy and have an already full agenda; they have the needs of their clients and cases to manage and move forward, as well as their own personal matters (e.g., family) that need their attention. Lawyers leading their firms are frequently challenged to prioritize an organizational matter when they are already juggling multiple issues presented by clients and other members of the firm.

Furthermore, many decisions require the consideration of external inputs (from experts and faculty reports, to government findings and the like) and cannot be rendered very expeditiously. Decisions affecting groups of people and entire organizations and firms—for example, decisions about personnel retention and promotions, real estate and office acquisitions, client practice areas, and so on—may sometimes, under unforeseen and unfortunate circumstances, have to be made quickly; but more often they will require extended deliberation, negotiations, even dispute resolutions, and the involvement by many parties (committees and departments).

Solutions to Indecision

To preempt indecision, leaders must create a culture of decisive behavior, one that ensures that effective decisions are made promptly and correctly. Leaders must pay particular attention to how they act and communicate that the importance of prompt and effective action is clearly part of the firm's DNA, as it is of each of the individual lawyers involved. Normative signals are sent via "social operating mechanisms" such as meetings, decision-making "trees," formal and informal email, and similar communication systems to promote productive dialogue and influence the perceptions and actions of others in the organization.

In these ways, having an effective decision-making process in place serves to create an organization that is collaborative, efficient, and productive.[4] Moreover, candid feedback and strenuous follow-through characterizes organizations that fully engage their people and teams, and mitigate against indecision paralysis.

Effective Change and Leadership

You are very unlikely to get any better than you are without doing something differently than you are now doing. This truth applies to both individuals and organizations. If "better than today" is a desired end state, then change is required, and effective change is all about leadership and changing the business-as-usual environment. Don't get us wrong—there are no guarantees that change will result in improvements. However, without making any changes, the probability of improvement is quite unlikely. After all, the other truth is that if you are not growing, then, just like fruit on the vine, you will eventually rot. As former US Army Chief of Staff Eric Shinseki observed, "[If] you don't like change, you're going to like irrelevance even less."[5]

Components of Change

There are a number of critical components for successfully initiating change. These include establishing a sense of urgency, selecting an appropriate "guiding coalition" to effect change, articulating a shared vision for change, identifying and communicating the actions necessary to address the challenge, generating an environment where it is safe to experiment and learn from experience (and mistakes), and integrating the changes into the organization's processes and culture.[6]

Need for Change

If an organization is doing well or if a client's legal needs are routine, then the attorney's tasks are modest. However, if the challenges are great and the need to improve, modernize, or advance is critical, then those lawyers must implement a process of change, and leadership will necessarily be required.

Law firms have experienced unprecedented pressures in recent years from several forces. These pressures include talent issues in the firm, such as hiring new lawyers and managing unproductive older partners; client demands for reduced costs of legal services; and the inability of senior lawyers and firm leaders to effectively manage technology, both their own as well as that of their clients.[7] In addition, the industry is facing increased globalization of legal services, a decline in the number of lawyers in law practice, and a growing number of alternative law service providers.

Such seismic fluctuations are endangering legal organizations these days, and most firms are neither effectively managing them nor leading transitions.[8] Surveys have found that over 70 percent of lawyers believe that the pace of significant change affecting law firms will continue to increase, yet only 38 percent of them indicate that their firms are actively engaged in rolling out innovative changes. They further report that the resistance to change efforts comes mostly from firm partners (ostensibly the leadership team).[9]

Clearly, responding to the trends and challenges of these times is necessary, and that won't happen without leadership. The responsibility for creating the energy and conditions for firm adaptation rests with those leading legal organizations. In fact, in order to adapt to ongoing social, political, economic, and technological developments, firms must be making moderate changes annually and be prepared for major changes in the way they operate every four to five years.[10]

Essays written by law students in our leadership classes have recognized that regardless of whether an organization is a student group or a law firm, change is a critical element of survival. These students described the challenges of leading change when the student organizations they led hit a dead end—a double whammy when fewer students were joining and attendance at meetings was declining (even the free pizza was not getting them out!). These student leaders realized that extinction was a distinct possibility, and they found themselves needing to quickly understand the causes of the problem, inspire others to respond to these concerns, and enable their colleagues to implement the necessary innovations.

Student organizations that don't survive very long are the ones led by those who discount the data and push concerns aside because, after all, "it's only a law school student organization!" Importantly, students have seen firsthand that law firms they have worked for have similar challenges, that is, motivating people to do more than show up, as well as perennial problems of retention.

The process of moving others in the law firm forward is not all that different in that every organization requires leadership for effective change.

Incremental versus Disruptive Change

Management is mostly about dealing with the status quo; change, and getting better than today (the status quo), requires leadership. The more significant and disruptive the changes, the more leadership plays a pivotal role.

Disruptive change occurs when a highly novel and unanticipated demand (often exogenous to the industry) or an immediate threat forces attention to the problem. Some examples of disruptive changes would be the discovery of a radically new and different technology that renders many of a firm's assets (such as intellectual property or talent pools) obsolete or otherwise subject to a quick write-off.

Incremental change still requires leadership, but at a much slower pace. It occurs where industries or market participants are making continuous improvements—for example, making the firm's assets more efficient and productive or gradually increasing the demand for the industry's products. The client-driven demands for different billing practices (e.g., billable hours and value billing) are representative of more incremental challenges requiring changes in how law firms operate.

Regardless of whether the change is disruptive or incremental, all effective changes require leadership and begin with clear decisions and directions from leaders.

Change and Innovation

Approaching change in difficult and challenging circumstances requires leaders to be innovative and challenge the process. This is not always easy for law school students, especially because their educational experience in law school seems to be mostly built on understanding precedent. Leadership at the individual client or case level, or organizational level, will often require thinking outside of existing paradigms.

Innovative Decision Making versus Traditional Problem Solving

People often confuse innovative problem solving and decision making with other, more traditional business thinking, such as strategic or long-range planning. These different approaches to problem solving have their place in legal organizations faced with ambiguity about future directions.

Traditional business thinking tends to be logical, requires proof, looks for precedent, is binary ("there is right and wrong"), is uncomfortable with ambiguity, and desires immediate results. There is nothing wrong with traditional business thinking in most organizations, but it is incomplete or inadequate for many situations that require more transformative action.

Innovative thinking is different from traditional forms of problem solving, being much more collaborative and value-added.[11] Innovative thinking tends to be intuitive and future oriented, asking "what if" questions. It is unconstrained by the past, embraces multiple possibilities, and relishes ambiguity. Innovation requires an agility and quickness that is not generally prized in traditional planning and business decision-making routines and environments.[12]

In terms of incremental versus disruptive change, incremental change can usually be addressed by institutional strategic planning, while disruptive change often requires innovation to address the challenges presented by the disruptive threat. Nonetheless, innovation certainly can be—and might need to be—employed to address incremental change; although in terms of disruption, firms' response time is much shorter, and often participants in the industry or market may not understand all of the factors that caused or led to the disruptive force.[13]

Importantly, providing innovative leadership entails creating an organizational climate where people are both free and encouraged to apply innovative thinking in addressing contemporary challenges for their clients and organizations.[14]

Components of Innovation

There are three components in the process of innovation that are particularly important to consider. These are (1) collaboration, (2) investments in people and processes, and (3) assessment and evaluation.

Effectively addressing change typically involves mobilizing a collective, rather than individual, response. Success at addressing the need for change, and implementing those changes, requires that you make sure an appropriate, diverse, and representative group of people are involved in the decision-making process. Frequently, this takes the form of creating a task force that is charged with generating ideas and alternatives.

Similarly, innovation occurs through team effort, when people are engaged with one another and share a common purpose, along with a sense that resolving challenges requires collaborative, rather than individual, efforts. To this end, leaders bring people together and create teams to process possibilities, which at the same time requires nurturing and sustaining a climate within the team and organization that values and pursues experimentation and risk taking.

Successful innovation needs an environment that fosters and permits not only experimentation but also learning, meaning that some setbacks, stumbles, mistakes, and failures will be an inevitable part of the experience. The people and teams charged with finding creative solutions to difficult problems must feel that they can consider alternative perspectives and try different solutions without fear of being embarrassed or penalized for not getting it absolutely right the first time. In this sense, perfection, as Winston Churchill best put it, is the enemy of progress.

Studies show that successful innovation processes involve participants who see themselves as pioneers and explorers. They are flexible thinkers, comfortable with ambiguity, and open to new ideas and ways of making things happen.[15] In harnessing this energy, leaders must build trust among the participants through building relationships, promoting cooperation, insisting on open communication, and inspiring a shared vision that builds commitment to persevere through setbacks and hardships.[16]

Effective innovation also means that leaders and their organizations must be prepared to make investments in both their people's abilities to innovate and in the tools and processes needed to be imaginative and creative. For example, an organization might try out new ideas in one office or region and iron out the kinks before launching any company-wide initiatives.

Innovative processes can make the difference in the current era of legal services outsourcing, overwhelming technological advances and changes, and increasing client demands for greater law firm efficiency and better service delivery.

Finally, a successful innovation process doesn't stop with results but, similar to the after-action reviews conducted by the armed services, requires assessment and evaluation in order to foster learning and build future capacity. People will not struggle for long without knowing how they are doing and what progress they are making toward their shared aspirations. Researchers have found that a feeling of making progress is one of the essential factors that motivates people and keeps them focused on the target ahead.[17] Leaders create ways to provide milestones along the journey (and, certainly, litigation has many of these steps built into the process), as well as dashboards (modeled after automobiles) to give people a sense of how they are doing.

Roadblocks to Innovation

Many law firms, typical of most organizations, face internal challenges that inhibit support for truly creative action. Almost by their nature, organizations favor stability and are unprepared for, and perhaps even unaware of the need for, innovation and continuous process improvement. Global studies have found that only about thirteen percent of employees are truly engaged in the work of creatively responding to major problems and that fifty percent of employees feel that they are too busy or otherwise blocked at work from being creative and innovative.[18]

These results underscore two critical issues for organizations facing the need for major change. First, for change to happen, a perceived urgency is necessary to spur innovative thinking. Second, this urgency needs to be so significant that leaders can essentially compel the creation of an innovation methodology that will get results (that is, lead to substantive changes). The coalescing of these two elements are the special value that leaders add to the organization—they recognize and embrace the challenge and clearly articulate the need for change—and they persuade others to engage in creative steps to address the challenge.

Innovation and the Need for Leadership

Neither innovation nor creative change just happen on their own; inertia and continuation of the status quo are the default. Leadership is needed to drive the organization through innovative analysis, ideation, exploration of ideas for change, and adoption of the needed change.

Your aspiration to initiate and lead innovation will require expertise, commitment, and direction. The organizational climate for creativity is directly attributable to how leaders behave, with studies showing that twenty percent to as much as sixty-seven percent of the variance in creativity depends on the example set by leaders.[19] If leaders inspire people in such a way that they can grasp both the need and the urgency for change, then people will most likely enlist in the cause and want to be part of the solution.

FOLLOWING THROUGH

- Decision making is a critical skill for lawyer leaders—necessary for effecting change and inspiring innovation within an organization.
- Decision making impacts every aspect of the legal profession: clients, law firms, and public service.
- The foundation of good decision making is good judgment, and the foundation of good judgment is learning from experience.
- Decision making is a deliberate process, but it is not necessarily a rigid, step-by-step undertaking. Rather, it involves a blend of skills, abilities, and actions.
- Successful innovation requires collaboration, an investment in people and processes, as well as assessment and evaluation. Judgment and decision making, like leadership, are learned skills. Law students and new lawyers should develop and hone these skills as early in their careers as possible.

REFLECTIONS

1. Think about a time when indecision paralyzed either you or someone with whom you worked. What factors contributed to the indecisiveness? What can help eliminate the chances that a decision is stalled or can't be made?

2. Pinpoint a particular situation in which you exercised good judgment, and how was that judgment shaped by experience? How did that judgment reflect your values? What lessons do you take away from this analysis?

3. What are the major challenges that law firms or particular law service groups (for example, the district attorney's office or a legal services program) face these days? For each, what innovations can you imagine that would ameliorate or eliminate the problem or challenge? How would you suggest these innovations be implemented?

4. What goals do you have for your first job or the early stages of your career, and how do you see yourself exercising leadership? How can you develop your skills in offering innovative ideas?

ELEVEN

Becoming a Team Leader

There is a fundamental difference between working individually with a group of people and leading a team.

THE LEAD-IN

- Collaboration: What It Is, What It Isn't
- Collaboration: The Foundation of the Legal Profession
    - Areas of Collaboration
    - Collaboration: A Reflection of Societal Trends
    - Collaboration: A Learned Skill
- Persuasion in the Process of Collaboration
    - Persuasion and Communication Skills
    - Persuasion and Listening Skills
    - Persuasion in Group Situations
    - Persuasion: A Learned Skill
- Lawyer Leaders: Building Teams
    - Building Consensus
    - Clearly Defining Plans
    - Getting the Right People on the Team
    - Choosing and Developing Team Players
- Lawyer Leaders: Leading Teams
    - Incorporating The Five Practices of Exemplary Leadership®
    - Addressing Problems that Plague Teams
- Following Through
- Reflections

Popular culture films tend to treat lawyers either as intelligent introverts, preferring the monastic life of pouring over complex provisions of law, or as swashbuckling courtroom crusaders. These themes may make for good movies, but they do not draw an accurate picture of what lawyers do for others or how they conduct their professional and business lives.

In actuality, lawyers' work as counselors, negotiators, and advocates is quite people intensive and frequently involves working in groups to successfully accomplish shared goals. Lawyers participate on many different teams and often are called on to lead them. For lawyers to successfully build, participate on, and lead teams, they must effectively collaborate.

Collaboration: What It Is, What It Isn't

A truly collaborative work group, or team, is composed of members who engage with each other toward a shared understanding and mutually beneficial resolution of the issues they address. A good definition of a team is "a small number of people with complementary skills who are committed to a common purpose, set of performance goals, and approach for which they hold themselves mutually accountable."[1] Successful collaborative relationships require commitment and expertise to achieve the desired outcomes. Long-term collaboration may involve attention to or resolution of multiple projects (such as the foci of the management or litigation committee in a law firm), or they address an ongoing issue (partner compensation, for example). Litigation or deals may require shorter term collaboration among a diverse group of professionals.

There is a fundamental difference between working individually with many individuals and leading a team. You could conduct your business by simply tapping into the experience and expertise of one or more individuals on a one-on-one transaction basis. You seek an opinion on a specific matter of law, and the person you contact may not need to know about the actual case or people involved. Although, you consult with many people, none of them feels any sense of personal responsibility or accountability for the outcome. This group is composed of individuals who are each essentially independent of one another, and while you may be coordinating their efforts, they don't really constitute a *team*.

Collaborative groups, or teams, also differ from mere assembly projects wherein each participant prepares a report and someone collects and collates them into a final statement. Collaborative teams are characterized by all members assembling together to jointly work on all aspects of a project; assembly projects, by contrast, are characterized by subject-matter experts working independently to contribute to a group report. These reports can be useful, but they are not the product of truly collaborative processes and generally lack sufficient joint input and consensus to be considered a collaborative effort.

Furthermore, a collaborative team effort is different from a sequential work situation, wherein a series of successive groups each picks up a project where an antecedent group left off and carries the project further along. Such work groups have their own use, but they are not truly collaborative. True collaborative groups involve lawyers and other professionals working substantively together throughout the entirety of a project rather than individual groups working separately on different phases of a project.

The power of a team (versus a mere assemblage of people) emanates from its strong sense of being an interdependent community, which exerts a strong influence on people's attitudes and behaviors. Noncollaborative groups utilize individual strengths to get work done with the members focusing on their own goals, while people on a team see themselves as connected and dependent on one another and utilize each other's abilities to achieve a common goal. The resulting products of these two types of groups are quite different—a reflection of the fact that greater insights, knowledge, research, and thoughtfulness come from the act of collaborating with others.

Collaboration: The Foundation of the Legal Profession

From the very early stages in people's education and socialization processes, they are expected to "play well with others." This dictate extends into all facets of adulthood, where the ability to collaborate is especially valued.

The legal profession is no exception. In fact, the foundation of the legal profession is collaboration. Teams are assembled for purposes that cannot be realized by a single individual or a group of individuals working either independently or sequentially with one another, including addressing an issue (partner and associate compensation, for example), a problem (balancing the concerns and challenges of parenthood while practicing law), or an opportunity (moving into a new practice area). In addition to the work-product benefits of collaboration, research shows that when lawyers have strong collaborative skills on top of their technical skills, their firms earn higher profit margins, their clients remain more loyal to the firm, and their billing rates are higher.[2] But the importance of strong collaboration skills by lawyers transcends their impact on the bottom line of law firm profitability.

Areas of Collaboration

Collaboration comes into play in all facets of lawyering: lawyer–client relationships, litigation, transaction work, and firm or organizational administration and management..

Lawyers must be able to collaborate with others to best serve their clients and get their work done. In today's complex environments, collaboration across disciplines requires lawyers to combine their knowledge and skills and tailor them to the needs of the client in a manner such that the outcome is more than the sum of individual participants' contributions. The practice of law has become increasingly specialized, and lawyers are often selected because of their subject-matter expertise. They work in environments that are increasingly complex, volatile, and uncertain; and clients rely on their lawyers' abilities to help navigate those conditions. General counsel with a Fortune 50 firm noted that, "[The] lawyer's core skill of understanding how values, rules, and institutions interrelate with social, economic, and political conditions is central to the demands of [their] leadership."[3] Research has found that lawyers who can collaborate across practice fields and clients generate the highest revenues from client services fees.[4]

In particular, lawyers team up with others for litigation and transaction work, and lawyers collaborate in teams comprised of people with expertise that cuts across many technical and functional arenas. Much of the litigation and transaction work for business clients involves working across divisions or lines within an organization, involving, for example, accounting and engineering and, of course, general counsel or the legal department. On mergers and acquisitions work, lawyers with Securities and Exchange Commission and finance experience collaborate with functional specialists from the client's organization (marketing, finance, regulatory compliance) and technical experts from other fields. In terms of litigation, lawyers work on teams for settlement negotiations, trial preparation sessions, and client counseling meetings.

Furthermore, the work of most legal organizations—including midsized to larger law firms, corporate counsel offices, risk-management and compliance departments—is structured to be conducted by teams. Good examples of teams within a law firm are the firm's management, compensation, and associate committees. These teams are how the business of managing contemporary law firms happens. The reality for most law organizations is that teams function everywhere, are critical to their operations and success, and affect most aspects of lawyers' daily work.

Collaborative skills are also important outside the firm in dealings with opposing counsel, where the abilities to be candid and professional are critical to the successful completion of the case. It may seem counterintuitive to view the adversarial lawyers in deals and in litigations as "collaborators," but the truth is that all lawyers must work together to conclude the transaction or contract for their clients or resolve the dispute in litigation. Many judges express their exasperation with the inability of lawyers in a matter of litigation to resolve seemingly routine discovery matters and forcing the judge into resolving motions to compel or for sanctions.

Collaboration: A Reflection of Societal Trends

The prevalence of teamwork in the law practice industry reflects broader economic and social influences, because law jobs and legal projects are becoming increasingly complex, less time-bound, and more global in scope. Organizations that cut across disciplines, industries, and businesses must rely on teams to handle multifaceted issues as well as the more mundane aspects of working in an organization. Work in mergers and acquisitions, for example, utilizes expertise and experience across fields of increasing sophistication and knowledge; and even a really savvy and technically proficient lawyer cannot individually demonstrate expertise in international finance, cross-border licensing requirements, and the economics of an acquiring firm's premerger and post-merger performance necessary to complete a complex deal. Rather, in order for that lawyer to successfully conduct the transaction or conclude the litigation, the principal skill is pulling together the right people to be on the team.

Furthermore, in a crisis situation, aggressive and collaborative work within the firm is needed to identify the real and likely impacts of various scenarios and then devise appropriate ways to address them. Financial and economic pandemics in past decades have painfully shown how many law firms reacted slowly and ineffectively, and subsequently failed.

Collaboration: A Learned Skill

Nearly all (97 percent) of the nearly 1,200 global leaders surveyed by the Center for Creative Leadership indicated that collaboration is essential to the success of their organizations.[5] Unfortunately, only 30 percent of the respondents felt that those leading their organizations were very skilled at collaboration. This gap between the need for strong collaboration and the lack of those skills by the organizations' leaders, argues that for greater collaborative skills education and development, including as early as law school.

Collaboration is a skill that can be learned and honed. To that end, more and more law schools have been emphasizing team projects and collaboration. Law schools' curricula, as well as continuing professional development programming for lawyers, increasingly focus on collaborative skills, such as negotiation, teamwork, and dispute resolution.

Persuasion in the Process of Collaboration

Bringing people together requires persuasive abilities. Influencing the behaviors and decisions of others is a critical skill for any lawyer. Persuading people to work together for the common good of everyone involved is fundamentally similar to how leaders Inspire a Shared Vision. Lawyers influence and motivate others, including clients, opposing counsel, and, importantly, judges from whom a favorable decision is desired. Persuading others is central to the work that lawyers perform in gaining support for a legal position or inducing a witness to provide necessary information. People will follow a leader, just as clients will follow lawyers, when they clearly communicate a shared goal or purpose, supported by common values, and articulate why such a pursuit is in their best interests.

Persuasion and Communication Skills

Neither lawyers nor leaders are often successful when they are inadequately prepared to persuade others. Preparation starts with identifying the key objectives that both the lawyer (leader) and the client (follower) want and need to achieve. This requires developing a heightened sense of awareness of the situation and the message that you need to send in that context, making it the right message at the right time.[6] In other words, lawyers and leaders must be masters of communication skills in their roles as advocates and in their interpersonal interactions.

Success, regardless of profession or position, requires being able to effectively communicate with specificity of purpose and clarity of message. People in leadership and managerial roles spend seventy to ninety percent of their time every day communicating with others.[7] Leadership is very much a person-to-person business, and so often the messages must be at a personal level—for example, explaining how the proposed change or action will benefit people personally even when the change is at a group or organizational level. Persuading others to shift their behavior from one lane to another requires an appreciation that people find it challenging to give up what they are currently doing (even if they are unhappy) unless they can see how they will be better off by pursuing a different path.

Persuasion and Listening Skills

Excellent listening skills, as we discussed in earlier chapters, are also essential to being effective at both persuasion and communications. Listening and understanding a client's or law firm associate's situation enable you to clearly appreciate the client's goals, to empathize with the difficulties that the legal problem is causing, and to articulate a set of shared objectives and a vision for moving forward.

Since persuading others to act differently may involve reciprocity, listening plays an important role. Reciprocity describes the situation where two parties agree that if you take this action for me now, I will, in the future, return the favor and benefit you. This is a common and important form of persuasion between lawyers as they seek, for example, to resolve litigation or an impasse in a transaction. In these situations, the client's interest is advanced because the lawyer is able to move the transaction along to a successful conclusion or garner something more beneficial to the client by trading off something less valuable.

Persuasion in Group Situations

Most situations where lawyers use persuasion to advance their clients' interests involve interpersonal interactions. However, sometimes you will have to persuade groups, such as a jury panel or a corporate board of directors, to reach agreement or take a difficult, possibly less than optimal, course of action. Situations like these require additional skills in (a) shaping a message that appeals to the group and (b) communicating that message to a group that may likely include some dissenting viewpoints.

To influence groups, you need to be extra vigilant in developing a good sense of the audience's needs, wants, and interests and then crafting a message that fosters a sense of meaning for them. As their lawyer and leader, you want them "to get it"; sometimes that requires a nuanced message, while at other times it requires a message that may be quite blunt.

Persuasion: A Learned Skill

Given that most law school curricula lack developmental opportunities in persuasion means that you will need to find ways on your own to develop the skills to influence others in an effective and ethical manner. The good news is that persuading others is a skill that can be learned, and practice in law school trial and appellate advocacy courses is an excellent way to hone this ability at an early stage in your career.

Persuasion begins with having a firm, clear commitment to the achievement of the intended goal. You must muster cogent arguments for the sought-after goals, including marshaling sufficient and supportive facts, justifications, and reasons. You must consider how to clearly communicate the rationale through skillful presentation, often in a face-to-face setting, and sometimes quite spontaneously.

Lawyer Leaders: Building Teams

By the time you arrive at law school, no doubt you have had many experiences—some more successful and satisfying than others—with participation on teams, be they in school, sports, social and political organizations, or the workplace. In fact, some of your most significant leadership experiences no doubt have come from these early occasions to work with others in groups to make decisions and take actions—that is, to collaborate. For example, one student described leading a high-technology project team, which involved members from engineering, accounting, and legal. They were tasked with a product development and rollout that had a revenue projection of over $7 million. Another student reported about leading several teams of lawyers and experts in handling class member notifications about litigation settlements and securing documentation of class members' agreements to settle.

In taking on leadership roles for these teams, these students and others had to understand and pay attention to what it takes to build an effective team in the first place. There are at least three important considerations in creating teams: building consensus, creating a clearly defined plan, and getting the right people onboard.

Building Consensus

To start, there must be a shared understanding or consensus among the people involved regarding purpose—that is, why the team was formed—otherwise it is just a group of individuals. Without agreement on the purpose of why people are being brought together as a team, the resulting collaborative efforts are likely to fail—they might simply be an answer in search of a problem. Consensus is more than a fancier word for agreement because it typically involves a decision-making process that seeks to ensure widespread support among the people involved for a specific course of action.

Consensus also entails agreement on the goals or outcomes of the team's project. Like purpose as a guiding element for a successful team, consensus of what a good outcome looks like is critical to the team members' acceptance of the group's work.

Reaching consensus is not a matter of just taking a head count to see where everyone is on a particular issue. Rather, it usually requires thoughtful persuasion to get everyone thinking in the same way about how to solve a problem. This means setting an example by listening carefully to what everyone is saying, inducing silent members to speak, and incorporating and integrating multiple viewpoints into the dialogue. It also requires reflecting on points others are making, not just to win them over but to evaluate the validity of the ideas and arguments being advanced, regardless of their source, and how they will lead the team to successfully complete the task.

Clearly Defining Plans

Another essential effective team component is a clearly stated plan of action to achieve the team's goals. That planning requires special attention—by a leader—early in the process. To make the most efficient use of resources, effective teams will agree on, and assign, areas of responsibility so that every team member knows what each is expected to contribute. Clear expectations are absolutely necessary to ensure commitment to (not simply compliance with) the project's achievement. Most team projects have expectations, whether developed internally or in their charge, about successfully delivering recommendations and reports.

A defined plan includes specifics about the project's timeline. Team members need to know that the project has a beginning as well as an end—in other words, how to know when success has been achieved. You should begin with the end point in mind, effectively focusing the team on what information, data, and evidence will be required. Many projects require evaluation of data before a fact-based set of recommendations can be made. For example, if the compensation committee wants to determine associates' compensation by national or regional standards, it needs sufficient information on the compensation levels of other law firms.

Similarly, law firm efforts to put together the most attractive associate hiring packages will miss the mark if they are not based on detailed marketplace information.

Another essential in the action plan is a clear articulation of follow-up steps and implementation actions associated with the team's conclusions. Unfortunately, this critical step is often overlooked because the recommendations and action plans of many teams are not self-executing. The team itself, its leader, or the managing partner must ensure that recommendations and/or action plans are followed through.

Often within the defined plan is an understanding of and appreciation for how the team's project fits within the structure of the organization of which the team is an integral part. A team that is viewed in the organization as strong, positive, and necessary is most likely to have its recommendations or conclusions accepted by others in the organization.

Getting the Right People on the Team

A third essential consideration is the composition and representativeness of the team. At a basic level, composition involves size and expertise. Is the team the right size to get the task done efficiently? Does the team have people with the necessary skills, experience, and clout?

How the team leader is selected, whether by statute, appointment, or election, is another critical consideration. Selection of the team leader by democratic methods generally fosters greater buy-in by team members, but sometimes an individual, based on expertise and/or connections and representation, needs to be brought in to lead the team.

Team composition also involves issues of representativeness. Do the people on the team reflect the diversity of the organization? Diversity can refer to whether there is sufficient participation from the affected parties as well as from underrepresented groups. Designing and leading successful teams involves considerations that stem from the uniqueness of the challenge facing the team. Sufficient and appropriate representativeness on teams is about more than "political correctness" or the organization's group dynamics. Diversity can bring important perspectives, without which any proposed solutions may be doomed to fail, since the team simply missed and didn't consider issues necessary to the solution's eventual success.

In situations where the organization has multiple constituencies, the composition of the team may need to reflect the interests and needs of many or all of the constituencies. For example, the American Bar Association's Section on Legal Education represents and responds to several interest groups within legal education, including law school deans and administrators, legal clinic directors and faculty, law students, law librarians, and others. The composition of that section's standing committees, task forces, and other governance or problem-solving groups often reflect these constituent interest groups.

Representativeness helps achieve commitment from the audience that you represent or to which you respond as well as providing necessary expertise to the team's mission. In law firms, a cross section of participants from the major constituencies (senior associates, associates, senior partners, equity partners, etc.) are often involved on teams, especially in connection with internal governance issues. Representation considerations are important, and sometimes more significant than the particular competencies being brought to the team. Constituency-based selection criteria can also facilitate implementation of the team's recommendations. A good example would be the composition of a team addressing working parent lawyer issues in successfully navigating toward partnership. A team assembled to address this set of difficult issues that doesn't include any members who have children at home would not be very credible to the employees at whom the firm's initiative is aimed. In addition, such a team is likely to be insensitive to and/or miss many issues central to successfully implementing any solution.

Choosing and Developing Team Players

Research about high-performing teams has illuminated the essential traits of individuals, and their actions, which materially contribute to the team's success.[8] You need to understand the characteristics of good team players so that, if you have a choice, you can select the best people to be on your team. If you don't have a choice, then you can consider how to develop participants into good team players. Five characteristics that matter in how people within a team behave are: (1) having a shared mindset, (2) feeling invested in the outcome, (3) communicating respectfully, (4) accepting responsibility, and (5) experiencing appreciation. Of course, what is true about what others need is also true about how you also must be acting, whether as the team's leader or simply as a good team member setting an example for others (and in this way providing leadership).

In putting a team together, select people who are energetic and expressive and generally interact on a positive basis with others because these characteristics facilitate trust, curiosity, confidence, and motivation within the teams with which they participate.[9] They encourage others to be open minded, resilient, and persistent and promote a sense that "we're all in this together." When team members feel respected by one another on the team, they contribute more to the team's efforts by developing a shared mindset that fosters commitment to the team's purpose and goals.[10]

Similarly, you'll want to find people that are comfortable with arriving at decisions by consensus and don't feel that they need to personally win every point or argument. Obviously, teams are not successful when everyone is expected to be a "yes person" and "toe the line" or when groupthink becomes the dominant theme of discussion. However, the ability to disagree and then accept and commit to the team's decision not only is critical for every person but also is a clear indication of embracing shared aspirations.

The best team players will have a strong, positive connection to the goals of the team. They feel "invested" in the outcomes of the project. When those firms wrestling with the challenges of working parents achieving partnership included one or more working parent lawyers on the team formed to look into the problem, these lawyers became quite invested in the outcomes of the team's recommendations and how the firm followed through. This was not simply because they could personally benefit, but also because they had been involved and they had become passionate about the equity aspects of those challenges.

Another important team player characteristic is strong communication skills, especially the capacity for candid reflection. Engaging in respectful dialogue is a necessity for highly effective team participation, and avoiding personal attacks and disruptive comments is crucial. Team members who monopolize the conversation during discussions, feeling compelled to restate a point or drone on, are oblivious to the impediments they are creating to effective communication among group members.

Emotional intelligence skills, such as self-awareness and empathy, generally go along with being a good communicator. Some people can sense discomfort or emotional difficulties by others on the team, and they act accordingly. They are good listeners and respect their colleagues on the team. Your leadership is required to identify when emotions are getting out of hand and becoming counterproductive and tactfully bringing the focus back to the task at hand, and reinforcing the importance of collaboration.

On the best teams, people come to meetings prepared and on time. Sounds like a rather simple matter, doesn't it? However, in working with law students, their top disappointments with their classmates, whether in study groups or student organizations, is voiced in comments like, "He is always late to meetings, and that is disruptive because we need to catch him up with the discussion" and "She is always making meetings difficult because she didn't read the agenda or other materials we were planning on discussing." Good team members don't waste people's time. They stay on track and focus themselves and their colleagues on what the team is doing and why, the progress that has been made, and what lies ahead to the finish line.

Furthermore, on the best teams people appreciate and recognize the contributions of their teammates. They not only express appreciation, but they also help find ways for the team to celebrate, both through the achievement of milestones along the way but also with some public acknowledgment of the project's progress and completion. These actions reinforce the feeling that "it is all for one and one for all" and that everyone is contributing to the group's objectives. Without that feeling the sense of being on a team, rather than simply a group project, is minimized and even lost.

Lawyer Leaders: Leading Teams

Being a team means that the people involved see themselves sharing a collective and common purpose, with mutual commitment and accountability to one another. Without effective leadership this team mentality will fall apart, and collaboration will not occur. What constitutes successful team leaders is that they incorporate The Five Practices of Exemplary Leadership® (discussed in detail in part II) and address common problems that plague teams.

Incorporating The Five Practices of Exemplary Leadership®

One of The Five Practices of Exemplary Leadership specifically focuses on collaboration: Enable Others to Act. This practice stresses the importance of collaboration for implementing a shared vision. Certainly, therefore, this practice is necessary for leading a team—but it is not the only one. Leaders inspire team members to collaborate toward a common goal by employing a variety of leadership behaviors, which cover the gamut of the five leadership practices.

Model the Way: Lead by example through your decisions and actions. Be the first person to follow you, and be certain not to undermine your credibility by mismatching your actions with your words and by not keeping the commitments and promises that you make. Let people know why you care about the team members and their work and the reasons that they should also be willing to put in the long hours required for success. By sharing your own thinking, you can set the tone for others to more freely share their thoughts and ideas and to search and find shared aspirations.

Inspire a Shared Vision: In envisioning the future, imagination, which has often been touted as even more important for success than intelligence, is likely to be the factor that helps you and your colleagues see what is just beyond the horizon and get there ahead of others. Curiosity goes hand in hand with imagination. Be contagiously curious about what is going on—and do so in a way that gets others interested in knowing how all the parts fit together. Being curious sets an example about being open minded and interested in more than just what you yourself are thinking and doing.

You also need to get others on board, and you can do this by showing them how they can make a difference. Keep people focused on the purpose behind the work itself and the higher meaning involved with the tasks being performed. Make sure that the team understands what difference their efforts and outputs make toward the bigger picture, as often their contributions may not be realized for several years into the future.

Challenge the Process: When you encourage people in your team to "think outside the box" and experiment, you should mean it by fostering a team environment that supports such creative thinking and rewards it where appropriate. Creating psychological safety allows people to take a risk and innovate. You need to provide support and also encourage supportive behavior among the members of your team. Team members need to feel respect from their peers and affirmation that they are competent and making contributions to the greater good. People become more open minded, resilient, motivated, and persistent when they feel safe participating in a group.[11]

Research has found that modes of positive emotion and interaction help establish trust, curiosity, confidence, and inspiration in team participants.[12] Feeling psychologically safe, people will share their experiences for the benefit of others, admit their mistakes, be open to feedback, and look for ways to help others. In such an environment, people will stretch themselves and encourage their teammates to "reach high" in creating both new knowledge and ways of thinking about problems and their resolution.

Enable Others to Act: You have to build relationships, based on trust, in order to foster collaboration. And the trust must flow both ways. People on your team must be able to trust your word and believe that you have their best interests at heart, and you must extend the same trust to the people on your team. Leaders demonstrate trustworthiness by showing empathy. Being empathetic means understanding and appreciating the needs of others and what they are experiencing (although it doesn't necessarily mean agreeing with the way they see things).

Empathy has always been an important interpersonal skill for leaders, and its importance gained increasing attention during the coronavirus pandemic and accompanying economic and social unrest. Empathy during these challenging times was demonstrated by those leaders who were knowledgeable about and sensitive to what their colleagues were experiencing in their day-to-day lives. Get yourself into the habit of listening attentively to those around you, paying attention to their verbal and nonverbal cues. Be so attuned that you can provide the support and assistance they need to press ahead and deal with the challenges, and setbacks, that might be holding them back.

Take actions that engage people, where you can provide them with choices and latitude in making decisions. What responsibilities can you share, and even delegate? Look to the full range of talents, interests, and knowledge that individual team members bring. The best performing teams are those that have a clear appreciation and inventory of their members' competencies as a group. They are most likely to use their knowledge to devise strategies for solving problems because the process of gathering the information from all team members about their interests and competencies increases their understanding of the task to be addressed and range of alternatives and strategies for dealing with it.[13]

Encourage the Heart: You can't take people on the team for granted. You have to expect the best of them, be willing to get close to people, and create a spirit of community. In particular, you need to ensure that team members feel that their contributions to the team matter and are critical to the team's mutual success. Express your commitment to and enthusiasm about both the team's capability and goals. Public acknowledgment of achievements, including in the form of celebrations, is optimal for making certain that people feel appreciated for who they are and for what they contribute.

Addressing Problems that Plague Teams

There are, unfortunately, any number of problems that can derail even the best constituted teams. Effective leaders, though, can anticipate, recognize, and be prepared to handle at least three problems that often plague teams: unproductive team dynamics, irresponsibility, and insufficient direction.

MANAGE TEAM DYNAMICS

Some impediments to collaborative teamwork result from poor group dynamics. A familiar problem to which some otherwise effective working groups fall prey is groupthink. Groupthink means that everyone agrees with or otherwise parrots the first speaker's comments, resulting in a *cascade effect*, and no new or additional insights come from the participants—even while it is apparent that diversity of thinking and sharing of experiences will lead to better decisions. Repetition of a well-made point doesn't make it any better, and repetition of the same point can impede new, creative thoughts.

Team members can also fall into a pattern of focusing on the insights, data, and conclusions they had when they started their participation on the team rather than offering unique data and insights or challenging one another's perspectives. By focusing on what everybody already knows, team members can fail to assess and evaluate critical insights and information held by others in the group.[14] Involving people with diverse backgrounds on the team pays dividends in accuracy because these individuals tend to process information more carefully.[15]

In addition, team members may become polarized and dig into their positions with firm and unyielding conviction. The best decisions may not emerge because of the persistence of a few dominant (or "elite") group members. Another shortcoming to watch out for is when teams amplify the errors of their members instead of correcting them. As the old saying goes, those who do not learn from the mistakes of the past are doomed to repeat them.

Effective leaders confront issues such as these by deftly moderating meetings to ensure that they are robust, with open and respectful discussion in which everyone is expected to contribute and listen to one another. Leaders who have earned the trust of their colleagues will more easily be able to extract optimal performance from group members.

ADDRESS IRRESPONSIBILITY

Let's face it: Some (sometimes many) team members are irresponsible in that they don't turn in their work on schedule, or they don't show up for meetings on time or come prepared. Such irresponsibility needs to be acknowledged and dealt with.

You earn the respect of the team when you make the most of their time and ensure that team meetings are efficient and well run. When you are leading the team, formulate a work plan. Carefully plan work flow and meetings.

Work around team members' individual schedules, when possible. Make work assignments that ensure that people are engaged and remain positive. You must be fearless about directly confronting difficulties and, where necessary, having candid conversations with underperforming team members. Holding slackers accountable is how you let others know that the standards and shared values of the team are taken seriously.

PROVIDE SUFFICIENT DIRECTION

Another problem that can affect successful team performance is insufficient direction and governance at the top—from the team leader or leadership group—which causes dysfunctionality, mistakes, false starts, conflicts, and possibly failure. The team leader's importance cannot be overstated.

Clear and effective leadership at the top of the team is especially critical in cross-functional teams that span the organization—for example, teams from across multiple departments in a law firm or teams that include disparate membership (that is, from the law firm, various departments within the client's organization, a marketing research firm, an outside expert, and so on). A study involving ninety-five teams across twenty-five leading companies revealed that nearly seventy-five percent of cross-functional teams experienced serious problems.[16] They were unable to get the job done because they lacked "governance support," that is, being able to prepare budgets, stay on schedule, or follow specifications and requirements. Even project teams with moderate levels of governance support were still four times less successful than teams with strong governance support.

Effective teams do not just happen. It takes concerted leadership efforts to reap the benefits of teams and achieve the synergies of teamwork over individual efforts. The good news is that leadership, like collaboration and persuasion, is a skill you can learn and a set of behaviors that can be cultivated and honed through leadership development classes and experiences.

FOLLOWING THROUGH

- The ability to collaborate is a critical skill for today's lawyers because so much of their work involves collaboration on teams, with clients and many internal and external parties.

- A truly collaborative team is one in which members engage with each other toward a common goal. Groups of individuals working independently or sequentially with one another are not collaborative teams.
- Persuasion is a key competency in fostering collaborative efforts, requiring the ability to clearly communicate a shared purpose and articulate why pursuing it is in people's best interests.
- In building collaborative teams, lawyer leaders must establish components of effective teams (such as consensus, a defined plan, and composition/representativeness) and select and develop good team players.
- Leadership plays an essential part in the success of high-performing teams. These skills, behaviors, and attitudes can be identified, and lawyers must learn and apply them to the most important collaborative activities and initiatives of their organizations.
- In addition to incorporating The Five Practices of Exemplary Leadership®, lawyer leaders must address problems that plague teams in order to maximize their effect as successful leaders.

REFLECTIONS

1. Compare and contrast your experiences working in a group with working on a team. What were the characteristics of the teams that were most effective, and what were the most unsatisfactory behaviors and actions? What did a team leader do, or what could a team leader have done, to avoid or prevent such disappointment?

2. To what extent are you a collaborative person? Under what circumstances have you been collaborative, or not? What behaviors do you recognize in the most collaborative team members?

3. As a leader, how can you ensure that people are "invested" in the team?

4. In thinking about your various acquaintances, friends, and colleagues, which ones would you pick for a team that you wanted to lead? Which ones would you definitely not pick? Explain your choices.

TWELVE

Developing Emotional Intelligence and Handling Adversity

Research has shown that lawyers with strong indicators of emotional intelligence generally outperform their less emotionally intelligent colleagues.

THE LEAD-IN

- Beyond Intelligence (IQ)
- Emotional Intelligence (EQ) and the Legal Profession
- EQ and Leadership
    - Expert Views
    - EQ and Organizational Success
    - EQ: Leading Self and Others
    - EQ: An Entrepreneurial Mindset
- EQ Skills and Managing Adversity
    - Adversity and the Legal Profession
    - Methods of Coping
    - EQ Skills and Crisis Leadership
    - Resilience and Grit
- EQ: A Learned Skill
- Following Through
- Reflections

It is widely recognized that success, however defined in today's complex world, requires more than strong cognitive abilities. One estimate is that only fifteen percent of people's financial success is due to technical ability, and the remaining eighty-five percent is due to personality and ability to negotiate with and lead people.[1]

Emotional intelligence (EQ) is the facility for identifying, processing, and regulating emotions within yourself and others. It is the ability to recognize and appropriately react to your emotions and those of others around you, and emotional sensitivity is a critical component of effectively interacting with others. While technical skills and cognitive abilities are quite important in law practice, EQ skills, especially during times of adversity, are the accelerant taking a good lawyer to an exceptional one—just as they transform a good leader into an exemplary one.[2]

Beyond Intelligence (IQ)

You will need more than content "tools" in your tool kit to be successful in the practice of law and the administration of justice. You need to be able to think and act beyond the day-to-day tasks performed in litigation, client advising, and transactions and be able to employ leadership skills, which will carry you forward to success both as a lawyer and as a leader.

Prior chapters have emphasized many critical practice-specific capabilities required of lawyers and how these are especially important and necessary for providing exemplary leadership. Being able to lead a team of peers or direct reports, effectively making timely and appropriate decisions, navigating crises with creative and innovative processes, and persuading others to follow your vision are all preeminent skills for today's lawyer leaders.

Still, there are additional abilities that lawyers need to possess, develop, and demonstrate in order to be successful, especially in environments that are volatile, challenging, and uncertain, as is the case with much of the work that lawyers do. A survey of hundreds of senior lawyers, corporate counsels, and law firm leaders regarding the most important skills that lawyers need to successfully lead their law organization revealed a demand for five specific strategic leadership skills.[3] The first two are quite relevant for lawyers just entering their firms, and while the latter three concern more senior members of the firm, it is worthwhile to keep them in mind as you envision moving ahead:

1. Intensely understanding clients' needs and effectively responding to them in a timely manner. Law is a *people business*, and the emphasis of the firm and its members must be on client satisfaction.
2. Remembering to take care of one's self while also taking care of the firm and all of its members.
3. Effectively dealing with the organization's "talent," including attracting new members of the firm and managing existing members. The major cost on the balance sheets of most legal organizations involves people, their care, and retention.
4. Making sound decisions and establishing the organization's strategic direction. Respondents agreed that this is a core function of leadership and is all the more important in uncertain times.
5. Responding to change and addressing the need for growth in the organization and its personnel. The ability to anticipate economic, legal, and law practice changes, according to the survey, is a critical factor in fast-changing times. The organization must have the capacity and commitment to respond to those changes by developing and expanding new and existing markets and practice areas.

These findings are helpful in highlighting the behaviors, attitudes, and abilities required of lawyers to effectively lead, guide, and develop their organizations in challenging times. You will note that "knowing more law" or "developing greater mastery of the rules of civil procedure," while important, are not at the top of the list. In fact, nearly all of the top-of-mind concerns require emotional intelligence, not greater legal competency.

Emotional Intelligence (EQ) and the Legal Profession

Social science research has identified factors essential for success in professional positions and careers: cognitive abilities, technical skills, and interpersonal (EQ) skills.[4] Cognitive abilities include intelligence, reasoning skills, and most analytic skills. These skills are often the most immediately valued and the primary "evidence" for making decisions about hiring, as well as entrance into professional degree programs such as law school. Technical skills, such as job knowledge and law practice abilities (e.g., taking a deposition and preparing a strategy for litigation discovery), are also often valued in placement and career promotion decisions. The third area of professional skills is emotional intelligence, including an understanding of one's strengths and limitations, self-confidence, and the ability to work with and lead others.

This third area is quite often undervalued as evidence of a lawyer's worth to the law firm or practice group. However, an increasing number of law firms are viewing coaching and developing of emotional intelligence as a competitive edge.[5] Research shows that lawyers with strong indicators of emotional intelligence generally outperform their less emotionally intelligent colleagues.[6] For example, lawyers with the necessary EQ skills to effectively collaborate generate the highest revenues within their firms.[7]

Emotional intelligence sharpens abilities to assess risk, as evidenced by a greater understanding about ethics, recognizing when and how others are making ethical choices, and consciously strengthening personal ethical choices. EQ makes lawyers better communicators, especially during difficult conversations with clients or colleagues in which tough choices must be made. People who have strong emotional intelligence are also more empathetic, which is critically important for lawyers in their client-counseling role. Moreover, lawyers who are strong in emotional intelligence are more credible to their clients, adversaries, colleagues, and judges because they are aware and in control of their emotions, and place a premium on positive interactions with others.

The findings from a study carried out in a large, nationwide insurance company, have important implications for practicing attorneys. Their sales agents who were strong in emotional areas such as self-confidence, initiative, and empathy sold policies with an average premium that was over fifty percent more than those of their counterparts who were weak in such areas.[8] The fact that people want to do business with a person whom they like and trust rather than with someone whom they don't like is significant for lawyers in terms of clients as well as juries.

The challenge, notes Ronda Muir, author of *Beyond Smart: Lawyering with Emotional Intelligence*, is that while lawyers score high in cognitive abilities, they tend to score poorly in emotional intelligence—which has a huge impact on the public's low opinion of the legal profession overall.[9] We have been impressed in our leadership classes that law students quickly grasp the importance of EQ behaviors and abilities, but they often come to this conclusion by pointing to the poor interpersonal and self-management skills of lawyers they have worked with. The legal profession, the students readily concede, needs considerable improvement in the area of emotional intelligence.

EQ and Leadership

The linkage between emotional intelligence and effective lawyering is clear, but does emotional intelligence help in being a leader, too? Research shows that emotional intelligence is the barometer of excellence in virtually any job,[10] and the most successful lawyers and leaders have well-developed EQ capabilities.

Expert Views

In speaking about lawyers' need for more and better EQ skills, one noted expert on lawyer leadership reported that "though technical excellence and intellect are critical factors for success as a lawyer, emotional intelligence is the differentiating factor for successful leadership."[11] As well as being important to lawyers in their personal and professional lives, EQ skills influence and advance the ability to engage in the practices of exemplary leadership.

Daniel Goleman, an internationally renowned psychologist, has studied and written extensively about emotional intelligence in the workplace, and he indicates that technical abilities and cognitive skills provide a "threshold" capability or capacity for success but that EQ skills are twice as important.[12] He contends that the ability to use emotional intelligence is one of the hallmarks of truly effective leaders. Self-aware people know that their feelings, beliefs, and abilities affect others, and they use this knowledge to inspire and implement change in the organization.

EQ and Organizational Success

Emotional intelligence on the part of leaders plays an important role in an organization's performance and productivity. Emotionally intelligent supervisors, for instance, are able to sense how their direct reports feel about their work situation and intervene effectively when those employees begin to feel discouraged, dissatisfied, and frustrated. When supervisors are self-aware and able to manage their own emotions, people will trust them and feel good about working with them. Studies show that employees who rate the quality of their immediate supervisor as *poor* are four times more likely to leave their organizations compared with those who rate their immediate supervisor as *excellent.*[13] Retention is directly tied to the EQ of the organization's leadership.

EQ is the "driver" of a healthy, productive, effectively functioning workplace. Look deeply at almost any factor that influences organizational effectiveness, and you will find that emotional intelligence plays a role:[14]

- *Opportunity for growth.* People seek a work environment where there is the potential for development in their position; employees desire the freedom to innovate and grow personally and professionally. Second- and third-year law firm associates voice this same refrain about the importance they place on the opportunity to grow their skill sets, influence firm decisions, and develop their professional skills with clients.
- *Responsibility.* Employees who believe that they have responsibility to get things done in their organizations feel most invested and positive about the workplace. Delegation shows that their supervisors trust them and value their work.
- *High standards in terms of integrity and quality work.* Employees who believe that their organization has high standards and that those standards are clearly spelled-out report the highest levels of satisfaction with their organization.
- *Reward systems.* Employees who perceive a clear, achievable, and relevant system of rewarding good performance are much more motivated and satisfied with the organization than those who aren't certain about how their work is valued. Lawyers who work hard, smart, and "win" expect their organization to reward them accordingly.
- *Clarity of organizational purpose, values, and goals.* Among the most likely to express pride in telling others about their organization are those employees who are most clear about whom, and what, they are working for. Likewise, employees who feel the most positive about their workplace are the most committed, not only to their clients but also to the company.

All of these drivers of workplace motivation and retention are relevant to most professional workplaces but especially law, where there are great mutual dependencies on other lawyers in the firm to maintain high standards of ethical conduct and professional comportment. The key point is that workplace satisfaction does not happen by accident or without effective leadership, and such leadership reflects the characteristics associated with strong emotional intelligence. Research abounds that high levels of emotional intelligence "create climates in which information sharing, trust, healthy risk-taking, and learning flourish."[15] In contrast, "[L]ow levels of emotional intelligence create climates rife with fear and anxiety... their organizations may post good results, but they never last."[16]

We have asked law students to reflect on the exceptional leadership skills demonstrated by a lawyer or judge, and, without exception, it was their EQ skills that made the greatest impact on the students' perceptions of a desirable, effective workplace. For example, students who either served as interns for or joined the staff of a particular district attorney's office commented on the DA's leadership: "He told the truth, to them and to the public, he was highly ethical, and his principles were evident and inspiring in the way he led the office. His value-driven leadership and his highly effective interaction with everyone in the office made it a place with which they wanted to be associated."

EQ: Leading Self and Others

Consider for a moment the attributes of colleagues, supervisors, or organizational leaders with whom you have worked and whom you highly admire. What are the behaviors and personal attributes that characterize them that made your work together positive and productive? We suspect that your list will include, in some fashion, the characteristics associated with emotional intelligence. Some of those characteristics relate to a leader's ability to lead oneself; others relate to a leader's ability to lead others.

The first two aspects of emotional intelligence—awareness and regulation—focus on the individual and the ability to lead oneself. If you do not know who you are and what you stand for, or if you don't know how to control your impulses and harness your emotions for the good of the group, then why would someone choose to follow you?

- *Self-awareness* requires a deep understanding of your emotions, your strengths and weaknesses, needs and wants. Being self-aware means that you understand how your feelings and attitudes not only affect you but also impact other people. For example, if working on a tight deadline brings out the worst in you, then you adjust your work routine to get your work done ahead of schedule. Self-aware attorneys will know what difficult or demanding clients do to their moods and levels of frustration and act in a manner that moderates or avoids those moods and feelings. They know themselves well enough to know what difficult situations and people do to their emotions and behaviors. They have developed the skill of self-reflection—the ability to examine how their own motivations, beliefs, and values affect their thoughts and actions, and the capacity to adjust or change them in light of other's actions and thoughts and to do so in future experiences.[17] When you experience strong emotions, slow down and think about why you are feeling what you are feeling, and be more intentional in how you choose to react.

- *Self-regulation* requires continuous attention and personal growth because most people are impulsive and emotional about things that are relevant and important to them. People generally learn at an early age that they must control many of these impulses and emotions in order to function well in their jobs, classes, and personal relationships. For lawyers and leaders, this ability is critical because people who are in control of their feelings and impulses are able to create an environment of trust and fairness, which is highly desired by coworkers, direct reports, and others. People who can regulate their behaviors also tend to avoid improper conduct (e.g., rarely verbally attack others) and demonstrate higher integrity (e.g., don't stereotype people) than those who succumb to temptation and take the "low road." Lawyers with a high degree of self-control are generally reflective and thoughtful, and they are comfortable with ambiguity and the need for change.

There is an outward focus to EQ's second dynamic—the ability to work well with others—and it is evident in lawyers related to attracting and keeping clients, retaining talent in the firm, and working with others who actually want to interact with you. This aspect of emotional intelligence addresses your ability to lead others and has two critically important *social* attributes:

- *Social awareness* is your ability to sense and respond to the feelings, difficulties, and attitudes of those around you. When you say that someone doesn't have a clue about what's going on, you are really saying that they are not aware of how their behavior and statements affect others. Saying that they are "tone-deaf" is another way of saying that they are unable to put them self into someone else's situation. Both of these expressions refer to a lack of empathy. Active listening is an antecedent of empathy—that is, thoughtfully considering the feelings and concerns of others. Take the time to look at situations from other people's perspectives (not just argue for your own). Respond to, rather than avoid, feelings; and seek to understand the *why* behind how people are expressing themselves and their viewpoints.
- *Social skills* refer to your ability to manage relationships with other people, and these skills are closely associated with communications

skills. Leaders and lawyers with strong social skills build common ground and can develop rapport with a wide range of people. Many of these skills are the team-building skills described in the previous chapter. Be purposeful and attentive when networking, making connections, and creating projects and situations that bring people together. Generate alternatives when disagreements arise, and promote a cooperative climate in which everyone feels welcome and invited to contribute.

EQ is a necessary part of any leader's portfolio. You have to lead yourself first, and then you need to be able to lead others, while recognizing that success in any endeavor comes about through the intersection of these two facets of EQ and leadership. Because leadership ultimately involves doing something that has never quite been done that way before, developing the mindset of an entrepreneur also has special relevance to lawyer leaders.

EQ: An Entrepreneurial Mindset

The lament of a young practicing attorney in a large law firm about how he "wished someone had told me in law school about how I would need to be an entrepreneur in order to be a successful lawyer," echoes what a growing number of practicing attorneys and law firms are also coming to terms with.[18] As with successful entrepreneurs, lawyers with strong EQ can leverage empathy, handle ambiguity, and see challenges from various perspectives, which improves problem solving, create strong relationships, and ultimately wins people over. A meta-analysis (looking at nearly forty studies, involving more than sixty-five thousand entrepreneurs) found that while both IQ and EQ were important to entrepreneurial success, EQ had twice the influence of IQ.[19]

Entrepreneurship, defined as "the pursuit of opportunity beyond the resources you currently control,"[20] requires an internal drive to make the most of possibilities, a willingness to experiment coupled with the ability to quickly pivot and adapt as circumstances change, and the ego strength to overcome and learn from setbacks. Assessing an entrepreneurial opportunity requires discerning how you can capitalize on that prospect, candidly calculating what resources you will need and how to gain control over them, and determining the best structure to take advantage of an opening.[21]

Lawyers, just like successful entrepreneurs, should have a growth mindset and believe in themselves. What follows is being unafraid of making mistakes, being in touch with your feelings, and carving out your own path forward. This self-awareness contributes to a bias for action and favors decisiveness—taking to heart the wisdom from one entrepreneur who explained that he had never met a rich person who hadn't ever lost any money, but he had met lots of poor people who had never lost a dime.[22] Adopting an entrepreneurial mindset means believing more in the possibilities than in the probabilities, becoming comfortable with discomfort, and actually being on the lookout for problems so that you can fix them.

Bring these entrepreneurial qualities to your practice of the law, and within the organizations you associate with. This entrepreneurial spirit and process are important in the ways that lawyers effectively turn adversity into opportunity within their legal firms and environments.[23] The most successful lawyers have an entrepreneurial mindset as they evaluate and then seize new business opportunities, including market expansions, adoption of new technologies, development of new practice areas, and launch of a new law practice group.

EQ Skills and Managing Adversity

Lawyers make their living dealing with adversity. You are educated from your earliest days in law school to anticipate conflicts and disagreements and deal with setbacks and disappointments. In the legal profession, you can't take anything for granted, you must expect the unexpected, and there are wild cards in every deck. Of course, such observations apply to everyone, no matter their occupation or status, but they take on special importance when you are a lawyer leader dealing with significant circumstances, such as handling a client's liberty or wealth—and just another reminder about why emotional intelligence is essential for lawyers and lawyer leaders.

Adversity and the Legal Profession

There is a powerful scene in the film *The Paper Chase* when the iconic Professor Kingsfield dryly remarks to a classroom of new law students, "Look to your left, look to your right. One of you won't be here next year." This comment highlights the fact that law is a profession rife with adversity.

Lawyers' professional lives are complicated by regular setbacks, unanticipated circumstances, difficult people that disrupt an established plan or strategy, and the vagaries of luck. Drawing a judge with a history of opposition to a major element or point in your case is a modest example of adversity; having the entire mergers and acquisitions department in your corporate defense firm leave (with associates) to form a boutique firm is a more significant one. The sudden, unanticipated death of the top rainmaker in the firm is another significant example, as would be an economic recession that causes the firm to seek the protection of the federal bankruptcy laws.

Law organizations have been experiencing significant changes and challenges from a variety of sources in recent years.[24] They have to overcome, or manage, significant threats to their business, including competitive pressures from international law firms and alternative legal services providers; dramatic escalation in the use of technology in the practice of law; challenges associated with attracting and retaining young, as well as experienced, talent; and increasing demands from clients for reducing the cost of legal services.[25]

On an individual level, too, adversity is ubiquitous. Setbacks such as an adverse jury decision, a case dismissed on summary judgment, or unfavorable arbitration award all create stresses and pressures on the attorney of record. Additional stress and pressures to succeed come from law school debt, possible new family responsibilities, managing people (e.g., administrative personnel), and overhead costs, to name a few.

Methods of Coping

Leaders, as well as lawyers, need to understand and plan for adversity and crisis. Whether from the perspective of a leader or a lawyer, the issue is not whether you will face adversity but rather how you will deal with it when it happens.

A great deal of research on mental and emotional hardiness and coping has shown that every person has a distinct, consistent pattern of thinking about life's ups and downs and also that most people are unaware of their particular pattern.[26] A classic study examining how different people reacted to the identical challenge or stress found that it does not affect every person in a similar fashion.[27] During the coronavirus pandemic, for example, while everyone experienced the same storm, they were not all in the same boat.

Some people seem to handle a crisis or bad outcome easily, while others experience great difficulty coping with it. The difference is not attributable to a character flaw but rather the variances in the way people process, manage, and rebound from a challenging episode or situation. For some people, adversity is viewed as an opportunity for change and growth rather than as a situation warranting anger, disappointment, and despair due to the challenge or failure.[28] Those with the strongest EQ skills cope most successfully with adversity.

Trial lawyers, for example, know that in litigation there is always one side that wins and one side that loses, so some appreciation of how to handle a defeat and help a client understand a loss is vitally important. Much of the work that lawyers do involves a stark divide between winning and losing and that more than "a tough skin" is needed. What's required is a finely tuned ability for managing self, built by experience and strong EQ skills.

EQ Skills and Crisis Leadership

There is little question that lawyers are living in tumultuous times—economic upheavals, medical pandemics, social unrest, political polarization, and climate calamities are likely to continue. Thus, lawyer leaders need the skills and attitudes that will permit them to function well in those uncertain times, and equally important, they need to survive and prosper with their spirit and self-confidence in good shape. In other words, they need strong EQ skills to lead through crises and adversity.

A VUCA world does not favor taking a business-as-usual attitude, even though people are looking to their leaders to set the path forward, providing "marching orders" through a vision for the future. More is necessary. Here are six EQ-inspired strategies that you can consider for reframing crisis and adversity as opportunity:[29]

- Broaden the context in which you find yourself by reminding people that the situation is not personal and that many others are trying to cope with the same disruption and dislocation. While that doesn't address the steps that must be taken to deal with the crisis, it does provide a mental framework within which to consider the problem.
- Be up front and candid with your colleagues and/or team about the situation, about what actions must be taken, and what is or is not working. Many Americans saw this played out poorly with the federal government's early reaction to the coronavirus outbreak: confusion, obfuscation, disregard for medical science, and intentional misstatements of fact. People don't blame leaders for adverse outcomes over which they had no control, but they do blame them, and cease to trust them, if the leaders don't tell it like it is.
- Reach out to others and engage even more with them. If you perceive that difficult times lie ahead, then your colleagues are also experiencing those challenges, uncertainty, and possibly even isolation. Those

are the feelings and reactions that people experience in a crisis, and you need to be fully engaged in leading your team through it. Get started by asking people about their conditions and situations; express empathy but also give assurances that by working together, this calamity can be turned into a positive opportunity to improve the team or organization. This is the time to demonstrate compassion and caring for others so they know that you have their best interests in mind and will do your best to get everyone through the crisis.

- Act quickly and boldly. Depending on the nature of the crisis, prompt action is usually necessary and expected; strive for strategic decision making with speed over precision of impact.[30] Speed over precision is preferred because during a crisis people become cognitively overwhelmed, useful information is incomplete or unavailable, and there is a tendency to shut down. Therefore, effective crisis leadership requires prompt, but thoughtful, action to assess the scope and extent (and cause) of the threatened harm and then engage in active decision making and responses.
- Do what you say you will do—don't make promises that you can't keep. Keep reminding people about the progress that is being made. One of the most disappointing aspects of the federal government's initial handing of the COVID-19 pandemic was that there was no national mandate or plan of action, and each state and municipality was on its own; consequently, when actions were eventually taken by government agencies, they appeared to be chaotic and quixotic. People admire those who stick to their commitments and set an example for others to emulate. Be both candid (realistic) and optimistic in offering a pathway forward.
- Prepare yourself to lead in a crisis. Many of the demands of leadership are predictable, but most crises spring on the leaders and their constituents with little notification. In such circumstances, prompt and confident responsive action is needed. It will be quite helpful if you have already identified how you will communicate and how roles and responsibilities will be allocated in the event of a sudden and significant event. Think of this as a fire drill, or liken this to the emergency response exercises that first responders conduct. Each challenge requires its own playbook, but leaders can prepare in general ways for a crisis and then adapt to the challenge that prompts action by the group.

Resilience and Grit

Life doesn't come with a road map, and there is no freeway to the future. Every life path (personal as well as organizational) has twists and turns, road-blocks and delays, and unexpected detours, some of which will be graver, more challenging, or even more joyous than others. Each change affects people differently, and yet people generally adapt well over time to life-changing situations and stressful situations—in part thanks to resilience and grit. While resilience involves the ability to get back up when you've been knocked down or to come back fighting stronger after a loss, grit is your passion for and perseverance in reaching a long-term goal. Lawyer leaders can use their EQ skills to transform adverse situations into opportunities by fostering and promoting both resiliency and grit in themselves and their teams.

RESILIENCE

Psychologists define *resilience* as the process of adapting well in the face of adversity, trauma, tragedy, threat, or significant sources of stress—such as family and relationship problems, serious health problems, or workplace and financial stressors. Resilience can be thought of as a kind of solitary internal "grit" that allows individuals to rebound, often stronger than before, from setbacks and sustain their drive and commitment over time.

As much as resilience most often involves "bouncing back" from these difficult experiences, it can also involve profound personal growth (actually bouncing forward).[31] Resilient people look at the world in a very realistic way, and, as such, they act in ways that permit them to face head-on the problems, challenges, and opportunities that come their way. They may be disappointed with the situation they are facing, but they have prepared themselves for adversity and even great success. Resilience positively influences people's work satisfaction and engagement, lowers their levels of depression, and improves overall well-being. Resilient people are generally healthy, productive, and dependable. They have the capacity to respond quickly and constructively to crisis and adversity, and resiliency has been shown to explain differences between highly successful and unsuccessful people.[32]

GRIT

Grit helps to explain why some people accomplish more than others despite similarities in talent and resources.[33] Grit is the motivational drive that keeps you going on a difficult case over a sustained period of time.

Research involving a large, international sample found that grit was related to The Five Practices of Exemplary Leadership®, with the grittiest more likely to lead by example (Model the Way) and to support others in challenging the status quo (Challenge the Process). From a practical view, grit enables you as a leader, and as a lawyer, to be more willing to stick with, stand up for, and live by your principles, as well as be more comfortable taking risks and learning from experience.[34]

BUILDING RESILIENCE AND GRIT

The way that you envision situations and explain setbacks to yourself (and to others) is important to building resilience and grit. For example, resilient people view a difficulty as a challenge, not as a paralyzing event. They see the effects of setbacks as temporary rather than permanent and view them as experiences from which to learn and as opportunities from which to grow and develop. Resilient people recognize that they won't win in every situation, so they don't blame themselves or consider themselves victims when that happens but rather focus on what they can learn to propel themselves forward the next time.

Furthermore, when you have a purpose for what you are doing and a commitment to make the most of every relationship and the causes you care about, resilience and grit are built and fostered. Focus your time and energy on situations and events over which you have some control and where you can have an impact because this strengthens your resolve and confidence, overcoming feelings of helplessness, loss, and powerlessness.

One of the strongest ways to build personal resilience and grit is to forge connections and relations with others. This helps you remember the meaning in your work, maintain perspective with confidence, and clearly focus on the "path forward" so that your colleagues and team members share your confidence and strategic vision for solutions.[35] Take a look at the Grit Project, created by the ABA Commission on Women in the Profession, to develop and enhance the grit and growth mindset of women lawyers. However, the articles, videos, case studies, and activities are all foundational for lawyers of any shape, size, preference, or color.[36]

EQ: A Learned Skill

While identifying and describing the significant pressures and demands on themselves and their law firms, a rather substantial percentage of law firm leaders readily admit that they and their firms are not undertaking substantive actions to handle these challenges; and, consequently, they were losing talent, clients, and market share.[37] Firm leaders report deep concerns about the large number of American law firms that, in the last two decades, have experienced an existential crisis caused by an economic recession or a collapse of a practice area and have gone out of business.[38] The causes for law firm closings and failures are varied, but most of them can be traced back directly to the failure of leadership.

In order to adequately prepare for adversity, lawyer leaders must develop EQ skills. Strong EQ skills and aptitude are very important in the work that lawyers do. They are not, however, genetic, which means that they can be learned, developed, and mastered. While emotional intelligence often increases with age and maturity, a conscious commitment to advancing these abilities can considerably improve your effectiveness as a lawyer and as a leader even early in your career. Like building a muscle, doing so takes time and intentionality. As with building muscles, though, building EQ skills is worth the time because the end result is strong and healthy leadership.

FOLLOWING THROUGH

- Cognitive and technical skills are important, but even more essential are emotional intelligence (EQ) skills. This is true for lawyers and even truer for lawyer leaders.
- EQ skills are important for leading self, others, and organizations.
- The legal profession is characterized by adversity, but lawyer leaders can best handle adversity and crisis situations with EQ skills.
- EQ helps leaders foster resilience and grit—two key factors in handling adversity—in themselves and in their followers.
- Leaders with EQ provide leadership that turns adversity into opportunity.
- EQ abilities are not innate and may not come naturally to many lawyers, but can be learned and developed, so all lawyers can add this skill to their tool kit of effective leadership.

REFLECTIONS

1. What EQ qualities do you have that will prepare you to be a better lawyer? A better leader? Describe times when you could have been more emotionally present or aware, and what you wish you could have done or said.

2. What prepares lawyers to handle dramatic or difficult change? What are the roadblocks or obstacles to doing so?

3. Does the preponderance of adversity in the lives of lawyers (e.g., losing cases, losing clients, managing difficult personalities, etc.) contribute to negative perceptions about being a lawyer? What pause does it give you to know that attorneys have said, "I wouldn't become a lawyer again if I had it to do over"?

4. Identify instances in your experience that have demonstrated grit. When you've been knocked down, what caused you to get back up?

THIRTEEN

Leading the Charge for Diversity, Equity, and Inclusion

Lawyers interpret for their clients the national policies promoting equality in opportunity for all Americans—yet they have often failed to lead their own organizations . . . to meet those goals.

THE LEAD-IN

- A Diversity Problem in the Legal Profession
- Foundational Concepts
    - Diversity, Equity, and Inclusion (DEI)
    - Implicit Bias
- Advantages of Greater DEI
    - Performance Benefits
    - Cultural Draw
- Leading DEI Change
    - Self-Analysis of Implicit Bias
    - Current Level of Inclusiveness
    - Ubiquitous Diversity Training
    - Vision for Change
    - DEI Change: A Win–Win Situation
- Following Through
- Reflections

The American Bar Association (ABA) recognizes that the profession has a diversity problem. They have led initiatives promoting greater diversity in the legal profession and have established goals for the enhancement of diversity in the profession and the elimination of bias throughout the profession and the judicial system.[1] The association's goals stress three fundamental components to achieve a more diverse profession and the elimination of bias: diversity, equity, and inclusion (DEI). The ABA has established a center for the advancement of diversity in the profession as well as sponsored programs to assist law organizations to achieve their goals of greater diversity and inclusion. The ABA's Diversity and Inclusion 360 Commission articulated its commitment that "all providers of legal services, including law firms and corporations,... expand and create opportunities at all levels of responsibility for diverse attorneys" and urged "clients to assist in the facilitation of opportunities for diverse attorneys, and to direct a greater percentage of the legal services they purchase, both currently and in the future, to diverse attorneys."[2] Particular challenges for women and people of color were highlighted by the coronavirus pandemic, which make DEI efforts all that more significant.[3]

A strong institutional commitment to greater inclusiveness in the profession is an excellent starting point, but more must be done. What it will take to move the legal profession and its institutions and organizations (from the organized bar to law schools and law firms) toward a state of equality in opportunity and equity in outcomes is leadership.

The work that lawyers do requires a great awareness of the need for a more inclusive society and far more diverse workplaces (usually expressed in terms of racial, ethnic, gender, and sexual orientation). Lawyers are at society's front line in addressing problems of discrimination and justice. They routinely advise clients on legal and business problems stemming from their less-than-inclusive workplaces—yet lawyers largely work in just those workplaces themselves. Lawyers interpret for their clients the national policies promoting equality in opportunity for all Americans—yet they have often failed to lead their own organizations (e.g., law firms, corporate counsel offices, and government legal departments) to meet those goals.

A Diversity Problem in the Legal Profession

Becoming a lawyer is an aspiration for many Americans. Surveys show that being a lawyer is a career goal for many people, and, in recent years, over sixty thousand people have applied annually to American law schools.[4] Accordingly, you might think that the ranks of lawyers are as diverse and representative as is the United States at large. But the facts suggest that the legal profession is largely White and male; relatedly, this is also true for the federal and state judiciary.

Although about forty-five percent of law school applicants identify as *not* White/Caucasian,[5] demographics of practicing lawyers tell a different story. Black people constitute twelve percent of the US population but only six percent of American lawyers.[6] Hispanic/Latinx people constitute eighteen percent of the national population yet less than six percent of its lawyers. Asians make up about seven percent of the US population and less than five percent of American lawyers.[7] Notably, White people in America account for sixty percent of the population but an overwhelming eighty-seven percent of lawyers.[8] Furthermore, according to contemporary surveys, males in America account for only forty-nine percent of the population, yet they constitute sixty-three percent of practicing lawyers.[9] Even a cursory examination of the factual data indicates that there is racial and gender disparity in the legal profession.

The diversity gaps are again quite apparent among the most venerable and important group of lawyers—those who serve on the bench in judgment of others. The judiciary is the most significant segment of American lawyers due to the impact that judges have on setting national policy and providing a "face" for the civil and criminal justice systems as well as the overall legal profession. Some illustrative data on the diversity issue: Approximately eighty percent of all sitting federal judges in the United States are White.[10] Only one in three federal judges is female.[11] And more than half of all state court justices are White and male, while only fifteen percent are people of color, even though White males constitute only about thirty percent of the US population.[12]

In addition to the diversity problem in the legal profession, there is the problem of people in the legal profession questioning whether a diversity issue even exists. In any legal environment, there will be a range of opinions, with some people taking polar-opposite positions: some will claim, "We don't have a diversity problem; everything is okay," and some will exclaim, "All this diversity stuff is just political correctness!" One survey highlighted strong differences in perceptions among lawyers about the extent to which their firm's professionals experienced or perceived bias and uneven access to opportunities and benefits: Only eleven percent of White male lawyers in the survey believed that diversity efforts were failing to address subtle racial or gender bias, compared to forty percent of the White women and about fifty percent of the women of color in the survey.[13]

Clearly, there is a need for diversity and inclusiveness in the legal profession, and there also is a need to address the pushback and skepticism surrounding this issue. These needs highlight the necessity for lawyer leaders.

Foundational Concepts

In order to understand how to address diversity issues and how leadership can help in this regard, it is critical to grasp some foundational concepts. Mastering key terminology is the starting point for any discussion of diversity. Second, understanding the problem of implicit bias is the starting point for any solution to the diversity problem. Finally, understanding that discrimination is systemic, and often inheres in the structures of the American legal profession, and is not simply the product of individual animus, is fundamental to increasing diversity in the profession.

Diversity, Equity, and Inclusion (DEI)

What the term *diversity* and its close cousins' *equity* and *inclusion* mean and entail is often misconstrued. Each of these terms play an important role in combating bias and discrimination in the legal profession and the practice of law, as well as in strengthening the vitality and culture of an organization.

Diversity is basically the presence of differences within a given setting. A person is not diverse; diversity is a relational construct based on some collective whole. It is typically described by a numerical representation of different types or groups of people, such as how many Latinx people are admitted to law school, how many females are recruited to the firm, and how many Black people are getting promoted and advanced in the office. The measurement of diversity is usually captured in fairly traditional characteristics, such as age, gender, and ethnicity, or as identities of people (such as by disability or by sexual orientation). The representation of women lawyers in the firm or the percentage of Asian American lawyers and paralegals in a particular office, for example, permits comparisons over time or with various organizational factors (for example, compensation and rates of retention and advancement to partner status). This is useful information to the firm's leaders who are advancing diversity goals.

Equity recognizes that in most settings there is not an equal starting place; it's like a Monopoly game where someone doesn't get to begin playing until most of the other players have already purchased properties and built houses. Equity acknowledges this context, makes a commitment to address the gaps and imbalances, and takes corrective actions. Equity refers to institutional efforts that ensure that all people, especially those from historically marginalized identities, have access to opportunities, resources, and support from the organization. Equity does not mean equality—as in each person is treated equally—but rather strives to eliminate any constraints on individuals' ability to access an open position or a promotion, or the resources of the organization to support their personal goals and ambitions.

Inclusion focuses on the "how" of diversity—that is, the behaviors and social norms, along with policies and decisions, that contribute to or hinder the involvement and sense of belonging that people feel with regard to the group, team, or organization. Inclusion can be tangible and visible, as in who gets invited to meetings, whose opinions are heard, how offices are physically organized and allocated, or even who gets access to particular information and resources. Inclusion is what new lawyers are thinking when asking themselves questions such as the following:

- How well do I fit in this place?
- How welcome do I feel in this situation?
- How valued does this place make me feel when decisions are made?

An analogy is often used to describe the relationship among these three concepts: diversity is being invited to the party, equity is being asked to plan the dance, and inclusion is being asked to dance. Stated another way, equity is a goal for the organization with diversity being a first (and quite important) step and inclusion referring to the effort, actions, and environment that are necessary to achieve the goal.

Implicit Bias

Perhaps the greatest challenge to lawyers and their organizations is the underlying reason that DEI efforts are necessary: implicit bias and the effects it has on the structure and operation of law firms and law organizations.

Social scientists have firmly established that people employ two cognitive reasoning systems—one that is rapid, intuitive, and prone to errors, and a second that is more calculated and deliberative and more likely to be error free.[14] It is the first type of reasoning in which implicit perceptions, attitudes, and stereotypes occur and affect social judgments without conscious awareness or control. These implicit thoughts and feelings leak into many behaviors and attitudes, including how you perceive others and what you value. Within this type of reaction, behavior is the result of unconscious mental processes that are based on these implicit attitudes and stereotypes formed by life experiences. They occur below the surface of your conscious thinking.

Researchers have documented certain almost-spontaneous perceptions by particular groups when they encounter members of other particular groups—for example, perceptions by White males when they encounter African American males or Asian American women. These biases and prejudices, if unchecked, cause a great deal of the discrimination and exclusion directed toward—and resulting lack of opportunities for—racial, gender, and ethnic group members as well as other groups of marginalized and disadvantaged people.[15]

The inability to corral implicit bias has dramatic, and usually negative, implications for law firms. Consider the well-documented case of a national law firm that actively recruited (at considerable expense) and hired more than thirty African American associates in an eight-year span but was then unable to retain any of them. These associates cited implicit bias of the firm's lawyers as the reason that they left.[16] The legal profession is concerned that implicit bias affects attorney hiring practices and evaluations of "minority" lawyers by senior colleagues.[17] These forms of bias in hiring, retention, and promotion make it difficult to ensure fair, equitable access to the benefits of the law firm for diverse associates.

Implicit bias also affects other areas of the law and the administration of justice, such as the noteworthy perception in many communities of color that the court systems are racist, treating Black and Latinx parties adversely compared to White parties in the system. Furthermore, recent events have shown that implicit bias is a persistent problem among law enforcement personnel, leading one group of researchers to conclude "that [police] officers might be *implicitly* biased against minorities and more likely to use force against them as a result."[18] The researchers noted that although there is a perception of a disproportionately greater number of police killings of people of color, there was no centralized database of officer-related deaths until the police killing of Michael Brown in Ferguson, Missouri, in 2014.[19] The negative impact of these perceptions of racism and bias is decreased trust in these important institutions of justice.

There is clear evidence that law firm leaders tend to underestimate the impact of unconscious bias in their firms and to overestimate the effectiveness of their current policies.[20] However, research has shown that efforts to mitigate the perceptions of unequal treatment of diverse parties can be successful in ameliorating the effects of implicit bias.[21] Overcoming inertia or complacency with regard to identifying implicit biases often begins by collecting data and actually looking at various metrics connected with diversity, equity, and inclusion within the organization, and by being familiar with the research studies on these issues across the profession as a whole.[22] Thoughtful and appropriately aggressive measures by the leadership of legal firms can improve the working environment for diverse lawyers and level the playing field in terms of hiring, retention, mentoring, pay, and promotion.

Lawyers and law organizations must remain vigilant in their efforts to combat expressed or implicit bias not only in their own workplaces but also in the "halls of justice" and the legal profession in general. Lawyers have not been blameless in the centuries of systemic bias and racism in the United States: They drafted racial and ethnic exclusion clauses in millions of real property deeds; helped landlord clients to implement redlining practices; and actively counseled clients on racist, and often illegal, practices that held back communities of color for many years. Certainly, lawyers should seek to learn from that history and strive not to repeat it. Even more, it is incumbent on them to lead toward positive change now.

One area that lawyers can begin to attack is the problem of systemic bias toward women and minorities in their own law organizations. There has been considerable analysis of how hiring, retention, and partner decisions have discriminated again women and lawyers of color within the firm and how the discrimination occurs in myriad ways.[23] The pyramidal structure of attorney hiring and progression in the firm is often insensitive to the demands on women lawyers who need personal leave time for children and who are often called on to provide caregiving to other members of the family. These individual and personal interests of many lawyers are challenging law firms to move to more flexible structures for promotion and retention policies that reflect these demands of the law firm's talent.[24] Solutions to these challenges requires thoughtful attention and leadership across the organization to harmonize the firm's interests with attorneys' personal needs.

Advantages of Greater DEI

While it is fair to conclude that the legal profession has a diversity problem, it is more accurate to state from a leadership perspective, that the legal profession has a diversity "opportunity." Why are diversity, equity, and inclusion in the legal profession and the judicial system important from an opportunity standpoint?

The answer to this question requires a clear examination of the institutional and professional benefits of more inclusive law organizations. For example, the increasing importance that law students and young lawyers and even corporate clients place on greater diversity, and the acceptance and embracement of differentness in the institutions with which they choose to associate.

Performance Benefits

There is considerable research that supports DEI institutional goals. Advancing diversity and inclusion ameliorates many basic organizational goals such as optimizing recruitment, increasing retention, enhancing institutional reputation, and driving client development.[25]

Why aren't law firms more diverse and inclusive if doing so would make them so much better? To be fair, diversity can create conflicts among different perspectives, which are shaped by people's upbringing, cultural differences, and biases, which are hardwired into their thinking and beliefs. Studies show that efforts to promote diversity and a more inclusive workplace environment may "simultaneously produce more conflict and employee turnover as well as more creativity and innovation."[26] Cultural, racial, or ethnic biases, often implicit, are powerful headwinds to overcome in efforts to achieve the positive influences of diversity.

Despite the challenges, the evidence clearly establishes that diverse teams and organizations are higher performing and get better results, generating more creative thinking and greater innovation. Most senior executives, including law firm managers, indicate that organizational policies and practices promoting diversity and inclusion are important for several reasons, but mainly because they improve the organization's performance.[27] This was precisely the conclusion from a Boston Consulting Group study: "[I]ncreasing the diversity of leadership teams leads to more and better innovation and improved financial performance."[28] Research into team performance has generally concluded that diverse and "nonhomogeneous teams are simply smarter."[29] People on these teams generally bring more information to the table, more carefully scrutinize the available data, don't rush to judgment, listen to one another, generate more alternatives, and reach better decisions.[30]

The findings also show that people working in diverse organizations tend to be more aware of their own biases. Not surprising is that rates of discrimination and harassment claims decrease in direct relation to positive assessments of DEI workplace culture.[31]

Cultural Draw

A law firm culture characterized by inclusiveness appeals to the culture at large. In particular, it is a draw for young lawyers, as well as corporate clients. Law firms, like many enterprises these days, are undergoing a significant transition in their ranks from older, baby boomer generations to younger, millennial employees. These generations lack an overlap in common life experiences (just think how law school studies have changed from spending hours in the library stacks tracking down documents to streams of information now accessible directly at one's desk), an understanding of each other's needs (for example, today all law school graduates are seriously impacted by student loan debt, causing nearly half of them to delay or abandon marriage plans and having children, and correspondingly putting more emphasis on work–life balance), and different ways of communicating (with baby boomers preferring face-to-face conversations while graduates today favor "speaking" via text or email).

Millennials (now representing over forty percent of the workforce) rate the importance of work culture at 8.5 on a ten-point scale,[32] and reports indicate that they are happier working in creative and inclusive cultures compared to authoritarian, rule-based ones.[33] Young lawyers want to feel included, valued, and listened to, and they respond more favorably to workplace culture than to financial rewards. In fact, organizational culture and fit are rated as more important than compensation in their decision regarding which firm to join and whether or not to stay rooted in that firm.[34] A law firm that responds to the interests and values of its younger lawyers, especially as the baby boomer partners are moving toward a less active status or retirement, is more likely to best utilize and retain their talent.

Consider the experience of one second-year law student who was struggling with the question of whether as a Latinx person she should seek an internship with the district attorney's office. She posed this question to a BIPOC (Black, Indigenous, and people of color) deputy district attorney, who impressed on her the importance of having a more diverse group of prosecutors. While he admitted at times struggling with the loneliness of being a person of color working in a predominantly White field, he was actively engaged in the recruitment process to help other people of color join the team. His explanation and encouragement convinced her to accept the internship. If individuals do not see people who "look" like them in the classroom, in the firm or profession, they neither aspire to be part of that occupation nor envision a path to leadership and success.

This cultural appeal, which applies not only to millennials but also to corporate clients, is interwoven with questions about the purpose of diversity. In approaching issues of equity and inclusion in the workplace and in society, lawyers often ponder why efforts to enhance diversity are important. They will likely begin with a legalistic approach: Does the law require a broadscale effort to create more inclusive and more diverse organizations, or does the law simply prohibit discrimination and exclusion from public rights? They may ask if the firm should increase diversity because it is a priority of the national organization of lawyers (i.e., the ABA) or because it is the "right" thing to do in a moral or ethical sense. In other words, should the firm promote the goals of equity and inclusion because it has to or because it wants to? A convenient landing point for this decision often comes down to "because it is good for business."

Indeed, many large corporate clients require that the law firms that they contract with have active diversity plans and outcomes, and often the corporation's general counsel will be driving efforts to improve diversity in law firms through their selection of outside firms. By having a diverse organization that values differences across a number of dimensions as well as accommodates them, a law firm increases the likelihood of retaining its younger lawyers—the firm's talent of the future. This is a substantial boon considering that, according to one estimate, losing an associate can cost the law firm between $200,000 and $500,000.[35] So, the right thing to do becomes the smart thing to do.

Besides being the "right thing to do," supporting and advancing greater efforts at inclusion and diversity has legal and policy implications for law firms and lawyers. Rule 8.4(g) of the American Bar Association's Model Rules of Professional Conduct prohibits lawyers from engaging in conduct that discriminates against another on the basis of protected categories (e.g., race, sex, religion, sexual orientation, gender identity, etc.) "in conduct related to the practice of law."[36] About two dozen states have adopted rules like Rule 8.4(g) prohibiting discriminatory actions by licensed attorneys. This remains a complicated and controversial area of the regulation of lawyer conduct, but the key takeaway is that lawyers must be mindful of the barriers to inclusion and equity in society and particularly in the practice of law.

Leading DEI Change

The talent (human resources) of a law firm is the most important asset in their path to success—and that talent is more productive, successful, and satisfied if they feel that they are included, that their opinions are valued by the organization, and that decisions are fair and equitable. Clearly, finding a solution to the diversity problem is essential—and that solution lies in leadership. Leading legal organizations to enhance inclusion and promote equity is not unlike leadership efforts around many other major initiatives. Good leadership skills, behaviors, and attitudes are required in order to influence the organization constructively, and strong emotional intelligence abilities are what those effective leaders need to lead themselves and others in the organization toward more inclusive workplaces.

The pernicious influence of implicit bias makes this a daunting task. For example, a leader committed to positive change must both perceive the need for change and persuade followers of that need and how to accomplish it. Consider the leadership challenge implicit in surveys that indicate only twenty-seven percent of White males feel strongly that it is important to improve diversity in their law firms, compared with eighty-seven percent of women of color and sixty-one percent of White women in those same firms.[37]

Nonetheless, there are several actions that leaders can employ to effect changes in their organization's culture of inclusiveness. These include assessing and addressing one's own biases, including identifying blind spots in one's own thinking; determining the current level of inclusiveness in the organization, which entails being open to feedback from others; extending diversity training throughout the organization; and creating and articulating a vision for change.

Self-Analysis of Implicit Bias

The first, and perhaps most obvious, step for lawyers leading change in their organization's culture is to address their own biases, implicit or otherwise. It is difficult to lead change if you don't believe it's needed and can't acknowledge how you have been complicit in the problem. Racism scholar Ibram X. Kendi explains that everyone is either racist or antiracist. There is no room for neutrality, and there is no such thing as a "non-racist."[38] Antiracism is an active and conscious effort to work against multidimensional aspects of racism. Similarly, becoming an "ally" is being recognized by the people you are being an ally for by involving yourself in the promotion and advancement of an inclusive culture through positive and intentional action.[39]

Because everyone has biases, law firm leaders need to set an example in identifying and dealing with them, beginning as leaders do by "going first" before asking others to also step forward. They should seek implicit bias training for themselves as an indication of their sincere interest in these issues, acknowledging their own potential shortcomings, and demonstrating that the issues involve everyone in the organization. Self-administrated tests are readily available—for example, the Harvard Implicit Association Test,[40] which can form the basis for efforts across the organization to assess the extent of implicit bias and take measures to address it.

Part of assessing and addressing implicit biases involves identifying blind spots in interactions with others and being open to both new and difficult information. For example, more than conceptually acknowledging that everyone doesn't think like you, you must appreciate the value of perspectives and experiences different from your own. Reflect on your interactions with others, much like viewing a videotape, to evaluate how your unconscious biases may have led you astray in your understanding of what they were saying. Leaders must, in addition, determine if they are trapped in a bubble of thinking and consequentially only hear preprocessed messages from their experiences. People generally hear only what they want to hear (not unlike the "selective hearing" of children when their parents admonish them), and this blocks critical thinking and more rational or realistic evaluations. Escaping this trap demands deep listening and really hearing what others are saying and feeling.[41]

Current Level of Inclusiveness

In addition to assessing themselves, leaders determined to enhance the culture of the team or organization must assess what level of inclusiveness currently exists. It's been shown that the "behaviors of leaders (be they senior executives or managers) can drive up to seventy percentage points of difference between the proportion of employees who feel highly included and the proportion of those who do not."[42] Taking stock of the organization's culture requires commitment by the firm's leadership to find out how others in the organization feel about their workplace environment. Indeed, leaders interested in improving the culture of inclusion and equity must actively seek input; they can't work in their offices waiting for someone to make an appointment and let them know what is going on. Leaders are out and about; to quote John le Carré, the British author of numerous espionage novels, "a desk is a dangerous place from which to view the world."[43]

For leaders to be successful in gathering feedback about inclusiveness, members of the team must feel that their leaders are approachable and interested in learning about how their behavior is impacting the performance of others. They must take steps to find out the extent to which people believe that they are treated with dignity, respect, civility, and decency. And, they must determine if people feel a sense of belonging in the organization, feeling valued and appreciated for who they are and what they contribute. Law firm leaders and their firms can move the inclusiveness needle by actively promoting mentoring opportunities for women and lawyers of color. Mentoring relationships, whether formal or informal, can provide junior lawyers with access to people who can help them learn the ropes and navigate the organizational culture.[44]

One of the best, and simplest, questions to ask is, "How can I (or the firm) do better?" You might not like the feedback you receive, but it is the only way that you (and the firm) can improve. Listen carefully—and without judgment—to what others have to say, especially if you disagree with some parts or premises of the others' viewpoints. Also, listen to what people are not saying, and make sure that the really important clues are not being overlooked. For the famous detective Sherlock Holmes, in one case, it was the "dog not barking" that completely shifted his perspective. No matter what the initial data reveals, feedback is always "friendly" if the intention is to use the information to make improvements. It becomes the foundation on which to build and offers a forward-looking perspective rather than a backward descent into the past, assigning blame or shame.

Ubiquitous Diversity Training

Another step in DEI leadership is extending diversity training beyond the formal hierarchical ranks. An organization won't benefit if only the most senior people engage in training to address biases, but it will profit greatly if implicit bias training and education about the advantages of greater workplace inclusion are extended throughout the organization, and as appropriate to the needs and experiences of various constituencies. Many law firms have realized tangible benefits from creating a diversity function, often called a chief diversity officer, or a diversity committee or group within the firm. These firm leaders develop and promote diversity and inclusiveness goals and strategies, assist with recruiting more diverse lawyers and staff, and provide guidance and expertise to other firm leaders in advancing a more diverse and inclusive environment.[45]

Vision for Change

A critically important step in leading the move toward DEI is the creation and articulation of a vision for change, including why it is important to the organization and its members *and* how they and the organization will be better off as a consequence of the change. Two critical aspects are a "recognition of leadership *for* diversity, which would increase the range of people who are leaders, and leadership *with* diversity, to ensure that leadership is beneficial to everyone and the organization as a whole."[46] Effective leadership in law organizations requires thoughtful attention to both dynamics of leading change—with and for diversity and toward a more inclusive workplace.

The need for visionary leadership is often overlooked by lawyers and their firms because they have concluded that "vision" is not in their wheelhouse; this is something that others, including their clients, do—but not them. This is a rather narrow and limited perspective on the roles of lawyers—in all positions, but especially in managerial and leadership roles. The top-performing and most effective lawyers (especially those in their organizations' senior hierarchical positions), according to a survey of a cross section of many types of law firms, are "more visionary, provide their teams with much-needed perspective, and engage associates and peers in critical discussion and decisions."[47] These leaders are able to accelerate their firm's transformation to a more inclusive work environment because they are able to provide perspective and persuade others to embrace the change.

DEI Change: A Win–Win Situation

Initiatives to create a more diverse and inclusive workplace, and generate equitable opportunities, enhance the legitimacy of the organization both internally and externally. Of course, simply instructing people to be respectful of others does not necessarily result in a workplace where people feel respected; rather, leadership must be proactive about inclusion. And leaders themselves must display inclusive behaviors and manifest attitudes that suggest they highly value inclusiveness of others; without that, diversity efforts are perceived as simply window dressing. It is important to note that inclusion is not a zero-sum game where any gains by one group of employees are offset by losses to another. Everyone wins when the workplace culture becomes more inclusive, welcoming, and fair to all employees. The organization is more profitable and has less turnover, and people are proud to say that this is the organization to which they belong.

FOLLOWING THROUGH

- Diversity issues in the legal profession are a problem—but also represent a leadership opportunity.
- Diversity, equity, and inclusion are related concepts. Diversity refers to differences in an environment. Equity refers to efforts to ensure an even playing field of opportunities for all team members. Inclusion refers to the ways in which members of a group are accepted.
- Implicit bias is a roadblock to achieving DEI, as are various structural biases.
- Law firms benefit greatly from DEI in terms of performance and results but also in the ability to attract and retain talent and corporate clients.
- Because of the many benefits, the right thing to do—greater DEI—becomes the smart thing to do.
- Lawyers and law firms need to take the helm of leadership in incorporating DEI into their environments. The leadership effort begins with a self-analysis of implicit bias, moves on to assessment of the current DEI culture and diversity training for everyone in an organization, and culminates with the creation and articulation of a vision for change.

REFLECTIONS

1. Closely consider and evaluate your current law-related work or academic environment in terms of the following questions:

   - How strongly do the leaders in your situation value the attitudes and viewpoints of all employees?
   - To what extent do underrepresented groups feel there's a good fit and experience a sense of belonging?
   - To what degree would you say that decisions are made in an impartial and equitable manner?

2. After taking the Harvard Implicit Association Test, identify and describe three instances of observed bias. How did you feel about these situations, and how did you react then? How would you now react to them?

3. What are some additional areas of bias (beyond race and gender) that could and should be included in any DEI effort?

4. What actions can you take to be an ally and antiracist?

Part IV

This final part, consisting of one chapter, serves as a bookend to the first part. It focuses on achieving a mindset for leadership development, leading in challenging times, and being a lawyer leader who impacts the legal profession and the world in a positive way. It also advocates for life-long leadership development just as lawyers must continue their development and growth as lawyers throughout their careers.

FOURTEEN

Leadership Development for Lawyers

To move forward successfully, lawyers must develop their professional and personal leadership abilities to thrive in a turbulent and complex world sustaining their growth as lawyers and as individuals.

THE LEAD-IN

- Leadership Development in Challenging Times and Circumstances
    - Professional Challenges
    - Personal Challenges
- Lawyer Leadership Development of the Future
- Appreciating Leadership Styles
    - Authoritative Style
    - Affiliative Style
    - Democratic Style
    - Pacesetting Style
    - Coaching Style
    - Mix and Match
- Self-Development: Basis of Leadership Development
    - Inner Quest
    - Too Much of a Good Thing
    - From Selfish to Selfless
- Following Through
- Reflections

Complexity in practicing law is not a recent phenomenon but rather a long-standing conundrum that began in law school, with the challenges presented by adapting to the study of law ("thinking like a lawyer") and then navigating the bar exam. Likewise, the legal profession has been subjected to a turbulent environment over the past two decades, including major financial meltdowns, law firm mismanagement and alleged fraud, technological disruptions and substitutes, and most currently a catastrophic worldwide health and safety crisis, rallies for social justice, and increasing political polarization. These days, it is noted that "lawyer-leaders must be as agile as white-water guides in treacherous rapids."[1] The more than one million practicing lawyers (as well as many who work in law-related fields) have been experiencing a succession of challenges that have dramatically affected the legal profession, including most lawyers and every law student. Unprecedented shifts are the reality of the contemporary practice of law.

As the old adage goes, "extraordinary times call for extraordinary measures"—and that saying speaks directly to the necessity of paying greater attention to leadership both for lawyers and for their organizations, regardless of size or geography. Lawyers must navigate their environment and grow as professionals in whatever context they practice law, and growing their leadership skills will contribute substantively to their success in the legal profession overall. We have maintained throughout this book that leadership education and development are essential to lawyers and to their organizations in contemporary times. We believe that leadership development is the single greatest tool for today's lawyers to align their aspirations for success and happiness with the realities of the very complex and uncertain environment of law practice.

Becoming a lawyer in a leadership position is not the objective, though. Becoming a lawyer with leadership skills, attitudes, and behaviors is the aspiration. This final chapter aims to provide a path for your personal and professional development as a lawyer and as a leader—and consequently as an individual that makes a difference.

Leadership Development in Challenging Times and Circumstances

There are several guideposts to pay attention to and understand in your leadership development journey: the context in which leadership should occur, the environment in which leadership must be exercised, and why leadership skills are necessary to address the challenges and opportunities in that environment. Once you've recognized and understood the landscape in your path, then the process for leading forward begins with creating a plan for leading yourself and others through the resolution of those obstacles, switchbacks, and detours associated with being a lawyer and in the practice of law.

To move forward successfully, lawyers must develop their professional and personal leadership abilities to thrive in a turbulent and complex world and sustain their growth as lawyers and as individuals. Law school is a great place to have already started on this journey.

Professional Challenges

A second-year associate with a national law firm aptly described the challenge facing every new attorney: "I'm navigating an environment that is extremely complex and, in many ways, lacking transparency. The firm hasn't caught up to the leadership needs of new lawyers like me, so it is definitely a struggle." This statement reflects a common and profound concern: More leadership, both individually and by lawyers in their firms, is needed to address the complexities of modern law practice. Moreover, it has been noted that "law firms can no longer assume that leaders will simply emerge from the ranks."[2] Rather, attention to the development of leadership must be intentional rather than implicit, and this is true not only for law school educators but also throughout the entire legal profession.

VUCA PROBLEM

A frequent description of the world today and into the foreseeable future is aptly captured by the term *VUCA*, an acronym standing for the following:[3]

- Volatile: Change happens rapidly and often on a large scale.
- Uncertain: The future cannot be predicted with any certainty or precision.
- Complex: The challenges are complicated by many factors, and there are seldom single causes or easy solutions.
- Ambiguous: There is little clarity on what the underlying adverse events mean or the effect that they are likely to have.

In particular, *VUCA* is quite descriptive of the practice of law and much of the legal profession.

For example, the 2007–08 economic recession and the 2020 coronavirus pandemic presented grave challenges to the legal profession, law firms, and even law schools. Law school job postings dropped off, associate and new attorney hiring dwindled, and law firm hiring of laterals declined appreciably. And preceding these catastrophic events were ongoing threats to law firms from the growth of alternative service providers offering lower-cost service models, as well as the introduction of the services of international law firms. Similar threats to the law practice organization model stemmed from a decrease in the overall demand for legal services accompanied by a glut in the number of lawyers, which created an oversupply of providers.

Simply put, these past two decades have prompted clients to reassess their need for legal services and to become more selective in choosing their service providers, thus adding considerable competition among law firms. In addition, clients have been demanding greater cost efficiencies and greater value in the delivery of legal services.

These sudden, difficult, and unanticipated events and recent trends in law practice constitute significant VUCA demands, some of which are disruptive and some of which are incremental. Disruptive changes occur, for example, when a new technology renders most of the firm's current technology obsolete. A recent disruptive change occurred when the COVID-19 pandemic closed down most in-person law practices, which required a sudden shift to remote lawyering and greater, more complicated interpersonal interactions. The movement from hourly billing to value billing by law firms is an example of an incremental change that has been occurring slowly over time. Disruptive changes require quick, innovative responses, while incremental changes require institutional and strategic planning and action.

ADDRESSING THE VUCA PROBLEM

Change is what leaders eat for breakfast, for leadership is what is required in responding to both disruptive and incremental challenges and trends. Unfortunately, as noted previously, law firms in particular, as well as other legal organizations, have too often failed to step up to these challenges—the result being that many of those groups suffered, some gravely by moving into bankruptcy and insolvency. Many of these woes can be traced back to insufficient or failed leadership at the firm level. At the same time, a number of firms during this period, through innovative leadership, have been able to take on those challenges and difficulties and build new opportunities for both lawyers' and firm growth.[4]

These complexities of modern law practice are manageable and, indeed, provide inflection points for lawyers and their organizations to innovate, develop, and thrive through effective leadership. The currents and headwinds that lawyers must face have been described at several points in this book in the context of acquiring the leadership skills needed to handle these blustery conditions.

The greatest challenge in these times, though, is whether lawyer leaders are developing their skills and attitudes quickly enough and in the right ways to effectively handle VUCA environments.[5] A survey of law firm leaders by the Center for Creative Leadership asked what skills were needed to lead contemporary law firms. Respondents generated a list of over thirty skills that lawyers need to have or must develop, ranging from "how to motivate underperforming partners" to "how can I be a more effective communicator."[6] The survey results identified the skills that today's lawyer leaders need while highlighting the urgency that law organizations face in finding ways to effectively develop these skills. Lawyers need an extensive "toolbox" of skills, attitudes, and behaviors to manage the frequently shifting, technology-driven environment that is the modern practice of law.

Personal Challenges

Being a lawyer and practicing law are seldom mundane or easy. Clients make unreasonable demands, documents multiply, workloads are unending. The dread of being unprepared, making a mistake and losing a client's case, costs ranging from livelihood to life itself, add great pressure. Frequent travel, late evening and weekend sessions, and nights away from home all augment the stress that many lawyers experience. Then there are the financial challenges: paying off law school debt, covering overhead, managing the administration of their firm, and the like.

All of these ingredients make for a potent, and sometimes deadly, cocktail, resulting in lawyers experiencing a very stressful occupation and lifestyle. However, leadership can be an effective antidote.

WELLNESS PROBLEM

Due to the combination of stresses inherent in lawyering, the legal profession has a well-documented wellness problem. There are rehabilitation centers that specialize in working with lawyers who are substance abusers and in treating the stress, depression, disability, and addiction that are prominent in the legal profession. Every state offers Lawyer Assistance Programs, which provide confidential services and support to legal professionals who are struggling with substance use or mental health issues.[7]

A report sponsored by the American Bar Association and the Betty Ford Foundation found that twenty-one percent of licensed, employed attorneys qualify as problem drinkers; twenty-eight percent experience depression, and nineteen percent have anxiety symptoms.[8] The Centers for Disease Control and Prevention found that lawyers have among the highest rates for suicide as well as drug and alcohol abuse. Lawyers also rank high in divorce rates as well as illnesses exacerbated by stress.[9] Furthermore, nearly seventy percent of legal malpractice suits are associated with substance abuse.[10]

These problems actually begin in law school and are then exacerbated throughout much of lawyers' careers.[11] Significant stress is reported by ninety-six percent of law students, nearly forty percent higher than medical students, and more than twice that of graduate students in general. Depression rates at the end of the first semester of law school are approximately four times higher than that of the general population.[12] Postgraduation, younger lawyers, those in their first ten years of practice, have the highest incidence of these problems.[13]

ADDRESSING THE WELLNESS PROBLEM

There are steps or approaches that law students (and lawyers) can take to alleviate the challenges of stress in the profession of law. Leadership development is one key tactic.

One of the very first steps in addressing wellness—or thriving, even better—is going through a thoughtful process of evaluating your values, goals, strengths, weaknesses, passions, and the like as part of a career search process. Regardless of the profession, when people are in jobs that align with who they are, they are more satisfied with their lives, happier, and generally more productive. Again, leading yourself is a necessary precursor to being an effective lawyer leader for others.

Another wellness step in a legal career is preparing for the work of a lawyer by building a realistic mindset for practicing law. Wellness programs offered at law schools and through bar associations serve as a preventative for sliding into the core causes of lawyer unhappiness that may lead to unhealthy behaviors and attitudes. National, state, and local bar associations have implemented steps to identify and address lawyers' wellness problems, such as substance abuse and depression, and their implications for clients and the legal system.[14]

Furthermore, opportunities for public service outside of the law firm, such as pro bono representation, and for peer support and advice through sections of bar associations and groups, provide avenues for lawyers to address many of the underlying causes of distress and dissatisfaction.

Last, but certainly not least, leadership training is another way to address the wellness problem. Throughout this book, we have stressed the value of leadership training for lawyers and the many positive benefits of leadership skills. Significantly, law school (and early career) leadership development of positive traits and competencies has been identified as an important way of dealing with the harmful aspects of lawyering. This is because "leadership training often includes competencies such as collaboration, teamwork, problem solving, inspiring others, creativity, transparency, humility, healthy conflict, goal setting, self-promotion, and marketing."[15] These educational experiences are instrumental in preparing lawyers for a healthy, professional work and life balance.

Self-care is important to your ongoing ability to make a difference, as a lawyer and as a leader. Doing so, one law firm partner told us, "is not a luxury, it is a requirement." If you aren't in a good place yourself, this will inevitably affect your relationships with others and your work. By analogy, if you do not refill your car's tank, you will run out of gas and never get to your destination as planned. Without question, now, while in school, is the time for you to begin planning for your future as a lawyer and a leader. Law students often defer the launch of this important process by saying "I'll get to the serious planning after the bar exam." But the exam is just one step forward, and you need to have a longer-term perspective of how you want to live your life, who you want to serve, and how you want to be remembered.

Lawyer Leadership Development of the Future

The contemporary practice of law and legal education have changed in dramatic ways due to both disruptive events and incremental trends. Lawyer leaders must be committed to having and developing the necessary skills to lead, and prosper, in such an environment.

Leadership development efforts must be directed toward complex and adaptive competencies such as greater agility in learning, robust self-awareness, increasing comfort with ambiguity, richer facility with strategic thinking, and an entrepreneurial mindset.[16] Looking ahead, surveys of law firm leaders and managing lawyers who were asked about what lies ahead for lawyers and, more particularly, what the main challenges are for lawyers who lead organizations and teams, are in agreement that law practice will be very different in at least three ways for the coming generation of lawyer leaders.[17]

First, law firms and legal organizations will be investing less in developing their human resources in traditional ways, such as hiring consulting experts and holding management and leadership workshops. Instead, they will be encouraging their employees to take greater responsibility for developing themselves as leaders and preparing themselves to take leadership responsibilities and roles in the future. Firms probably will not be abandoning their programs for associate professional development or succession planning for more senior lawyers, but you can anticipate that more individual initiatives on your part will be expected in developing your individual leadership abilities. Consequently, there will be more "vertical professional development" by lawyers as they seek to achieve greater levels of personal, professional, and leadership development.

What does this development look like, and what should law students and young lawyers today be thinking about to prepare themselves? One of the principal areas that will distinguish exceptional lawyer talent is the ability to enhance the range of their cognitive and emotional intelligence without being forced or instructed to do so. In terms of adult learning theory, this means moving through stages of cognitive development from being "socialized" to a more advanced level with the capacity for self-growth and transformative thinking.[18] Lawyers, more so than ever, must possess high levels of self-awareness, empathy, and the social skills to inspire others through their leadership and to move organizations forward in complex, uncertain, and volatile times.[19] These are key competencies and abilities that you need to be able to demonstrate.

Preparing yourself to lead others through the organization's challenges demands that you have a clear and deep knowledge of what others in the organization need and what it takes for the team to face those challenges.

Second, along with the changes in how leaders are developed in law organizations, organizations will value leadership that is more "networked," with a focus on leading through a collective process. Much of today's work is performed in highly networked environments, so it makes sense that those networks and collective groups will be the medium in which leadership is exercised. Leadership in law organizations will become less linked solely to one individual but rather will be distributed throughout the organization to many others. Leading teams and departments, great "followership," collaboration and teamwork, and excellent communication skills will be the characteristics that distinguish lawyer leaders in this contemporary environment.

Third, the exercise of leadership will place a premium on creative thinking and the ability to innovate around problems. Certainly, strategic planning skills will continue to be important for those charged with leading legal organizations, but there will be less and less top-down command-and-control tactics. Rather, the ability to lead change through a process of innovation that taps collectively into the talents of people at all levels will be a key competency of these forthcoming law leaders.

The legal profession got a glimpse of why these skills are in high demand during the 2007 recession that hit law firms hard—but also demonstrated that the hardy and nimble firms were able to focus intently on their clients' needs in the recession, to address gaps in knowledge and utilization of technology within their firms, and to adapt their hiring and retention practices to strengthen the commitment of their lawyers and staff to the pressing needs of the firm and their clients. The same agility was demanded by the pivot to virtual work during the 2020 coronavirus pandemic.

Both of these events also hit many lawyers and law students at a personal level as they demanded a great deal of entrepreneurial skills and behaviors. Many law school graduates saw their plans for the future (e.g., secure a position in a law firm) suddenly evaporate, and they shifted their thinking to opening up their own law offices. Starting your own law firm demands entrepreneurial abilities that law school graduates don't often have, nor do law schools necessarily prepare them for that possibility. In VUCA environments, everyone must be thinking like an entrepreneur.

This new vision for what leadership in law organizations will look like is neither fantastical nor cynical. Rather it reflects the ongoing changes in the complex environments that all professionals and their companies are facing.

Appreciating Leadership Styles

Regardless of how leadership development evolves in the future, one thing that will not change very dramatically is the importance of how you behave as a leader, as characterized by The Five Practices of Exemplary Leadership®. The Five Practices constitute a valid theory and set of operating principles that "are universally relevant and effective across various cultures, environments, settings, and populations."[20] A study involving over seventy-one thousand leaders and two hundred thousand of their direct reports from seventy-seven countries, concluded that this framework "is a 'safe bet' for how leaders should behave."[21]

Still, context matters. The robustness of this framework derives from its focus on behavior and hence its adaptability to various personalities and circumstances. That said, it is incumbent on you to reflect on and diagnose the situation and setting in which you find yourself and engage the various leadership practices appropriately—often referred to as leadership styles with which you utilize The Five Practices.

The most effective leaders are able to use more than one style, choosing a style or styles that suit the demands of the situation and the needs and interests of the people involved (be they colleagues and/or clients). There is not a one-style-fits-all, or an all-encompassing, approach to providing leadership or utilizing The Five Practices. Consider, for example, how the leadership behaviors associated with Challenge the Process would vary in "style" (and probably scope) if you were engaging with a law school intern versus a senior partner in the firm. Likewise, as a litigator, how would you Inspire a Shared Vision (tapping into the hopes and dreams of your constituents) when engaging with a client facing a misdemeanor versus with another facing a first-degree murder charge? As realized during the coronavirus pandemic, neither everyone's circumstances, consequences, and reactions were the same. No one can describe and prescribe what to do in every situation, whether describing either the law or leadership. You'll be responsible for scoping out and determining how to best apply the various leadership practices and behaviors depending on the situation. Both adaptability and flexibility on your part are required.

Scholars have suggested a variety of "styles" for how an individual might behave while leading a group.[22] Each style is only effective when it appropriately matches the requirements of the situation at hand, and being flexible is often the key to success.[23] You will find it informative to consider which of these styles described below seems not only most like you, but also to appreciate that one style doesn't fit all situations. You will always want to Model the Way, but how you do that in person will vary with how you do that virtually, just as it differs when dealing with someone you've had a long relationship with versus a new colleague or client.

Here's a brief look at several styles, and you might think about how well they reflect various personalities, including your own, and how to adapt your style and leadership behavior to the demands of the situation and nature of your audience.

Authoritative Style

Lawyer leaders in some circumstances may rely on their status or rank (such as managing partner) to employ an *authoritative leadership style*. There are legitimate circumstances in which hierarchical relationships require compliance—that is, there is a need for one person to make critical decisions and expect acquiescence from everyone. Meeting a tight deadline on the filing of merger or acquisition documents is an example where the partner calls the shots and others fall in line.

While a leader may need to resort to coercion (as in "it's my way or the highway"), this approach doesn't occur with great frequency in legal professional settings. Even when it is required, the most effective leaders will still take the time to explain the thinking behind their orders versus being autocratic and simply saying, "Do as I say." Otherwise, over time trust will be eroded.

Affiliative Style

Another style in legal organizations, at least among lawyers working on a project in litigation or a transaction, is an *affiliative style*. This style relies on strengthening interpersonal relationships, building mutual trust and respect, and using persuasive strategies for guiding colleagues toward accomplishment of agreed-on objectives. Affiliative leaders believe that "people come first," and with this style, the leader is often up close and personal with people, establishing team bonds, attending to emotional needs, clearly communicating goals, seeking buy-in, and encouraging everyone to work cooperatively to achieve shared objectives.

Democratic Style

In some workplace settings, especially with a highly educated and seasoned group, the leadership function is widely diffused, perhaps among a network of professionals, and the person in charge as the official leader will utilize a *democratic style* for taking actions and making decisions. In this fairly participative approach, the leader will ask questions like "What should we do?" or "What do you think?" and use people's input for making choices. For example, in a session of lead counsel in a multidistrict litigation proceeding or a meeting of class action counsel, the most useful approach to decision making would be more collaborative and inclusive.

This leadership style requires a high degree of trust and confidence by all members of the group not only in the leader but also among themselves. Everyone needs to be prepared and committed to the task and goal and comfortable with rewards being distributed on the basis of interdependence rather than independent contributions. The leader's emphasis is on collaborating, obtaining buy-in, and soliciting input and feedback from everyone involved.

Pacesetting Style

A leadership style that a lawyer leader may take can be called *pacesetting*. In this approach, the leader is literally saying, "Do as I do, and come along with me." This method can often achieve results quickly, especially if the team is highly motivated to accomplish the task.

This style can be very helpful when a partner, for example, is attempting to mentor a group of associates in a transaction, and the explicit message is, "If you want to know how to do this, then pay attention to what I do and how I handle this." This approach is also commonly seen in situations where a chief litigation partner is leading a group of associates in learning, for example, the ropes of trial preparation and witness cross-examinations. This style can fall short, however, if the team members sense that the leader is arrogant or hostile or if people involved don't share a common sense of purpose.

Coaching Style

Still another approach to leading others is a *coaching style*. With this style, leaders are prone to saying, "Consider this," and then provide individual attention to developing people through offering advice and mentoring. This approach has value, for example, in succession planning, where the leader wishes to prepare a person (or groom a number of people) for possible future leadership responsibilities in the firm. One downside is that this leadership style can be quite time consuming and also quite challenging, requiring considerable interpersonal competence, especially in the sense of being a role model. It is most appropriate, however, when seen as making an investment in the future of an individual and/or organization.

The coaching style is not the same as mentoring. Coaching tends to be more directive than mentoring and often involves expressed goals for the individual being coached. Mentoring is frequently accomplished in more of a question-and answer method—for instance, a new associate is encouraged to bring issues, concerns, or problems to their mentor for discussion, with the ultimate resolution left in the hands of the person being mentored.

Mix and Match

There are many typologies of leadership styles in the academic literature; this section presented just one continuum, ranging from authoritative at one end to coaching at the other end, with a variety of styles in between. Each style has its place in your leadership tool kit, just as carpenters need several types of saw blades and varieties of screw drivers in their toolbox. The most effective leaders are able to use more than one style, especially as situations shift and change. As the Chinese proverb wisely proclaims, "The wise adapt themselves to circumstances, as water molds itself to the pitcher." Armed with The Five Practices of Exemplary Leadership, you have a framework for going both wide and deep in how you behave as a leader.

Self-Development: Basis of Leadership Development

Wanting to lead, believing that you can lead, and understanding your style are important guide rails on the road to becoming an exemplary leader. However, you are the driver, and being an exemplary leader comes from being the best version of yourself. In the art of leadership, leadership development is fundamentally a process of self-development.[24]

Inner Quest

The quest for developing your leadership skills and behaviors is first an inner search to discover and be in touch with who you are. Through discernment and self-reflection comes the confidence needed to lead. Self-confidence is really awareness of and faith in your own powers. These capabilities become clear and strong only as you work to identify and develop them—and own them.

As you begin this inner journey, you must wrestle with some difficult questions. For example:

- How much do I care about making a difference, about justice, about fairness, about wealth, about influence, and about the people who are like me or different from me?
- What do I think is the proper role and responsibility of lawyers and the legal system?
- What kind of clients do I want to work with and serve?
- How do I feel about law enforcement officers, district attorneys, and opposing counsel; the prison system; and prospects of rehabilitation?

- How prepared am I to handle the complex problems that now confront the legal profession?
- What are my beliefs about how people should work with one another in an office, or on a case, with junior associates and partners?
- How committed am I to fostering and supporting an inclusive culture?
- How certain am I of my own conviction about my firm's stated vision and values? The conviction and commitment of my colleagues?
- How solid are my relationships with constituents? Are they built on a firm foundation of trust and good judgment?
- What are my strengths and weaknesses?
- What do I need to do to improve my abilities?
- Am I the right one to be taking the lead at this very moment?

The questions go on and on. Many of these questions are probably ones that you have discussed in class, reflected on regarding your own leadership experiences, and written about in various assignments and essays in the course on lawyer and leadership issues and behaviors.

Being in touch with who you are, by extension, also means that you must strive to improve how well you understand others near and far from you. While scholars may disagree on the origins of leadership, there is a strong consensus that leaders must be interpersonally competent. Explained one noted legal scholar: "Attempting to train leaders without focusing more effectively on interpersonal skills is, to borrow a colleague's metaphor, like trying to teach geology without the rocks."[25] You must be willing and able to listen and take advice, as well as sometimes lose arguments and follow others. Unless you can develop the trust and respect of others, you will be unable to mobilize people's energies toward higher purposes and motivate them to go with you to places they have never been before. In other words, you will be unable to lead.

Too Much of a Good Thing

Some fundamental contradictions in leadership, however, are revealed as you struggle to develop yourself as a leader.

First, you will realize that any leadership practice can become destructive if taken to extremes. Challenging the status quo to promote innovation and progressive change, taken to extremes, can create needless turmoil, confusion, and paranoia. The singular focus on one vision of the future can blind you and others to alternatives, as well as the realities of the present.

Exploiting your powers of inspiration can cause others to surrender their will. Overreliance on collaboration may indicate an unwillingness to make critical or unpopular decisions. An obsession with being seen as a role model can push you into isolation for fear of losing privacy or cause you to be more concerned with style than substance. Constantly worrying about who should be recognized and when you should celebrate can turn you into a gregarious minstrel.[26]

Far more insidious than all of these for leaders, however, is the treachery of hubris. It is exciting to be a leader, gratifying to have influence, and exhilarating to have scores of people hanging onto your every word. It is empowering to hand out directions and have people fired up to march at your command. In far more subtle ways than anyone would like to admit, you can be seduced by your own power and importance. History reveals that every *evil* leader has been infected with the disease of hubris: they were rulers and not leaders. They became bloated with an exaggerated sense of self and used the gifts of leadership to pursue their own sinister ends.

These contradictions in leadership highlight the fact that leadership practices are amoral, but the people who use the practices are moral or immoral. There is an ethical dimension to this discussion of leadership that neither leaders nor their followers should take lightly or ignore.

The conflicts and contradictions of leadership can only be resolved if you establish for yourself an ethical set of standards on which to base all of your actions. You can avoid excessive pride only if you recognize that you are human and need the help of others. All of your individual complexities are held together by a fundamental set of values and beliefs, and developing yourself as a leader begins with those key convictions. Clarifying your own values and visions is a highly personal matter; no one else can do it for you. To exhibit to others authentic leadership—where words and deeds are consonant—you must be in tune internally. When you clarify the principles that govern your life and the ends that you seek, you give meaning to your daily decisions and actions.

From Selfish to Selfless

The late John Gardner—former cabinet secretary of health, education, and welfare; adviser to four US presidents; founder of both Common Cause and Independent Sector; and recipient of the Presidential Medal of Freedom—wrote about the four *moral* goals of leadership: (1) releasing human potential, (2) balancing the needs of the individual and the community, (3) defending the fundamental values of the community, and (4) instilling in individuals a sense of initiative and responsibility.[27]

Attending to these goals will always lift your eyes to higher purposes, and leadership development through self-development is the way to attend to these goals. As you work to become all you can be, you can start to let go of petty self-interests. Similarly, as you reflect on these aspirations, keep in mind the ABA Model Rules—that lawyers should seek "to attain the highest level of skills, to improve the law and the legal profession, and to exemplify the legal profession's ideals of public service."[28] As in the biblical imperative, "To whom much has been given, much will be required,"[29] as you serve the values of justice, freedom, equality, and dignity, you will constantly renew the foundations of democracy.

FOLLOWING THROUGH

- The legal landscape is complex and constantly changing in what society and clients require from their lawyers. In order to navigate these headwinds, you must have a plan for developing yourself personally and professionally, and this must include leadership development.
- Maintaining a healthy outlook on professional work is particularly important for lawyers because the law profession is a high-stress occupation with high-pressure schedules, deadlines, and work hours where unhealthy reactions (e.g., excessive substance use) are all too common. Leadership skills can help lawyers deal with these stresses.
- The future of the legal profession requires lawyers to take greater individual responsibility for leadership development.
- Leadership encompasses many different styles, and the most effective leaders use a combination of these.
- Self-development is the key to leadership development as the leader is the embodiment of the self. Controlling baser instincts and cultivating selflessness are means of achieving success on both a personal and a societal level.

REFLECTIONS

1. What attributes and attitudes are necessary to succeed as a lawyer leader? How does your answer sync with your personal areas of strength and with opportunities for your personal and professional improvement?

2. What has given you the courage to continue acting in the face of uncertainty and adversity?

3. What is your advice on how your current or preferred law organization (e.g., law firm, law office, etc.) should advance the leadership training and development of new lawyers in the organization?

4. In what ways is leadership an art and in what ways is it a science? How do you find a balance between these two perspectives?

Endnotes

ONE

Educating Lawyers for Leadership

1. American Bar Association, "ABA Profile of the Legal Profession 2020," July 2020, https://www.americanbar.org/content/dam/aba/administrative/news/2020/07/potlp2020.pdf.

2. Joe Patrice, "The Most Lawyers in the World," *Above the Law* (blog), February 12, 2018, https://abovethelaw.com/2018/02/the-most-lawyers-in-the-world/.

3. Ben W. Heineman Jr., "Law and Leadership," *Journal of Legal Education* 56, no. 4 (2006): 596–614.

4. Donald J. Polden, "Leadership Matters: Lawyers Leadership Skills and Competencies," *Santa Clara Law Review* 52 (2012): 899–920, at 901.

5. According to Worldometers (using United Nations population data), in 2021 the United States had a population of 332,685,557. According to the American Bar Association's 2020 Profile of the Legal Profession report, there were 1.3 million active lawyers in the United States. By these figures, there is one active lawyer in the United States for every 255 people; lawyers constitute .0039% of the US population. See worldometers.info/world-population/us-population/#:~:text=The%20current%20population%20of%20the,the%20latest%20United%20Nations%20data.

6. US Library of Congress, Congressional Research Service, Jennifer E. Manning, "Membership of the 117th Congress: A Profile," R46705, November 8, 2021, https://crsreports.congress.gov/product/pdf/R/R46705.

7. Ballotpedia, "Governors and State Executives by Higher Education Background," *Ballotpedia*, updated February 2021, https://ballotpedia.org/Governors_and_state_executives_by_higher_education_background.

8. "Legislators Occupations 2015," National Conference of State Legislatures, 2015, https://www.ncsl.org/Portals/1/Documents/About_State_Legislatures/Occupations.pdf.

9. Alexis de Tocqueville, *Democracy in America*, trans. Henry Reeve (University Park, PA: The Pennsylvania State University, 2002), 307, and on lawyers generally, 302–09, http://seas3.elte.hu/coursematerial/LojkoMiklos?Alexis-de-Tocqueville-Democrary-in-America.pdf; see also Phil Neal, "De Tocqueville and the Role of the Lawyer in Society," *Marquette Law Review* 50 (1967): 607–17, at 609.

10. Leah Witcher Jackson Teague, "Training Lawyers for Leadership: Vitally Important Mission for the Future Success (and Maybe Survival) of the Legal Profession and Our Democracy," *Santa Clara Law Review* 58 (2018): 633–72, at 636, 643.

11. Ana Swanson, "How the Most Disliked—and Elected—Profession Is Disappearing from Politics," *Washington Post*, January 16, 2016, https://www.washingtonpost.com/news/wonk/wp/2016/01/19/how-the-most-disliked-and-elected-profession-is-disappearing-from-politics/.

12. William M. Sullivan, Anne Colby, Judith Welch Wegner, Lloyd Bond, and Lee S. Shulman, *Educating Lawyers: Preparation for the Profession of Law* (San Francisco: Jossey-Bass/Wiley, 2007), 185–90.

13. Leah Teague, "Growing Number of Leadership Progrms and Courses Supports Professional Identity Formation", 62 *Santa Clara Law Review*, 62 (2022):162–163; Teague, "Training Lawyers for Leadership," 655.

14. Ellen Van Velsor and Joel Wright, *Expanding the Leadership Equation: Developing Next-Generation Leaders* (Greensboro, NC: Center for Creative Leadership, 2012).

15. Teague, "Training Lawyers for Leadership," 651–56 (describing the formation of the AALS Section on Leadership and the 2018 survey of leadership courses, programs, and certificates at ABA-approved law schools). Leah Teague, "Growing Number", 162–163.

16. Leo J. Shapiro & Associates, *Public Perceptions of Lawyers: Consumer Research Findings* (Chicago: American Bar Association, 2002), https://www.americanbar.org/content/dam/aba/administrative/market_research/public_perception_of_lawyers_2002.pdf.

17. Susan T. Fiske and Cydney Dupree, "Gaining Trust as well as Respect in Communicating to Motivated Audiences about Science Topics," *Proceedings of the National Academy of Sciences* 111, no. 4 (September 16, 2014): 13593–97, https://www.pnas.org/content/111/Supplement_4/13593.full.

18. Michael Asimow, Steve Greenfield, Stefan Machura, Guy Osborn, Peter Robson, Robert Sockloskie, Cassandra Sharp, and Guillermo Jorge, "Perceptions of Lawyers—A Transnational Study of Student Views on the Image of Law and Lawyers," *International Journal of the Legal Profession* 12, no. 3 (2005): 407–36.

19. Robert MacCrate, *Legal Education and Professional Development—An Educational Continuum (Report of the Task Force on Law Schools and the Profession: Narrowing the Gap)* (Chicago: American Bar Association, 1992) (hereafter referred to as the *MacCrate Report*); Sullivan et al., *Educating Lawyers*, 185–90.

20. Barry Z. Posner, "Leadership Development in Law Schools: Myths, Principles, and Practices," *Santa Clara Law Review* 58 (2018): 399–409.

21. For example, see Scott A. Milner, Jennifer Mott Williams, and William Childers, "Tomorrow's Lawyers Must Embrace Innovation, Technology," *Bloomberg Law*, April 8, 2020, https://news.bloomberglaw.com/privacy-and-data-security/insight-tomorrows-lawyer-must-embrace-innovation-technology; see also Kristen Holmquist, "Challenging Carnegie," *Journal Legal Education* 61 (2012): 353–78.

22. Roland Smith and Paul Morrow, "The Changing Nature of Leadership in Law Firms," *New York State Bar Association Journal* 80 (2008): 33–38, at 34–35.

23. See Donald J. Polden, "Lawyer Leadership in the Practice of Law," *Tennessee Journal of Law and Policy* 14 (2020): 441–65.

24. For example, see Heineman, "Law and Leadership."

25. Ronit Dinovitzer, Bryant G. Garth, Robert Nelson, Gabriele Plickert, Rebecca Sandefur, Joyce Sterling, and David Wilkins, *After the JD III: Third Results from a National Study of Legal Careers* (Washington, DC: American Bar Foundation and NALP Foundation for Law Career Research and Education, 2014), http://www.americanbarfoundation.org/uploads/cms/documents/ajd3report_final_for_distribution.pdf; see also American Bar Association, "ABA Profile of the Legal Profession 2020."

26. James M. Kouzes and Barry Z. Posner, *The Leadership Challenge: How to Make Extraordinary Things Happen in Organizations*, 6th ed. (Hoboken, NJ: Wiley, 2017).

27. Id.

28. "Honesty/Ethics in Professions," Gallup, https://news.gallup.com/poll/1654/honesty-ethics-professions.aspx. Since 1976 this percentage has never been higher than 6 percent.

29. Robert Half Business, "Beyond Legal Expertise: What Makes a Lawyer a Great Leader," *The Robert Half Blog*, February 16, 2015, https://www.roberthalf.com/blog/management-tips/beyond-legal-expertise-what-makes-a-lawyer-a- great-leader.

30. Paula Monopoli and Susan McCarty, *Law and Leadership: Integrating Leadership Studies into the Law School Curriculum* (New York: Routledge, 2016), 1.

31. Larry Richard, *Leadership in Law Firms: An Expert Guide*, ed. Laura Slater (London, UK: Ark Group), http://www.lawyerbrain.com/sites/default/files/leadership_in_law_firms_by_lrr_ark_group.pdf.

32. Susan P. Sturm, "Lawyering Paradoxes: Making Meaning of the Contradictions," *Columbia Law Research Paper No. 14-642*, 2019, 62 Santa Clara Law Review 62 (2022): 175, 180–183.

33. Nick Petrie, *Future Trends in Leadership Development: A White Paper* (Greensboro, NC: Center for Creative Leadership, 2011), https://law.scu.edu/wp-content/uploads/leadership/Future-Trends-in-Leadership-Development.pdf.

34. Richard Susskind, "From Bespoke to Commodity," *Legal Technology Journal* 1 (2006): 4–9.

35. Donald J. Polden, "Lawyers, Leadership, and Innovation," *Santa Clara Law Review* 58 (2018): 427–52, at 444; see also Meghan Tribe, "Decade of Dissolution: The Top Law Firm Failures of the 2010s," *Bloomberg Law*, December 23, 2019, https://news.bloomberglaw.com/us-law-week/decade-of-dissolution-the-top-law-firm-failures-of-the-2010s.

36. Brian Holmes, "The Decade's Big Law Failures: Why do Big Law Firms Fail?" *Lawfuel* (blog), https://www.lawfuel.com/blog/the-decades-big-law-failures-why-do-big-law-firms-fail/ (quoting Brad Hildebrandt).

37. Daniel Goleman, *Emotional Intelligence: Why It Can Matter More Than IQ* (New York: Bantam Books, 2005).

38. Alli Gerkman and Logan Cornett, "Foundations for Practice: The Whole Lawyer and the Character Quotient," Institute for the Advancement of the American Legal System, July 26, 2016, https://iaals.du.edu/publications/foundations-practice-whole-lawyer-and-character-quotient.

39. Donald J. Polden and Leah Jackson Teague, "More Diversity Requires More Inclusive Leaders: Leading by Example in Law Organizations," *Hofstra Law Review* 48 (2020): 681–703, at 685–91; see also Rocío Lorenzo, Nicole Voigt, Miki Tsusaka,

Matt Krentz, and Katie Abouzahr, "How Diverse Leadership Teams Boost Innovation," Boston Consulting Group, January 23, 2018, https://www.bcg.com/publications/2018/how-diverse-leadership-teams-boost-innovation.

40. Tina Shah Paikeday and Jean Lee, "Unleashing the Power of Diversity through Inclusive Leadership," Harvard Law School Forum on Corporate Governance, May 20, 2019, https://corpgov.law.harvard.edu/2019/05/20/unleashing-the-power-of-diversity-through-inclusive-leadership/.

41. Id.

42. Katherine Memery, "The Importance of Resilience," REALM, May 13, 2019, https://www.realmrecruit.com/blog-news/blog/view/42/the-importance-of-resilience.aspx.

43. Petrie, *Future Trends*.

44. Lauren A. Keating, Peter A. Heslin, and Susan J. Ashford, "Good Leaders Are Good Learners," *Harvard Business Review*, August 10, 2017, https://hbr.org/2017/08/good-leaders-are-good-learners; Barry Z. Posner, "Understanding the Learning Tactics of College Students and Their Relationship to Leadership," *Leadership & Organizational Development Journal* 30, no. 4 (2009): 386–95; Lillas M. Brown and Barry Z. Posner, "Exploring the Relationship between Learning and Leadership," *Leadership & Organizational Development Journal* 22, no. 6 (2001): 274–80.

45. Melissa Berry, Kendra Brodin, Laura Friedman, Jerry Organ, and Debbie Shapiro, "What Firms Want: The Use of Competency Models in Associate PD," *NALP Bulletin*, May 2021, https://www.nalp.org/uploads/_bulletin_article_uploads/NALPBulletinPDQMay2021AssociateCompetenciesReport.pdf.

TWO

Leadership: What It Means to Law Students

1. Cambridge Dictionary, "leader," https://dictionary.cambridge.org/us/dictionary/english/leader.

2. Deborah L. Rhode, "Developing Leadership," *Santa Clara Law Review* 52 (2012): 689–724, at 690n.4.

3. James M. Kouzes and Barry Z. Posner, *The Leadership Challenge: How to Keep Getting Extraordinary Things Done in Organizations*, 2nd ed. (Hoboken, NJ: Wiley, 1995), 30.

4. Donald J. Polden, "Leadership Matters: Lawyers Leadership Skills and Competencies," *Santa Clara Law Review* 52 (2012): 899–920, at 903.

5. Robert H. Jerry II, "Leadership and Followership," *University of Toledo Law Review* 44 (2013): 345–54, at 353.

6. James M. Kouzes and Barry Z. Posner, *The Leadership Challenge: How to Make Extraordinary Things Happen in Organizations*, 6th ed. (Hoboken, NJ: Wiley, 2017), 26.

7. Dina Eisenberg, "What Clients Really Want from You," *Law Practice Today*, June 14, 2019, https://www.lawpracticetoday.org/article/what-clients-want/.

8. Melissa Berry, Kendra Brodin, Laura Friedman, Jerry Organ, and Debbie Shapiro, "What Firms Want: The Use of Competency Models in Associate PD,"

NALP Bulletin, May 2021, https://www.nalp.org/uploads/_bulletin_article_uploads/NALPBulletinPDQMay2021AssociateCompetenciesReport.pdf.

9. Id., 19.

10. American Bar Association, Rule 1.2, *Model Rules of Professional Conduct* (Chicago: American Bar Association, 2021), https://www.americanbar.org/groups/professional_responsibility/publications/model_rules_of_professional_conduct/rule_1_2_scope_of_representation_allocation_of_authority_between_client_lawyer/.

11. Id., Rule 1.4.

12. Id., Rule 1.2, which provides, "A lawyer shall provide competent representation to a client. Competent representation requires the legal knowledge, skill, thoroughness and preparation reasonably necessary for the representation."

13. Id., Rule 2.1.

14. Frigaliment Importing Co. v. B.N. International Sales, Corp., 190 F. Supp. 116 (S.D.N.Y. 1960).

15. Leslie A. Gordon, "Most Lawyers Are Introverted, and That's Not Necessarily a Bad Thing," *ABA Journal*, January 1, 2016, https://www.abajournal.com/magazine/article/most_lawyers_are_introverted_and_thats_not_necessarily_a_bad_thing; Ronda Muir, "The Unique Psychological World of Lawyers," *Law People Management* (blog), March 2006, https://www.lawpeopleblog.com/wp-includes/ms-files.php?file=2016/05/LPM-Unique-Psychological-World-of-Lawyers.final_.pdf; Larry Richard, *Leadership in Law Firms: An Expert Guide*, ed. Laura Slater (London, UK: Ark Group), http://www.lawyerbrain.com/sites/default/files/leadership_in_law_firms_by_lrr_ark_group.pdf; Larry Richard, "The Lawyer Personality: Why Lawyers Are Skeptical," *LexBlog* (blog), February 11, 2013, https://www.lexblog.com/2013/02/11/the-lawyer-personality-why-lawyers-are-skeptical/.

16. Larry Richard, "The Lawyer Types," *American Bar Association Journal*, July 1993, https://www.lawyerbrain.com/sites/default/files/the_lawyer_types_mbti.pdf.

17. James M. Kouzes and Barry Z. Posner, *Credibility: How Leaders Gain and Lose It, Why People Demand It*, 2nd ed. (Hoboken, N.J: Wiley, 2011); Barry Z. Posner, "The Influence of Demographic Factors on What People Want from Their Leaders," *Journal of Leadership Studies* 12, no. 2 (2018): 7–16.

18. Kouzes and Posner, *The Leadership Challenge*, 6th ed., 31.

19. Posner, "The Influence of Demographic Factors."

20. For example, see Lauren Morgan Roberts, Anthony J. Mayo, and David A. Thomas, eds., *Race, Work and Leadership: New Perspectives on the Black Experience* (Boston, MA: Harvard Business Review Press, 2019); Virginia Valian, *Why So Slow? The Advancement of Women* (Cambridge, MA: The MIT Press, 1999); Gabriella Gutierrez y Muhs, Yolanda Flores Nieman, Carmen G. Gonzalez, and Angela P. Harris, *Presumed Incompetence; The Intersections of Race and Class for Women in Academia* (Boulder: University Press of Colorado, 2012).

21. Carl I. Hovland, Irving L. Janis, and Harold H. Kelley, *Communication and Persuasion* (New Haven, CT: Yale University Press, 1953); James C. McCroskey, "Scales for the Measurement of Ethos," *Speech Monographs* 33 (1966): 65–72; David K. Berlo, James B. Lemert, and Robert J. Mertz, "Dimensions for Evaluating the Acceptability of

Message Sources," *Public Opinion Quarterly* 3 (1969): 563–76; Robert Cialdini, *Influence: The Psychology of Persuasion* (New York: Collins, 2007).

22. Kouzes and Posner, *The Leadership Challenge* 6th ed.; James M. Kouzes and Barry Z. Posner, *Everyday People, Extraordinary Leadership: How to Make a Difference Regardless of Your Title, Role, or Authority* (Hoboken, NJ: Wiley, 2020).

23. Barry Z. Posner, "Bringing the Rigor of Research to the Art of Leadership: Evidence Behind The Five Practices of Exemplary Leadership, http://www.leadershipchallenge.com/LeadershipChallenge/media/SiteFiles/research/our-research/tlc-our-research-bringing-the-rigor-of-research-to-the-art-of-leadership.pdf. Abstracts of over eight hundred studies can be accessed at http://www.leadershipchallenge.com/research/others-research.aspx.

24. Kouzes and Posner, *The Leadership Challenge*, 6th ed.

25. Kouzes and Posner, *Everyday People, Extraordinary Leadership.*

26. Frederick F. Reichheld, *The Ultimate Question 2.0* (Boston, NA: Harvard Business Review Press, 2011).

THREE

Model the Way

1. Barry Z. Posner, "Another Look at the Impact of Personal and Organizational Values Congruency," *Journal of Business Ethics* 97, no. 4 (2010): 535–41; James M. Kouzes and Barry Z. Posner, "Finding Your Voice," in *Servant Leadership in Action*, eds. Ken Blanchard and Renee Broadwell (Oakland: Berrett-Koehler, 2018), 109–14.

2. Deborah L. Rhode, "The Professional Responsibilities of Professional Schools: Pervasive Ethics in Perspective," in *Teaching and Learning Professionalism: Symposium Proceedings,* October 2–4, 1996 (Chicago: American Bar Association, 1997), 25.

3. Id., 36.

4. Ronda Muir, "The Unique Psychological World of Lawyers," *Law People* (blog), March 2006, https://www.lawpeopleblog.com/wp-includes/ms-files.php?file=2016/05/LPM-Unique-Psychological-World-of-Lawyers.final_.pdf.

5. Diane Curtis, "Loren Miller Winner Sid Wolinsky Sees No End to His Long Public Interest Career," *California Bar Journal*, September 2011, https://www.calbarjournal.com/September2011/TopHeadlines/TH5.aspx.

6. "2011—Todd L. Belcore," The Chicago Bar Foundation, updated 2021, https://chicagobarfoundation.org/fellowships/anderson-recipients/todd-belcore/.

7. Debra Cassens Weiss, "The Cost of Wilmer Hale's Gitmo Victory: $17M Worth of Pro Bono Hours," *American Bar Association Journal*, June 25, 2008, https://www.abajournal.com/news/article/the_cost_of_wilmer_hales_gitmo_victory_17m_worth_of_pro_bono_hours.

8. Paul Szoldra, "Seven Incredible Stories of Heroism on 9/11," *Business Insider*, September 11, 2017, https://www.businessinsider.com/7-incredible-stories-of-heroism-on-911-2015-9.

9. Dan Schawbel, "How to Use Storytelling as a Leadership Tool," *Forbes*, April 13, 2012, http://www.forbes.com/sites/danschawbel/2012/08/13/how-to-use-storytelling-as-a-leadership-tool/#3fdcf5277ac9. For more on how to write, tell, and use stories to convey important organizational lessons, see Paul Smith, *Lead with a Story: A Guide to Crafting Business Narratives that Captivate, Convince, and Inspire* (New York: AMACOM, 2012).

10. Steve Denning, *The Secret Language of Leadership: How Leaders Inspire Action Through Narrative* (San Francisco: Jossey-Bass, 2007); Harrison Monarth, "The Irresistible Power of Storytelling as a Strategic Business Tool," *Harvard Business Review*, March 11, 2014, https://hbr.org/2014/03/the-irresistible-power-of-storytelling-as-a-strategic-business-tool; Paul J. Zak, "Why Your Brain Loves Good Storytelling," *Harvard Business Review*, October 28, 2014, https://hbr.org/2014/10/why-your-brain-loves-good-storytelling; Sean R. Martin, "Stories about Values and Valuable Stories: A Field Experiment of the Power of Narratives to Shape Newcomers' Actions," *Academy of Management Journal* 59, no. 5 (2015): 1707–24.

11. Neha Sampat, "A Call to Deal with Impostor Syndrome," *American Bar Association Journal*, November 20, 2018, https://www.abajournal.com/voice/article/a_call_to_deal_with_impostor_syndrome_a_hidden_source_of_attorney_distress.

12. Brent D. Rosso, Kathryn H. Dekas, and Amy Wrzeniewski, "On the Meaning of Work: A Theoretical Integration and Review," *Research in Organizational Behavior* 30 (2010): 91–127.

13. Alison W. Brooks and Leslie K. John, "The Surprising Power of Questions," *Harvard Business Review*, May/June 2018, 60–67.

14. Douglas Stone and Sheila Heen, *Thanks for the Feedback: The Science and Art of Receiving Feedback Well* (New York: Penguin Random House, 2015).

15. Deborah Tanner, *Talking from 9 to 5: Women and Men at Work* (New York: HarperCollins, 1994).

16. Id.

17. Francesca Gino, "Research: We Drop People Who Give Us Critical Feedback," *Harvard Business Review*, September 16, 2016, https://hbr.org/2016/09/research-we-drop-people-who-give-us-critical-feedback; see also Hayley Blunden, Jennifer M. Logg, Alison Wood Brooks, Leslie K. John, and Francesca Gino, "Seeker Beware: The Interpersonal Costs of Ignoring Advice," *Organizational Behavior and Human Decision Processes* 150 (2019): 83–100.

18. Jack Zenger, "There Is No Feedback Fallacy: Understanding the Value of Feedback," *Forbes*, May 13, 2019, https://www.forbes.com/sites/jackzenger/2019/05/13/there-is-no-feedback-fallacy-understanding-the-value-of-feedback/#3da55df15368.

FOUR

Inspire a Shared Vision

1. Catherine Bailey and Adrian Madden, "What Makes Work Meaningful—or Meaningless," *MIT Sloan Management Review* 67, no. 1 (2016): 52–61.

2. Association of American Law Schools, *Before the JD: Undergraduate Views on Law School*, 2018, https://www.aals.org/wp-content/uploads/2018/09/BJDReportsHghlights.pdf.

3. Ronit Dinovitzer, Bryant G. Garth, Robert Nelson, Gabriele Plickert, Rebecca Sandefur, Joyce Sterling, and David Wilkins, *After the JD III: Third Results from a National Study of Legal Careers* (Washington, DC: American Bar Foundation and NALP Foundation for Law Career Research and Education, 2014), http://www.americanbarfoundation.org/uploads/cms/documents/ajd3report_final_for_distribution.pdf.

4. Association of American Law Schools, *Before the JD*; Hank Stout, "5 Reasons Why Law School Is Wrong for You (and 5 Reasons Why It Is Right)," American Bar Association *Student Lawyer* (blog), June 28, 2017, https://abaforlawstudents.com/2017/06/28/5-reasons-law-school-wrong-5-reasons-right/.

5. James M. Kouzes and Barry Z. Posner, *The Leadership Challenge: How to Make Extraordinary Things Happen in Organizations*, 6th ed. (Hoboken, NJ: Wiley, 2017).

6. Aaron Hurst, Adam Pearce, Cammie Erickson, Scott Parish, Lauren Vesty, Allison Schnidman, Meg Garlinghouse, and Andrea Pavela, "Purpose at Work: The Largest Global Study on the Role of Purpose in the Workforce," *Purpose at Work: 2016 Global Report*, LinkedIn and Imperative, 2016, https://cdn.imperative.com/media/public/Global_Purpose_Index_2016.pdf.

7. Jesse Newton and Josh Davis, "Three Secrets of Organizational Success," *Strategy+Business* 76 (2014), https://www.strategy-business.com/article/00271?gko=38cde; see also Simon Sinek, *Start with Why: How Great Leaders Inspire Everyone to Take Action* (New York: Portfolio, 2010).

8. Jamie Spannhake, "What Motivates Millennials? Ways Law Firms Are Retaining Young Lawyers," *Attorney At Work*, July 15, 2019, https://www.attorneyatwork.com/what-motivates-millennials-retaining-young-lawyers/.

9. John Beyer, "Startups and Millennials: The Perfect Fit," *Builtin*, April 19, 2019, https://builtin.com/company-culture/startups-and-millennials-perfect-fit.

10. Kouzes and Posner, *The Leadership Challenge*.

11. Daniel Goleman, *Social Intelligence: The New Science of Human Relationships* (New York: Bantam, 2006).

12. Barbara L. Fredrickson, *Positivity: Groundbreaking Research Reveals How to Embrace the Hidden Strengths of Positive Emotions, Overcome Negativity, and Thrive* (New York: Crown Publishers, 2009).

13. Bernard M. Bass, *Leadership and Performance Beyond Expectations* (New York: Free Press, 1985).

14. Fredrickson, *Positivity*.

15. Vanessa Van Edwards, "5 Secrets of a Successful TED Talk," *HuffPost*, December 6, 2017, https://www.huffpost.com/entry/5-secrets-of-a-successful_b_6887472.

16. Markus Koppensteiner, Pia Stephan, and Johannes Paul Michael Jäschke, "From Body Motion to Cheers: Speakers' Body Movements as Predictors of Applause," *Personality and Individual Differences* 74 (2015): 182–85.

17. Anayat Durrani, "Improving Your Nonverbal Performance in Front of a Jury," *Plaintiff*, October 2012, https://www.plaintiffmagazine.com/recent-issues/item/improving-your-nonverbal-performance-in-front-of-a-jury#:~:text=Lawyers%20should%20try%20to%20stay,any%20of%20those%20negative%20gestures.

18. Mark W. Johnson and Josh Suskewicz, "Does Your Company Have a Long-Term Plan for Remote Work?," *Harvard Business Review*, July 20, 2020, https://hbr.org/2020/07/does-your-company-have-a-long-term-plan-for-remote-work; see also Alison Hill and Darren Hill, *Work from Anywhere: The Essential Guide to Becoming a World-Class Hybrid Team* (Milton, Qld, Wiley, 2021).

19. Roy Strom, "This Big Law Firm Has Permanent Plans for Remote Working," *Bloomberg Law*, July 16, 2020, https://news.bloomberglaw.com/business-and-practice/this-big-law-firm-has-permanent-plans-for-remote-working.

FIVE
Challenge the Process

1. For a survey of the aftermath of the 2007–08 recession in the legal field, see Thomas S. Clay and Eric A. Seeger, "Law Firms in Transition: An Altman Weil Flash Survey," Altman Weil, Inc., 2018, http://www.altmanweil.com//dir_docs/resource/45F5B3DD-5889-4BA3-9D05-C8F86CDB8223_document.pdf.

2. Matthias Spitzmuller, Hock-Peng Sin, Michael Howe, and Shereen Fatimah, "Investigating the Uniqueness and Usefulness of Proactive Personality in Organizational Research: A Meta-Analytic Review," *Human Performance* 28, no. 4 (2015): 351–79.

3. Davide Nicolini, Maja Korica, and Keith Ruddle, "Staying in the Know," *Sloan Management Review* 56, no. 4 (2015): 57–65.

4. Thomas S. Bateman and J. Michael Crant, "The Proactive Component of Organizational Behavior: Measures and Correlates," *Journal of Organizational Behavior* 14 (1993): 103–18; J. Michael Crant, "Proactive Behavior in Organizations," *Journal of Management* 26, no. 3 (2000): 435–63; J. Michael Crant and Thomas S. Bateman, "Charismatic Leadership Viewed from Above: The Impact of Proactive Personality," *Journal of Organizational Behavior* 21, no. 1 (2000): 63–75.

5. Daniel H. Pink, *Drive: The Surprising Truth About What Motivates Us* (New York: Riverhead Books, 2011).

6. Ronit Dinovitzer, Bryant G. Garth, Robert Nelson, Gabriele Plickert, Rebecca Sandefur, Joyce Sterling, and David Wilkins, *After the JD III: Third Results from a National Study of Legal Careers* (Washington, DC: American Bar Foundation and NALP Foundation for Law Career Research and Education, 2014), http://www.americanbarfoundation.org/uploads/cms/documents/ajd3report_final_for_distribution.pdf, who identifies sources of job satisfaction for young lawyers.

7. Mihaly Csikszentmihalyi, *Flow: The Psychology of Optimal Experience* (New York: Harper & Row, 1990).

8. Milhaly Csikszentmihalyi, *Beyond Boredom and Anxiety: The Experience of Play in Work and Games* (San Francisco: Jossey-Bass, 1975), 30.

9. Gregory Berns, *Iconoclast: A Neuroscientist Reveals How to Think Differently* (Cambridge, MA: Harvard Business School Press, 2008).

10. Jeffrey H. Dyer, Hal Gregersen, and Clayton M Christensen, "The Innovator's DNA," *Harvard Business Review* 87, no. 2 (2009): 60–67.

11. Donald J. Polden, "Lawyers, Leadership, and Innovation," *Santa Clara Law Review* 58 (2018): 427–52, at 451n.102 (citing Ian Lopez, "Innovate to Eliminate Bad Ideas? Holland & Knight Leader on Changing the Business Model," *Legaltech News*, February 21, 2018.)

12. Jeffrey Rosen, *Conversations with RBG: Ruth Bader Ginsburg on Life, Love, Liberty, and Law* (New York: Henry Holt &. Co., 2019).

13. Douglas Brinkley, "The Man Who Kept King's Secrets," *Vanity Fair*, April 2006, https://archive.vanityfair.com/article/2006/4/the-man-who-kept-kings-secrets.

14. Peter Sims, *Little Bets: How Breakthrough Ideas Emerge from Small Discoveries* (New York: Free Press, 2011).

15. See, for example, Richard H. Thaler and Cass R. Sunstein, *Nudge: Improving Decisions about Health, Wealth, and Happiness* (New York: Penguin Books, 2009); B. J. Fogg, *Tiny Habits: The Small Changes that Change Everything* (New York: Houghton Mifflin Harcourt, 2020).

16. Karl E. Weick, "Small Wins: Redefining the Scale of Social Problems," *American Psychologist* 39, no.1 (1984): 40–49.

17. Teresa A. Amabile and Steven J. Kramer, *The Progress Principle: Using Small Wins to Ignite Joy, Engagement, and Creativity at Work* (Boston, MA: Harvard Business Review Press, 2011).

18. Amy C. Edmondson, *The Fearless Organization: Creating Psychological Safety in the Workplace for Learning, Innovation, and Growth* (Hoboken, NJ: Wiley, 2019).

19. David Rock, "Managing with the Brain in Mind," *Strategy+Business*, August 27, 2009, https://www.strategy-business.com/article/09306?gko=5df7f.

20. Daniel Kahneman, *Thinking, Fast and Slow* (New York: Farrar, Strauss and Giroux, 2011).

21. Edmondson, *The Fearless Organization*.

22. Charles Duhigg, "What Google Learned from Its Quest to Build the Perfect Team," *The New York Times Magazine*, February 25, 2016, https://www.nytimes.com/2016/02/28/magazine/what-google-learned-from-its-quest-to-build-the-perfect-team.html.

23. O. C. Tanner Institute, *2021 Global Culture Report*, 2021, https://www.octanner.com/content/dam/oc-tanner/images/v2/culture-report/2021/GCR-2021-sm.pdf.

24. Heidi K. Brown, "Fear and Lawyering: Create a Work Culture of 'Psychological Safety' that Encourages Taking Intellectual and Creative Risks," *American Bar Association Journal*, May 1, 2019, https://www.abajournal.com/magazine/article/fear-lawyering-psychological-safety.

25. Edgar H. Schein, *Humble Inquiry: The Gentle Art of Asking Instead of Telling* (Oakland, CA: Berrett- Koehler, 2013).

26. Edmonson, *The Fearless Organization*, 200.

27. James M. Kouzes and Barry Z. Posner, *The Leadership Challenge: How to Make Extraordinary Things Happen in Organizations*, 6th ed. (Hoboken, NJ: Wiley, 2017).

28. Paul J. H. Schoemaker and Robert E. Gunther, "The Wisdom of Deliberate Mistakes," *Harvard Business Review* 84, no. 6 (2006), 108–15.

29. Carol S. Dweck, *Mindset: The New Psychology of Success* (New York: Random House, 2006).

30. Albert Bandura and Robert E. Wood, "Effects of Perceived Controllability and Performance Standards on Self-Regulation of Complex Decision Making," *Journal of Personality and Social Psychology* 56 (1989): 805–14; see also Dweck, *Mindset*.

31. Tae Kyung Kouzes and Barry Z. Posner, "Influence of Managers' Mindset on Leadership Behavior," *Leadership & Organization Development Journal* 40, no. 8 (2019): 829–44.

32. See Salvatore R. Maddi, "The Story of Hardiness: Twenty Years of Theorizing, Research, and Practice," *Consulting Psychology Journal: Practices and Research* 54, no. 3 (2002): 175–85; see also Salvatore R. Maddi and Suzanne C. Kobasa, *The Hardy Executive: Health under Stress* (Chicago: Dorsey Press, 1984); Salvatore R. Maddi and Deborah M. Khoshaba, *Resilience at Work: How to Succeed No Matter What Life Throws at You* (New York: AMACOM, 2005).

33. For example, see Paul T. Bartone, Robert R. Roland, James J. Picano, and Thomas J. Williams, "Psychological Hardiness Predicts Success in US Army Special Forces Candidates," *International Journal of Selection and Assessment* 16, no. 1 (2008): 78–81; Reginald A. Bruce and Robert F. Sinclair, "Exploring the Psychological Hardiness of Entrepreneurs," *Frontiers of Entrepreneurship Research* 29, no. 6 (2009): 78–81; Paul T. Bartone, "Social and Organizational Influences on Psychological Hardiness: How Leaders Can Increase Stress Resilience," *Security Informatics* 1 (2012): 1–10; Banafshe Hasanvand, Mohamad Khaledian, and Ali Reza Merati, "The Relationship between Psychological Hardiness and Attachment Styles with the University Student's Creativity," *European Journal of Experimental Biology* 3, no. 3 (2013): 656–60; Asle M. Sandvik, Anita L. Hansen, Sigurd William Hystad, Bjørn Helge Johnsen, and Paul T. Bartone, "Psychopathy, Anxiety, and Resiliency—Psychological Hardiness as a Mediator of the Psychopathy-Anxiety Relationship in a Prison Setting," *Personality and Individual Differences* 72 (2015): 30–34.

34. See Susan Daicoff, "Lawyer, Know Thyself: A Review of Empirical Research on Attorney Attributes Bearing on Professionalism," *American University Law Review* 46 (1997): 1337–1427, at 1346–48.

35. Emily Esfahani Smith, "On Coronavirus Lockdown? Look for Meaning, Not Happiness," *New York Times*, April 7, 2020, https://www.nytimes.com/2020/04/07/opinion/coronavirus-mental-health.html.

36. Rebecca Aydin, "How 3 Guys Turned Renting Air Mattresses in Their Apartment into a $31 Billion Company, Airbnb," *Insider*, September 20, 2019, https://www.businessinsider.com/how-airbnb-was-founded-a-visual-history-2016-2.

37. Aysha Bagchi, "Big Law Associate Snags Rare Chance to Argue at Supreme Court," *Bloomberg Tax*, December 2, 2019, https://news.bloombergtax.com/daily-tax-report/big-law-associate-snags-rare-chance-to-argue-at-supreme-court.

SIX

Enable Others to Act

1. "Lessons from Practicing Lawyers: Why Attorneys Work Together," *The Practice* 1, no. 6, (Sept./Oct. 2015), https://thepractice.law.harvard.edu/article/lessons-from-practicing-lawyers/#:~:text=It%20requires%20bringing%20together%20individuals,as%20the%20individual%20la wyers%20themselves.

2. Michael B. Gurtman, "Trust, Distrust, and Interpersonal Problems: A Circumplex Analysis," *Journal of Personality and Social Psychology* 62 (1992): 989–1002; Glenn D. Grace and Thomas Schill, "Social Support and Coping Style Differences in Subjects High and Low in Interpersonal Trust," *Psychological Reports* 59 (1986): 584–86.

3. James A. Driscoll, "Trust and Participation in Organizational Decision Making as Predictors of Satisfaction," *Academy of Management Journal* 21 (1978): 44–56.

4. Larry Richard, "The Lawyer Personality: Why Lawyers Are Skeptical," *What Makes Lawyers Tick?* (blog), February 11, 2013, https://www.lawyerbrainblog.com/2013/02/the-lawyer-personality-why-lawyers-are-skeptical/.

5. Pamela S. Shockley-Zalabak, Sherwyn Morreale, and Michael Hackman, *Building the High-Trust Organization: Strategies for Supporting Five Key Dimensions of Trust* (San Francisco: Jossey-Bass, 2010).

6. James M. Kouzes and Barry Z. Posner, *Everyday People, Extraordinary Leadership: How to Make a Difference Regardless of Your Title, Role, or Authority* (Hoboken, NJ: Wiley, 2020).

7. David B. Sarnoff and Natalie W. Loeb, "The Case for Active Listening," *PLI Chronicle: Insights and Perspectives for the Legal Community*, April 2021, https://plus.pli.edu/Details/Details?rows=10&fq=title_id~3A2822~325651~2229202B~id~3A282B22~325651-ATL4~2229~&facet=true&qt=legal_boolean&mode=Group_By_Series.

8. Jack Zenger and Joseph Folkman, "What Great Listeners Actually Do," *Harvard Business Review*, July 14, 2016, https://hbr.org/2016/07/what-great-listeners-actually-do.

9. Id.

10. Lindsey P. Gustafson, Aric Short, and Neil W. Hamilton, "Teaching and Assessing Active Listening as a Foundational Skill for Lawyers as Leaders, Counselors, Negotiators, and Advocates," *Santa Clara Law Review*, 62, (2022): 1.

11. American Bar Association, "ABA Profile of the Legal Profession 2020," July 2020, https://www.americanbar.org/content/dam/aba/administrative/news/2020/07/potlp2020.pdf; Ronit Dinovitzer, Bryant G. Garth, Robert Nelson, Gabriele Plickert, Rebecca Sandefur, Joyce Sterling, and David Wilkins, *After the JD III: Third Results from a National Study of Legal Careers* (Washington, DC: American Bar Foundation and NALP Foundation for Law Career Research and Education, 2014), http://www.americanbarfoundation.org/uploads/cms/documents/ajd3report_final_for_distribution.pdf.

12. Ronit Dinovitzer, et al, "After the JD III".

13. Adam Grant, *Give and Take: Why Helping Others Drives Our Success* (New York: Penguin Group, 2013).

14. Id.

15. Robert Axelrod, *The Evolution of Cooperation*, rev. ed. (New York: Basic Books, 2006).

16. William Poundstone, *Prisoner's Dilemma: John Von Neumann, Game Theory, and the Puzzle of the Bomb* (New York: Doubleday, 1992).

17. Francis J. Flynn, "How Much Should I Give and How Often? The Effects of Generosity and Frequency of Favor Exchange on Social Status and Productivity," *Academy of Management Journal* 46, no. 5 (2003): 539–53.

18. John Thackray, "Feedback for Real," *Gallup Management Journal* 1, no. 1 (2001): 12–17; Marcus Buckingham and Curt Coffman, *First, Break All the Rules* (New York: Simon & Schuster, 1999); Gallup, *State of the Global Workplace* (New York: Gallup Press, 2017); Susan Rebstock Williams and Rick L. Wilson, "Group Support Systems, Power, and Influence in an Organization: A Field Study," *Decision Sciences* 28, no. 4 (1997): 911–37; Patty Azzarello, "Why Sharing Power at Work Is the Very Best Way to Build It," *Fast Company*, January 18, 2013, https://www.fastcompany.com/3004867/why-sharing- power-work-very-best-way-build-it; Edward L. Deci, Anja H. Olafsen, and Richard M. Ryan, "Self-Determination Theory in Work Organizations: The State of a Science," *Annual Review of Organizational Psychology and Organization Behavior* 4 (2017): 19–43.

19. Mauricio R. Delgado, "Reward-Related Responses in the Human Striatum," *Annals of the New York Academy of Science* 1104 (2007): 70–88; Dominic S. Fareri, Laura N. Martin, and Mauricio R. Delgado, "Reward-Related Processing in the Human Brain: Developmental Considerations," *Development & Psychopathology* 20, no. 4 (2008): 1191–1211; Mauricio R. Delgado, M. Meredith Gillis, and Elizabeth Phelps, "Regulating the Expectation of Reward," *Nature Neuroscience* 11, no. 8 (2008): 880–81; Mauricio R. Delgado and James G. Dilmore, "Social and Emotional Influences on Decision-Making and the Brian," *Minnesota Journal of Law, Science & Technology* 9, no. 2 (2008): 899–912; Bernard W. Balleine, Mauricio R. Delgado, and Okihide Hikosaka, "The Role of Dorsal Striatum in Reward and Decision-Making," *Journal of Neuroscience* 27 (2007): 8159–60.

20. Debra Cassens Weiss, "These Common Mistakes Can Lead to Lawyer Ethics Complaints," *American Bar Association Journal*, February 10, 2016, https://www.abajournal.com/news/article/these_common_mistakes_can_lead_to_lawyer_ethics_complaints.

21. See Dan Pinnington and Ian Hu, "2017 Practice Management," American Bar Association, *TechReport*, December 1, 2017, https://www.americanbar.org/groups/law_practice/publications/techreport/2017/practice_management/.

22. See, for example, Albert Bandura, *Self-Efficacy: The Exercise of Control* (New York: Freeman, 1997); James E. Maddux, "Self-Efficacy: The Power of Believing You Can," in *The Oxford Handbook of Positive Psychology*, 2nd ed., eds. Shane J. Lopez and C. R. Snyder (New York: Oxford University Press, 2011), 335–44; Eric Chester, *On Fire at Work: How Great Companies Ignite Passion in Their People Without Burning Them Out* (Shippensburg, PA: Sounds Wisdom, 2015).

23. Robert Wood and Albert Bandura, "Impact of Conceptions of Ability on Self-Regulatory Mechanisms and Complex Decision Making," *Journal of Personality and Social Psychology* 56 (1989): 407–15.

24. James M. Kouzes and Brian Z. Posner, *Learning Leadership: The Five Fundamentals of Becoming an Exemplary Leader* (Hoboken, NJ: Wiley, 2016).

25. Paul Leone, "Take Your ROI to Level 6," *Training Industry Quarterly* 1, no. 1 (2008): 14–18, http://www.nxtbook.com/nxtbooks/trainingindustry/tiq_2008spring/.

26. "The Frontline Leader Project: Exploring the Most Critical Segment of Leaders," Development Dimensions International, https://www.ddiworld.com/reports/frontlineleaderproject.

27. Robert J. Derocher, "Mentoring Helps New and Experienced Lawyers Make the Connection," *Bar Leader* 30, no. 6 (2006), https://www.americanbar.org/groups/bar_services/publications/bar_leader/2005_06/3006/mentoring/; David B. Sarnoff, Natalie Loeb, and David Robert, "Attorney Mentoring in the 21st Century," *PLI Chronicle: Insights and Perspectives for the Legal Community*, June 2021, https://plus.pli.edu/Details/Details?fq=id:(330315-ATL6).

28. Cynthia Pladziewicz, "Coaching and Career Development," in *The Art and Science of Strategic Talent Management in Law Firms*, ed. Terri Mottershead (St. Paul, MN: Thomson Reuters, 2010), 187, 190–91.

29. Andrew Sumitani, "These 4 Companies Totally Get Employee Recognition," *Tiny Pulse*, February 26, 2020, https://www.tinypulse.com/blog/these-4-companies-totally-get-employee-recognition.

30. Id.

31. "What 'Creative Perks' Boost Morale?" *Attorney at Work*, October 28, 2020 (quoting Nadia Wagner), https://www.attorneyatwork.com/creative-perks-morale/.

32. Id.

SEVEN

Encourage the Heart

1. Alison E. Smith, Lee Jussim, Jacquelynne Eccles, Michelle VanNoy, Stephanie Madon, and Polly Palumbo, "Self-Fulfilling Prophecies, Perceptual Biases, and Accuracy at the Individual and Group Levels," *Journal of Experimental Social Psychology* 34, no. 6 (1998): 530–61; Dov Eden, "Leadership and Expectations: Pygmalion Effects and Other Self-Fulfilling Prophecies in Organizations," *The Leadership Quarterly* 3, no. 4 (1992): 271–305.

2. R. J. Blitzer, C. Petersen, and L. Rogers, "How to Build Self-Esteem," *Training and Development Journal* 47, no. 2 (1993): 59.

3. David L. Cooperrider, "Positive Image, Positive Action: The Affirmative Basis of Organizing," in *Appreciative Management and Leadership: The Power of Positive Thought and Action in Organizations*, eds. Suresh Srivastva and David L. Cooperrider, and Associates (San Francisco: Jossey-Bass, 1990), 1–14.

4. David Scott Yeager, Valerie Purdie-Vaughns, Julio Garcia, Nancy Apfel, Patti Brzustoski, Allison Master, William T. Hessert, Matthew E. Williams, and Geoffrey L. Cohen, "Breaking the Cycle of Mistrust: Wide Interventions to Provide Critical Feedback across the Racial Divide," *Journal of Experimental Psychology* 143, no 2. (2014): 804–24.

5. Sari Fried-Fiori, "Competency-Based Development Programs," in *The Art and Science of Strategic Talent Management*, ed. Terri Mottershead (Eagan, MN: Thomson/West, 2011), 119–22.

6. Susan Manch, "Competencies and Competency Models: An Overview," in *The Art and Science of Strategic Talent Management*, ed. Terri Mottershead (Eagan, MN: Thomson/West, 2011), 77–83.

7. See Adrian Gostick and Chester Elton, *Managing with Carrots: Using Recognition to Attract and Retain the Best People* (Layton, UT: Gibbs Smith, 2001); S. J. Ashford and K. E. M. DeStobbeleir, "Feedback, Goal Setting, and Task Performance Revisited," in *New Developments in Goal Setting and Task Performance*, eds. E. A. Locke and G. P. Latham (New York: Routledge, 2013), 51–64.

8. See Gerry Riskin, "Leadership: Agility in the Face of Fragility," American Bar Association, November 1, 2020, https://www.americanbar.org/groups/law_practice/publications/law_practice_magazine/2020/nd20200/nd20riskin/.

9. Paulette A. McCarty, "Effects of Feedback on the Self-Confidence of Men and Women," *Academy of Management Journal* 29, no. 4 (1986): 840–47.

10. Elad N. Sherf, Ravi S. Gajendran, and Barry Z. Posner, "Seeking and Finding Justice: Why and When Managers' Feedback Seeking Enhances Justice Enactment," *Journal of Organizational Behavior* 42, no. 6 (2021): 741-766.

11. Terrence E. Deal and M. K. Key, *Corporate Celebrations: Play, Purpose, and Profit at Work* (San Francisco, Berrett-Koehler, 1998).

12. Tom Rath, *Vital Friends: The People You Can't Afford to Live Without* (New York: Gallup Press, 2006); Tom Rath and Jim Harter, *Well Being: The Five Essential Elements* (New York: Gallup Press, 2010).

13. Bob Nelson, *1001 Ways to Reward Employees*, 2nd ed. (New York: Workman, 2005).

14. Kerry Roberts Gibson, Kate O'Leary, and Joseph R. Weintraub, "The Little Things that Make Employees Feel Appreciated," *Harvard Business Review*, January 23, 2020, https://hbr.org/2020/01/the-little-things-that-make-employees-feel-appreciated.

15. Robert A. Emmons, *Thanks! How Practicing Gratitude Makes You Happier* (New York: Houghton Mifflin, 2008).

16. David Brooks, *The Social Animal: The Hidden Sources of Love, Character, and Achievement* (New York: Random House, 2011).

17. Wayne E. Baker, *Achieving Success Through Social Capital: Tapping the Hidden Resources in Your Personal and Business Networks* (San Francisco: Jossey-Bass, 2000).

18. Shawn Achor, *Happiness Advantage: The Seven Principles that Fuel Success and Performance at Work* (New York: Crown Business, 2010).

19. Susan Pinker, *The Village Effect: How Face-to-Face Contact Can Make Us Healthier and Happier* (New York: Penguin Random House, 2015).

20. Marcial Losada and Emily Heaphy, "The Role of Positivity and Connectivity in the Performance of Business Teams: A Nonlinear Dynamics Model," *American Behavioral Scientist* 47, no. 6 (2004): 740–65.

21. Leonard L. Berry, A. Parasuraman, and Valerie A. Zeithaml, "Improving Service Quality in America: Lessons Learned," *Academy of Management Executive* 8, no. 2 (1994): 32–45.

22. Olga Stavrova and Daniel Ehlebracht, "Cynical Beliefs about Human Nature and Income: Longitudinal and Cross-Cultural Analyses," *Journal of Personality and Social Psychology* 110, no. 1 (2016): 116–32.

23. Julianne Holt-Lunstad, Timothy B. Smith, Mark Baker, Tyler Harris, and David Stephenson, "Loneliness and Social Isolation as Risk Factors for Mortality: A Meta-Analytic Review," *Perspectives on Psychological Science* 10, no. 2 (2015): 227–37.

24. Robert C. Ford, Frank S. McLaughlin, and John W. Newstrom, "Questions and Answers about Fun at Work," *Human Resource Planning*, 26 no. 4 (2003): 18–33, at 22.

25. Robert Provine, *Laughter: A Scientific Investigation* (New York: Penguin, 2001).

26. Tiffany McDowell, Sheba Ehteshami, and Kyle Sandell, "Are You Having Fun Yet?" *Deloitte Review* 24 (2019): 133–44.

27. Young Gin Choi, Junehee Kwon, and Wansoo Kim, "Effects of Attitudes vs. Experience of Workplace Fun on Employee Behaviors," *International Journal of Contemporary Hospitality Management* 25, no 1 (2013): 410–27; Katerina Georganta and Anthony J. Montgomery, "Exploring Fun as a Job Resource: The Enhancing and Protecting Role of a Key Modern Workplace Factor," *International Journal of Applied Positive Psychology* 1 (2016): 107–31.

28. See, for example, Daniel Sgroi, "Happiness and Productivity: Understanding the Happy-Productive Worker," Social Market Foundation, October 2015, https://www.ciphr.com/wp-content/uploads/2016/11/Social-Market-Foundation-Publication-Briefing-CAGE-4-Are-happy-workers-more-productive-281015.pdf; Barry Chignell, "Six Reasons Why Fun in the Office is the Future of Work," CIPHR, May 22, 2018, https://www.ciphr.com/advice/fun-in-the-office/; Greg Winteregg, *Fun at Work: More Time, Freedom, Profit and More of What You Love to Do* (Clearwater, FL: Matterhorn Business Development, 2019).

29. "Performance Accelerated," O. C. Tanner Learning Group White Paper, April 24, 2020, https://www.octanner.com/content/dam/oc-tanner/documents/global-research/White_Paper_Performance_Accelerated.pdf.

30. Gary Klein, *The Sources of Power: How People Make Decisions* (Cambridge, MA: MIT Press, 1998); Gary Klein, *The Power of Intuition: How to Use Your Gut Feelings to Make Better Decisions at Work* (New York: Crown Business, 2004).

EIGHT

Professional Identity: Becoming a Lawyer, Becoming a Leader

1. "How Our Test Contributes to Comprehensive and Fair Law School Admissions," LSAC, June 19, 2019, https://www.lsac.org/blog/how-our-test-contributes-comprehensive-and-fair-law-school-admissions#:~:text=The%20results%20are%20consistently%20clear,%2Dpoint%20average%20(GPA).

2. Neil Hamilton, "The Major Transitions in Professional Formation and Development from Being a Student to Being a Lawyer Present Opportunities to Benefit the

Students and the Law School," *Baylor Law Review* 72 (Winter 2021), published ahead of print, https://www.baylor.edu/law/doc.php/362995.pdf.

3. Neil W. Hamilton and Louis Bilionis, *Law Student Professional Development and Formation: Bridging Law School, Student, and Employer Goals* (New York: Cambridge University Press, 2021).

4. Marjorie Shultz and Sheldon Zedeck, "Predicting Lawyer Effectiveness: Broadening the Basis for Law School Admissions Decisions," *Law and Social Inquiry, Journal of the American Bar Foundation* 36, no. 3 (2011): 620–61, at 661.

5. Hamilton and Bilionis, *Law Student Professional Development and Formation.*

6. William M. Sullivan, Anne Colby, Judith Welch Wegner, Lloyd Bond, and Lee S. Shulman, *Educating Lawyers: Preparation for the Profession of Law* (San Francisco: Jossey-Bass/Wiley, 2007).

7. Id.

8. Id.

9. Hamilton, "The Major Transitions in Professional Formation," 6.

10. Barry Z. Posner, "When Learning How to Lead, An Exploratory Look at the Role Models," *Leadership & Organizational Development Journal* 42, no. 5 (2021): 802–18.

11. See G. Andrew H. Benjamin, Alfred Kaszniak, Bruce Sales, and Stephen B. Shanfield, "The Role of Legal Education in Producing Psychological Distress among Law Students and Lawyers," *American Bar Foundation Research Journal* 11, no. 2 (1986): 225–52; Patrick Schiltz, "On Being a Happy, Healthy, and Ethical Member of an Unhappy, Unhealthy, Unethical Profession," *Vanderbilt Law Review* 52 (1999): 871–951.

12. Susan Daicoff, *Lawyer, Know Thyself: A Psychological Analysis of Personality Strengths and Weaknesses* (Washington, DC: American Psychological Association, 2004), 146–48.

13. John Bliss, "The Professional Identity of Lawyers," *The Practice* 2, no. 3 (2016), https://thepractice.law.harvard.edu/article/the-professional-identity-formation-of-lawyers/.

14. John Grisham, *The Rainmaker* (New York: Dell, 2011).

15. Id.

16. Donald G. McNeil Jr., "Fauci on What Working for Trump Was Really Like," *New York Times*, February 13, 2021 (updated), https://www.nytimes.com/2021/01/24/health/fauci-trump-covid.html.

17. Todd David Peterson and Elizabeth Waters Peterson, "Stemming the Tide of Law Student Depression: What Law Schools Need to Learn from the Science of Positive Psychology," *Yale Journal of Health Policy, Law, and Ethics* 9, no. 2 (2009), https://digitalcommons.law.yale.edu/yjhple/vol9/iss2/2/; Susan P. Sturm and Lani Guinier, "The Law School Matrix: Reforming Legal Education in a Culture of Competition and Conformity," *Vanderbilt Law Review* 60, no. 2 (2007): 515–54.

18. Jeannie Suk Gersen, "The Socratic Method in the Age of Trauma," *Harvard Law Review* 130 (2017): 2330–32; Cynthia G. Hawkins-Leon, "The Socratic Method-Problem Method Dichotomy: The Debate Over Teaching Method Continues," *BYU Education & Law Journal* (1998): 16–17.

19. Major, Lindsey & Africa, "2019 Millennial Attorney Survey: New Expectations, Evolving Beliefs and Shifting Career Goals," Above the Law, https://cdn2.hubspot.net/hubfs/209075/MLA_MillenialSurvey_040519_forWeb-1.pdf.

20. Lori Berman, Heather Bock, and Juliet Aiken, *Accelerating Lawyer Success: How to Make Partner, Stay Healthy, and Flourish in a Law Firm* (Chicago: American Bar Association, 2016), 46–58.

21. Deborah L. Rhode and Amanda K. Packel, *Leadership: Law Policy, and Management* (New York: Wolters Kluwer Law and Business, 2011), 163 (citing Arie de Geus, "Beware: Innovation Kills!" in *Leading for Innovation*, eds. Francis Hesselbein, Iain Somerville, and Marshall Goldsmith (San Francisco: Jossey-Bass, 2002), 225–38, at 226).

22. James M. Kouzes and Barry Z. Posner, *Everyday People, Extraordinary Leadership: How to Make a Difference Regardless of Your Title, Role, or Authority* (Hoboken, NJ: Wiley, 2020).

23. See Bill George, Peter Sims, Andrew N. McLean, and Diana Mayer, "Discovering Your Authentic Leadership," *Harvard Business Review*, February 2007, https://hbr.org/2007/02/discovering-your-authentic-leadership.

24. Daniel Goleman, *Emotional Intelligence: Why It Can Matter More than IQ* (New York: Random House, 2005).

25. See Mary Walsh Fitzpatrick and Rosemary Queenan, "Professional Identity Formation, Leadership and Exploration of Self," *University of Missouri-Kansas City Law Review*, 89 (2020): p. 539.

NINE

Becoming an Ethical Lawyer and Leader

1. Richard L. Hughes, Robert C. Ginnett, and Gordon J. Curphy, *Leadership: Enhancing the Lessons of Experience*, 7th ed. (New York: McGraw-Hill, 2012), 152–57.

2. Id.

3. Neil Hamilton and Louis Bilionis, *Law Student Professional Development and Formation: Bridging Law School, Student, and Employer Goals* (New York: Cambridge University Press, 2021).

4. Hughes, Ginnett, and Curphy, *Leadership*, 161–62.

5. Ronit Dinovitzer, Bryant G. Garth, Robert Nelson, Gabriele Plickert, Rebecca Sandefur, Joyce Sterling, and David Wilkins, *After the JD III: Third Results from a National Study of Legal Careers* (Washington, DC: American Bar Foundation and NALP Foundation for Law Career Research and Education, 2014), http://www.americanbarfoundation.org/uploads/cms/documents/ajd3report_final_for_distribution.pdf.

6. American Bar Association, Preamble para.7, *Model Rules of Professional Conduct* (Chicago: American Bar Association, 2020).

7. J. W. Gardner, *On Leadership* (New York: Free Press, 1990).

8. James M. Kouzes and Barry Z. Posner, *The Leadership Challenge: How to Make Extraordinary Things Happen in Organizations*, 6th ed. (Hoboken, NJ: Wiley, 2017).

9. Robert S. Bennett, *In the Ring: The Trials of a Washington Lawyer* (New York: Crown Publishers, 2008), 361.

10. Kouzes and Posner, *The Leadership Challenge*, 41.

11. Susan P. Sturm, "Lawyering Paradoxes: Making Meaning of the Contradictions," *Santa Clara Law Review* 62 (2022): 175.

12. American Bar Association, Rule 2.1, *Model Rules of Professional Conduct.*

13. Meinhard v. Salmon, 164 N.E. 545 (N.Y. 1928).

14. See Neil W. Hamilton, "Ethical Leadership in Professional Life," *University of St. Thomas Law Journal* 6 (2009): 358–96, at 361–65.

15. James M. Kouzes and Barry Z. Posner, *Everyday People, Extraordinary Leadership: How to Make a Difference Regardless of Your Title, Role, or Authority* (Hoboken, NJ: Wiley, 2020).

16. Kouzes and Posner, *The Leadership Challenge*, 114–15.

17. American Bar Association, *Model Rules of Professional Conduct.*

18. Id.

19. Roger C. Cramton, "On Giving Meaning to 'Professionalism,'" in *Teaching and Learning Professionalism: Symposium Proceedings, October 2–4, 1996, Oak Brook, Illinois* (Chicago: American Bar Association, 1997), 18–24.

20. Deborah L. Rhode, "Into the Valley of Ethics: Professional Responsibility and Educational Reform," *Law and Contemporary Problems* 58, no. 3/4 (1995): 139–51.

TEN

Making Decisions, Leading Innovation

1. Brian Tait, "Traditional Leadership vs. Servant Leadership," *Forbes*, March 11, 2020, https://www.forbes.com/sites/forbescoachescouncil/2020/03/11/traditional-leadership-vs-servant-leadership/?sh=52741e4d451e.

2. Noel M. Tichy and Warren G. Bennis, *Judgment: How Winning Leaders Make Great Calls* (New York: Portfolio, 2007), 9–10.

3. Peter Drucker, "The Effective Decision," *Harvard Business Review*, January 1967, https://hbr.org/1967/01/the-effective-decision.

4. Ram Charan, "Conquering a Culture of Indecision," *Harvard Business Review*, January 2006, https://hbr.org/2006/01/conquering-a-culture-of-indecision.

5. Peter J. Boyer, "A Different War," *New Yorker*, July 1, 2002, https://www.newyorker.com/magazine/2002/07/01/a-different-war.

6. John P. Kotter, *Leading Change*, rev. ed. (Cambridge, MA: Harvard Business Review Press, 2012); John P. Kotter and Dan S. Cohen, *Heart of Change: Real-Life Stories of How People Change Their Organizations* (Cambridge, MA: Harvard Business Review Press, 2012).

7. Donald J. Polden, "Lawyers, Leadership, and Innovation," *Santa Clara Law Review* 58 (2018): 427–52, at 442–43 (citing Thomas S. Clay and Eric A. Seeger, *2018 Law Firms in Transition: An Altman Weil Flash Survey* (Willow Grove, PA: Altman Weil, Inc., 2018), iii).

8. Polden, "Lawyers, Leadership, and Innovation," 443.

9. Clay and Seeger, *2018 Law Firms in Transition*, ii, v.

10. Deborah L. Rhode and Amanda K. Packel, *Leadership: Law, Policy, and Management* (New York: Walters Kluwer Law and Business, 2011), 163.

11. David Horth and Dan Buchner, *Innovative Leadership: How to Use Innovation to Lead Effectively, Work Collaboratively, and Drive Results* (Greensboro, NC, Center for Creative Leadership: 2014), 6–7, https://www.ccl.org/wp-content/uploads/2015/04/InnovationLeadership.pdf.

12. Polden, "Lawyers, Leadership, and Innovation."

13. Greg Satell, "The 4 Types of Innovation and the Problems They Solve," *Harvard Business Review*, June 2, 2017, https://hbr.org/2017/06/the-4-types-of-innovation-and-the-problems-they-solve.

14. Horth and Buchner, *Innovative Leadership*.

15. Glenn Llopis, "5 Ways Leaders Enable Innovation," *Forbes*, April 7, 2014, https://www.forbes.com/sites/glennllopis/2014/04/07/5-ways-leaders-enable-innovation-in-their-teams/#52e5ea948c4c.

16. Polden, "Lawyers, Leadership, and Innovation."

17. Theresa Amabile and Steven Kramer, *The Progress Principle: Using Small Wins to Ignite Joy, Engagement, and Creativity at Work* (Boston, MA: Harvard Business School Press, 2011).

18. Kristi Hedges, "How to Drive Innovation in Five Steps," *Forbes*, April 10, 2014, https://www.forbes.com/sites/work-in-progress/2014/04/10/how-to-drive-innovation-in-five-steps/#7fbf68a53d4b.

19. Horth and Buchner, *Innovative Leadership*, 13.

ELEVEN

Becoming a Team Leader

1. Jon R. Katzenbach and Douglas K. Smith, "The Discipline of Teams," *Harvard Business Review*, July/August 2005, https://hbr.org/1993/03/the-discipline-of-teams-2.

2. Heidi K. Gardner, "Collaboration in Law Firms," *The Practice* 1, no. 6 (September/October 2015), https://thepractice.law.harvard.edu/article/collaboration-in-law-firms/.

3. Ben W. Heineman Jr., "Law and Leadership," *Journal of Legal Education* 56 (2006): 596–614, at 607.

4. Gardner, "Collaboration in Law Firms"; see also Heidi K. Gardner, *Smart Collaboration: How Professionals and Their Firms Succeed by Breaking Down Silos* (Cambridge, MA: Harvard Business Review Press, 2017).

5. Andre Martin, *What's Next: The 2007 Changing Nature of Leadership Survey* (Greensboro, NC: Center for Creative Leadership, 2015), http://cclinnovation.org/wp-content/uploads/2020/03/whats-next-the-2007-changing-nature-of-leadership-survey_2015.pdf.

6. Mike Myatt, "10 Communication Secrets of Great Leaders," *Forbes*, April 4, 2012, https://www.forbes.com/sites/mikemyatt/2012/04/04/10-communication-secrets-of-great-leaders/?sh=7643b5ba22fe

7. Deborah J. Barrett, "Leadership Communications: A Communication Approach for Senior-Level Managers," in *Handbook of Business Strategy* (Emerald Group Publishing, 2006), 385–90, https://scholarship.rice.edu/bitstream/handle/1911/27037/Leadership+Communication++A+Communicatin+Approach+for+SeniorLeel+Managers++Barrett.pdf?sequence=2.

8. Neil Hamilton, "Fostering and Assessing Law Student Teamwork and Team Leadership Skills," *Hofstra Law Review* 48 (2019): 619–57; Lynda Gratton and Tamara J. Erickson, "Eight Ways to Build Collaborative Teams," *Harvard Business Review*, November 2007, https://hbr.org/2007/11/eight-ways-to-build-collaborative-teams; Martine Haas and Mark Mortensen, "The Secrets of Great Teamwork," *Harvard Business Review*, June 2016, https://hbr.org/2016/06/the-secrets-of-great-teamwork.

9. Amy C. Edmondson, *The Fearless Organization: Creating Psychological Safety in the Workplace for Learning, Innovation and Growth* (Cambridge, MA: Harvard Business Review Press, 2018); Amy Edmondson, "Teamwork on the Fly," *Harvard Business Review*, April 2012, https://hbr.org/2012/04/teamwork-on-the-fly-2.

10. Haas and Mortensen, "The Secrets of Great Teamwork."

11. Edmondson, "Teamwork on the Fly."

12. Edmondson, *The Fearless Organization.*

13. Bryan L. Bonner and Alexander R. Bolinger, "Bring Out the Best in Your Team," *Harvard Business Review*, September 2014, https://hbr.org/2014/09/bring-out-the-best-in-your-team.

14. Cass R Sunstein and Reid Hastie, "Making Dumb Groups Smarter: The New Science of Group Decision Making," *Harvard Business Review*, December 2014, 90–92, https://hbr.org/2014/12/making-dumb-groups-smarter.

15. David Rock and Heidi Grant, "Why Diverse Teams Are Smarter," *Harvard Business Review*, November 4, 2016, https://hbr.org/2016/11/why-diverse-teams-are-smarter.

16. Benham Tabrizi, "75% of Cross-Functional Teams Are Dysfunctional," *Harvard Business Review*, June 2015, https://hbr.org/2015/06/75-of-cross-functional-teams-are-dysfunctional.

TWELVE

Developing Emotional Intelligence and Handling Adversity

1. Keld Jenson, "Intellect Is Overrated: What You Really Need to Succeed," *Forbes*, April 12, 2012.

2. James M. Kouzes and Barry Z. Posner, *The Leadership Challenge: How to Make Extraordinary Things Happen in Organizations*, 6th ed. (Hoboken, NJ: Wiley, 2017); Ronda Muir, *Beyond Smart: Lawyering with Emotional Intelligence* (Chicago: American Bar Association, 2017).

3. Roland B. Smith and Paul Marrow, "The Changing Nature of Leadership in Law Firms," *New York State Bar Journal* 80, no. 7 (Sept. 2008): 33–38, at 33.

4. Daniel Goleman, "Leadership that Gets Results," *Harvard Business Review*, March /April 2000, https://hbr.org/2000/03/leadership-that-gets-results.

5. Natalie Loeb and David B. Sarnoff, "EQ versus IQ: What Smart Lawyers and Law Firms Need to Know about Emotional Intelligence," *PLI Current: The Journal of PLI Press* 4, no. 1 (2020), https://static1.squarespace.com/static/5c26b8695b409b7ff c6ca248/t/5e710003d98ddb7a3c013c12/1584463875317/Loeb+PLI+Article +EQ+v+IQ+_Vol.4_No.1_2020.pdf.

6. "How Emotional Intelligence Makes You a Better Lawyer," American Bar Association, October 2017, https://www.americanbar.org/news/abanews /publications/youraba/2017/october-2017/how-successful-lawyers-use-emotional -intelligence-to-their-advan/.

7. Heidi Gardner, *Smart Collaboration: How Professionals and Their Firms Succeed by Breaking Down Silos* (Boston, MA: Harvard Business Review Press, 2016).

8. Harvey Deutschendorf, "Why Emotionally Intelligent People Are More Successful," *Fast Company*, June 22, 2015, https://www.fastcompany.com/3047455/why -emotionally-intelligent-people-are-more-successful.

9. Muir, *Beyond Smart*.

10. Daniel Goleman, *Emotional Intelligence: Why It Matters More than IQ* (New York: Random House, 1995).

11. Roland B. Smith, "The Struggles of Lawyer-Leaders and What They Need to Know," *New York State Bar Journal* (March/April 2009): 38–40.

12. Goleman, *Emotional Intelligence*.

13. Amy Zipkin, "MANAGEMENT; The Wisdom of Thoughtfulness," *New York Times*, May 31, 2000, https://www.nytimes.com/2000/05/31/business/management -the-wisdom-of-thoughtfulness.html.

14. Cary Cherniss and Daniel Goleman, eds., *The Emotionally Intelligent Workplace: How to Select For, Measure, and Improve Emotional Intelligence in Individuals, Groups, and Organizations* (San Francisco: Jossey-Bass, 2001).

15. Daniel Goleman, Richard E. Boyatzis, and Annie McKee, "Primal Leadership: The Hidden Driver of Great Performance," *Harvard Business Review*, November-December 2001, https://hbr.org/2001/12/primal-leadership-the-hidden -driver-of-great-performance.

16. Id.

17. Our thanks to Professor Neil Hamilton for sharing his research on the skill of self-reflection and his "Assessment of a Student's Skill of Reflection Based on a Number of Experiences Where the Students Did Individual Reflection Writing Assignments."

18. Mark. A. Cohen, "The Golden Age of the Legal Entrepreneur—Why Now and Why It Matters," *Forbes*, June 1, 2018, https://www.forbes.com/sites/markcohen1/2018/06/01/the-golden-age-of-the-legal-entrepreneur-why-now-and-why-it-matters/?sh=55924f3d7803; Jonathan Marciano, "10 Lawyers-Turned-Entrepreneurs Creating a Revolution in Law," *Entrepreneur*, June 14, 2017, https://www.entrepreneur.com/article/295194.

19. Jared S. Allen, Regan M. Stevenson, Ernest H. O'Boyle, and Scott Seibert, "What Matters More for Entrepreneurship Success? A Meta-Analysis Comparting General Mental Ability and Emotional Intelligence in Entrepreneurial Setting," *Strategic Entrepreneurship Journal* (November 2020), https://onlinelibrary.wiley.com/doi/full/10.1002/sej.1377.

20. Thomas R. Eisenmann, "Entrepreneurship: A Working Definition," *Harvard Business Review*, January 10, 2013, https://hbr.org/2013/01/what-is-entrepreneur-ship; Howard H. Stevenson and David E. Gumpert, "The Heart of Entrepreneurship," *Harvard Business Review*, March 1985, https://hbr.org/1985/03/the-heart-of-entrepreneurship.

21. Stevenson and Gumpert, "The Heart of Entrepreneurship."

22. Robert Kiyosaki, *Rich Dad, Poor Dad: What the Rich Teach Their Kids about Money that the Poor and Middle Class Do Not*, 2nd ed. (Plata Publishing, 2017).

23. Bill J. Bonnstetter, "New Research: The Skills That Make an Entrepreneur," *Harvard Business Review*, December 7, 2012, https://hbr.org/2012/12/new-research-the-skills-that-m; Thomas J. Law, "Entrepreneurial Mindset: 20 Ways to Think Like an Entrepreneur," *Oberlo*, December 11, 2020, https://www.oberlo.com/blog/entrepreneurial-mindset.

24. Thomas S. Clay and Eric A. Seeger, *2018 Law Firms in Transition: An Altman Weil Flash Survey* (Willow Grove, PA: Altman Weil, Inc., 2018), iii.

25. Donald J. Polden, "Lawyers, Leadership, and Innovation," *Santa Clara Law Review* 58 (2018): 427–52; Clay and Seeger, *2018 Law Firms in Transition.*

26. Joshua D. Margolis and Paul Stoltz, "How to Bounce Back from Adversity," *Harvard Business Review*, Jan./Feb. 2010, https://hbr.org/2010/01/how-to-bounce-back-from-adversity.

27. Salvatore, R. Maddi, "The Story of Hardiness: Twenty Years of Theorizing, Research, and Practice," *Consulting Psychology Journal: Practices and Research* 54, no. 3 (2002): 175–85.

28. Margolis and Stotz, "Bounce Back from Adversity."

29. James M. Kouzes and Barry Z. Posner, *Turning Adversity into Opportunity* (San Francisco: Jossey-Bass, 2014); Barry Z. Posner, "Leadership Strategies for the Next Normal," *IEEE Engineering Management Review* 48, no. 3 (2020): 19-23; Chris Nicols, Shoma Chatterjee Hayden, and Chris Trendler, "4 Behaviors that Help Leaders Manage a Crisis," *Harvard Business Review*, April 2, 2020, https://hbr.org/2020/04/4-behaviors-that-help-leaders-manage-a-crisis.

30. Nichols, Hayden, and Trendler, "4 Behaviors that Help Leaders Manage a Crisis."

31. Donald Robertson, *Build Your Resistance: How to Survive and Thrive in Any Situation* (London: John Murray Press, 2012).

32. Margolis and Stoltz, "Bounce Back from Adversity;" Rob Cross, Karen Dillon, and Danna Greenberg, "The Secret to Building Resilience," *Harvard Business Review*, January 29, 2021, https://hbr.org/2021/01/the-secret-to-building-resilience.

33. Angela Duckworth, *Grit: The Power of Passion and Perseverance* (New York: Scribner, 2018).

34. Arran Caza and Barry Z. Posner, "How and When Does Grit Influence Leaders' Behavior?" *Leadership & Organizational Development Journal* 40, no. 1 (2019): 124–34; Arran Caza and Barry Z. Posner, "Mixed Associations Between Grit and Transformational Leadership Behavior", *Journal of Leadership Studies*, 15, no. 3 (2021): 6-20.

35. Cross, Dillon, and Greenberg, "The Secret to Building Resilience."

36. "21 Day Grit and Growth Mindset Challenge: Days 1–10," American Bar Association, https://www.americanbar.org/groups/diversity/women/initiatives_awards/grit-project/21-day-grit-challenge/#:~:text=The%20ABA%20Commission%20on%20Women,women%20lawyers%20have%20in%20common.%E2%80%9D&text=Do%20them%20on%20your%20own,the%20challenges%20and%20l earnings%20together.

37. Clay and Seeger, *2018 Law Firms in Transition*.

38. Polden, "Lawyers, Leadership, and Innovation," 442–43.

THIRTEEN

Leading the Charge for Diversity, Equity, and Inclusion

1. See, e.g., "Diversity and Inclusion Center Resources," American Bar Association, https://www.americanbar.org/groups/diversity/resources/about_us/; see also Eric Chung et al., "A Portrait of Asian Americans in the Law," *The Practice* 5, no. 1 (2018), https://thepractice.law.harvard.edu/article/a-portrait-of-asian-americans-in-the-law/.

2. "Report of Diversity and Inclusion 360 Commission," American Bar Association, August 2016, https://www.americanbar.org/content/dam/aba/administrative/diversity-inclusion-center/di-360-commission-executive-summary.pdf.

3. Jill Switzer, "Can Lawyers of Color and Women Get Ahead Now?" *Above the Law*, June 17, 2021, https://abovethelaw.com/2021/06/can-lawyers-of-color-and-women-get-ahead-now/.

4. "Admission Trends: ABA Applicants, Admitted Applicants & Applications," Law School Admission Council, 2021, https://report.lsac.org/View.aspx?Report=AdmissionTrendsApplicantsAdmitApps.

5. "Diversity in US Population & Pipeline to Legal Careers," Law School Admission Council, 2020, https://report.lsac.org/View.aspx?Report=DiversityPopulationandPipeline.

6. American Bar Association, "ABA Profile of the Legal Profession 2020," July 2020, https://www.americanbar.org/content/dam/aba/administrative/news/2020/07/potlp2020.pdf.

7. "ABA Profile"; Eric Chung, "Portrait of Asian Americans".

8. "ABA Profile"

9. "Diversity in US Population."

10. American Bar Association, "ABA Profile of the Legal Profession 2020."

11. "Women's History Month," US Courts, https://www.uscourts.gov/about-federal-courts/educational-resources/annual-observances/womens-history-month.

12. Alicia Bannon and Janna Adelstein, "State Supreme Court Diversity—February 2020 Update," Brennan Center for Justice, February 20, 2020, https://www.brennancenter.org/our-work/research-reports/state-supreme-court-diversity-february-2020-update; Nia Malika Henderson, "White Men Are 31 Percent of American Population. They Hold 65 Percent of All Elected Offices," *Washington Post*, October 8, 2014, https://www.washingtonpost.com/news/the-fix/wp/2014/10/08/65-percent-of-all-american-elected-officials-are-white-men/.

13. Deborah L. Rhode, "From Platitudes to Priorities: Diversity and Gender Equity in Law Firms," *Georgetown Journal of Legal Ethics* 24 (2011): 1041–77, at 1049.

14. Nicole E. Negowetti, "Implicit Bias and the Legal Profession's 'Diversity Crisis': A Call For Self-Reflection," *Nevada Law Journal* 15 (2015): 930–58, at 935–36.

15. Dolly Chugh, *The Person YOU Mean to Be: How Good People Fight Bias* (New York: Harper Collins, 2018).

16. See Luis J. Diaz and Patrick C. Dunican Jr., "Ending the Revolving Door Syndrome in Law," *Seton Hall Law Review* 41 (2011): 947–1003, at 977.

17. Negowetti, "Implicit Bias," 942–49.

18. Justin Nix, Bradley A. Campbell, Edward H. Byers, and Geoffrey P. Alpert, "A Bird's Eye View of Civilians Killed by Police in 2015," *Criminology and Public Policy* 16, no. 1 (2017): 309–40, at 310 (emphasis in original).

19. Id., 311, 315.

20. Rhode, "From Platitudes to Priorities"

21. See Leah Jackson Teague and Donald J. Polden, "More Diversity Requires More Inclusive Leaders Leading by Example in Law Organizations," *Hofstra Law Review* 48 (2020): 681–703, at 699–702; Donald J. Polden and Jenna M. Anderson, "Leadership to Address Implicit Bias in the Legal Profession", *Santa Clara Law Review* 62 (2022): 63.

22. One example is the National Association of Women Lawyers annual survey on the status of women in the profession (https://www.nawl.org/p/cm/ld/fid=2019), and another is the National Association of Law Placement and their 2020 Report on Diversity in US Law Firms (https://www.nalp.org/uploads/2020_NALP_Diversity_Report.pdf).

23. Negowetti, "Implicit Bias," 930; Rhode, "From Platitudes to Priorities."

24. Joan C. Williams, *Fair Measure: Toward Effective Attorney Evaluations*, 2nd ed. (Chicago: American Bar Association, 2008).

25. For a review of recent literature, see Teague and Polden, "More Diversity."

26. Thomas Kochan, Katerina Bezrukova, Robin Ely, Susan E. Jackson, Aparna Joshi, K. E. Jehn, D. Leonard, David Levine, and D. Thomas, "The Effects of Diversity on Business Performance: Report of the Diversity Research Network," *Human Resource Management* 42, no. 1 (2003): 3–21, at 5.

27. Ella Washington and Camille Patrick, "3 Requirements for a Diverse and Inclusive Culture," *Gallup*, September 17, 2018, https://www.gallup.com/workplace/242138/requirements-diverse-inclusive-culture.aspx; Molly Werhan, "3 Reasons Why Your Law Firm Needs to Care about Diversity+Inclusion," *Columbus Business First*, November 19, 2019, https://www.bizjournals.com/columbus/news/2019/11/19/3-reasons-why-your-law-firm-needs-to-care-about.html.

28. Rocío Lorenzo, Nicole Voigt, Miki Tsusaka, and Katie Abouzahr, "How Diverse Leadership Teams Boost Innovation," *Boston Consulting Group*, January 23, 2018, https://www.bcg.com/publications/2018/how-diverse-leadership-teams-boost-innovation.

29. David Rock and Heidi Grant, "Why Diverse Teams Are Smarter," *Harvard Business Review*, November 4, 2016, https://hbr.org/2016/11/why-diverse-teams-are-smarter.

30. Teague and Polden, "More Diversity."

31. Id.

32. Jonelle Lesniak, "The Millennial Perspective on Company Culture," *Thruue, Inc.*, September 21, 2017, https://www.thruue.com/thruue-points/culture/millennial-perspective-on-company-culture/.

33. "The 2016 Deloitte Millennial Survey: Winning Over the Next Generation of Leaders," *Deloitte*, 2016, https://www2.deloitte.com/content/dam/Deloitte/global/Documents/About-Deloitte/gx-millenial-survey-2016-exec-summary.pdf.

34. "Better Quality of Work Life Is Worth a $7,600 Pay Cut for Millennials," *Businesswire*, April 7, 2016, https://www.businesswire.com/news/home/20160407005736/en/Quality-Work-Life-Worth-7600-Pay-Cut.

35. Werhan, "3 Reasons Why."

36. American Bar Association, Rule 8.4(g), *Model Rules of Professional Conduct* (Chicago: American Bar Association, 2020).

37. "Visible Invisibility: Women of Color in Law Firms," ABA Commission on Women in the Profession, 2006, https://www.americanbar.org/content/dam/aba/administrative/women/visibleinvisibility-execsummary.pdf.

38. Ibram X. Kendi, *How to Be an Antiracist* (New York, Random House, 2019).

39. Nika White, "What Does It Really Mean to Be an Ally?," July 16, 2021, *Nika White Consulting* (blog), https://www.nikawhite.com/2019/07/16/what-does-it-really-mean-to-be-an-ally/; "What It Means to Be an 'Ally' and 8 Ways to Do It," Ben and Jerry's, https://www.benjerry.com/whats-new/2016/be-an-ally.

40. Project Implicit, https://implicit.harvard.edu/implicit/takeatest.html.

41. Adam Bryant and Kevin Sharer, "Are You Really Listening?" *Harvard Business Review*, March/April 2021, https://hbr.org/2021/03/are-you-really-listening.

42. Janet Foutty, Terri Cooper, and Shelley Zalis, "Shift/Forward: Redefining Leadership: The Inclusion Imperative," *Deloitte*, June 2018, https://www2.deloitte.com/content/dam/Deloitte/us/Documents/about-deloitte/us-shift-forward-redefining-leadership.pdf.

43. Cory Edwards, "Business Processes: Why Your Desk Is A Dangerous Place to Watch The Work," *Forbes*, November 29, 2011, https://www.forbes.com/sites

/dell/2011/11/29/business-processes-why-your-desk-is-a-dangerous-place-to-watch-the-world/?sh=d4e22a3105e6.

44. Lori Berman, Heather Bock, and Juliet Aiken, *Accelerating Lawyer Success: How to Make Partner, Stay Healthy, and Flourish in a Law Firm* (Chicago: American Bar Association, 2016), 65–66, 78–80.

45. Teague and Polden, "More Diversity."

46. Marianne Coleman, "Leadership and Diversity," *Education Management Administration and Leadership* 40, no. 5 (2012): 592–609.

47. Roland B. Smith and Paul Bennett Marrow, "The Changing Nature of Leadership in Law Firms," *New York State Bar Association Journal* 80, no. 7 (Sept. 2008): 33–38.

FOURTEEN

Leadership Development for Lawyers

1. Roland B. Smith, "The Struggles of Lawyer-Leaders and What They Need to Know," *New York State Bar Association Journal* 81 no. 3 (March/April 2009): 38–40.

2. Id.

3. Nick Petrie, *Future Trends in Leadership Development: A White Paper* (Greensboro, NC: Center for Creative Leadership, 2011), https://law.scu.edu/wp-content/uploads/leadership/Future-Trends-in-Leadership-Development.pdf.

4. Donald J. Polden, "Lawyers, Leadership, and Innovation," *Santa Clara Law Review* 58 (2018): 427–52, at 442–43.

5. Petrie, *Future Trends.*

6. Smith, "The Struggles of Lawyer-Leaders."

7. "Directory of Lawyer Assistance Programs," American Bar Association, https://www.americanbar.org/groups/lawyer_assistance/resources/lap_programs_by_state/; see also Priscilla Henson, "Substance Abuse Treatment Options for Lawyers," American Addiction Centers, last updated January 6, 2021, https://americanaddictioncenters.org/rehab-guide/workforce/white-collar/lawyers/treatment-options; "Drug Use Disorders," American Bar Association, May 8, 2018, https://www.americanbar.org/groups/lawyer_assistance/resources/drug_abuse_dependence/.

8. Patrick Krill, Ryan Johnson, and Linda Albert, "The Prevalence of Substance Use and Other Mental Health Concerns among American Attorneys," *Journal Of Addiction Medicine* 10, no. 1 (2015): 46–52, https://journals.lww.com/journaladdictionmedicine/Fulltext/2016/02000/The_Prevalence_of_Substanc e_Use_and_Other_Mental.8.aspx.

9. Mark A. Cohen, "Why Are Lawyers So Unpopular and Stressed?" *Bloomberg Law,* September 30, 2015, https://news.bloomberglaw.com/business-and-practice/why-are-lawyers-so-unpopular-and-stressed/.

10. Henson, "Substance Abuse Treatment."

11. Lawrence S. Krieger, "Institutional Denial about the Dark Side of Law School, and Fresh Empirical Guidance for Constructively Breaking the Silence," *Journal of Legal Education* 52, nos. 1 and 2 (2002): 112–29.

12. Rachel Casper, "The Full Weight of Law School: Stress on Law Students is Different," *Lawyers Concerned for Lawyers*, January 18, 2019, https://www.lclma.org/2019/01/18/the-full-weight-of-law-school-stress-on-law-students-is-different/.

13. Krieger, "Institutional Denial."

14. Susan Swaim Daicoff, "Expanding the Lawyer's Toolkit of Skills and Competencies: Synthesizing Leadership, Professionalism, Emotional Intelligence, Conflict Resolution, and Comprehensive Law," *Santa Clara Law Review* 52 (2012): 795–874, at 837–38.

15. Id.

16. Petrie, *Future Trends.*

17. Roland Smith and Paul Morrow, "The Changing Nature of Leadership in Law Firms," *New York State Bar Association Journal* 80 (2008): 33–38, at 34–35; Donald J. Polden, "Leading Institutional Change: Law Schools and Legal Education in a Time of Crisis," *Tennessee Journal of Law and Public Policy* 83 (2015/16): 949–81.

18. Robert Kegan and Lisa Lahey, *Immunity to Change: How to Overcome It and Unlock Potential in Yourself and Your Organization* (Cambridge, MA: Harvard Business Press, 2009).

19. Petrie, *Future Trends.*

20. Barry Z. Posner, "It's How Leaders Behave that Matters, Not Where They Are From," *Leadership & Organizational Development Journal* 34, no. 6 (2013): 573–87.

21. Arran Caza, Brianna Caza, and Barry Z. Posner, "Transformational Leadership across Cultures: Follower Perception and Satisfaction," *Administrative Sciences* 11, no. 32 (2021), https://doi.org/10.3390/admsci11010032.

22. Daniel Goleman, "Leadership that Gets Results," *Harvard Business Review*, March/April 2000, https://hbr.org/2000/03/leadership-that-gets-results; Bruna Martinuzzi, "The 7 Most Common Leadership Styles (and How to Find Your Own)," American Express, October 16, 2019, https://www.americanexpress.com/en-us/business/trends-and-insights/articles/the-7-most-common-leadership-styles-and-how-to-find-your-own/.

23. Susan Snyder and Sara Littauer, "Leadership Flexibility: How Outstanding Partners Gets Results," *Strategies: The Journal of Legal Marketing* 7, no. 3 (2005): 4–8.

24. James M. Kouzes and Barry Z. Posner, *The Leadership Challenge: How to Make Extraordinary Things Happen in Organizations*, 6th ed. (Hoboken, NJ: Wiley, 2017).

25. Deborah L. Rhode, "Lawyers as Leaders," *Michigan State Law Review* 2010 (2010): 413–22; R. Lisle Baker, "Character and Fitness for Leadership: Learning Interpersonal Skills," *Santa Clara Law Review* 58 (2018): 525–44.

26. Kouzes and Posner, *The Leadership Challenge.*

27. John W. Gardner, *On Leadership* (New York: Free Press, 1993).

28. American Bar Association, Preamble para 7, *Model Rules of Professional Conduct* (Chicago: American Bar Association, 2020).

29. Luke 12:48.

Acknowledgments

It gives us great pleasure, and a with sincere sense of appreciation, to acknowledge the many people who contributed to this book and our efforts to develop future generations of lawyer leaders. Of course, with deep humility, any errors or omissions remain with the authors!

First to a group of colleagues and friends who read the manuscript in an early form and contributed their insights and suggestions for improvement. We know that this book is better because of their thoughtfulness, and we hope the final product is one that they are proud to say that they made their important contribution:

Lori Berman, PhD
Director of Professional Development
Hogan Lovells US LLP
Washington, DC

Doug Blaze
Dean and Art Stoinitz and Elvin E. Overton Distinguished Professor of Law
University of Tennessee

Ausra Deluard
Partner, Co-chair, US Antitrust Practice
Dentons US LLP

Neil W. Hamilton
Thomas & Patricia Holloran Professor of Law
Co-director of Holloran Center for Ethical Leadership in the Profession
St. Thomas University

Susan R. Jones
Professor of Law
Director of Small Business & Community Economic Development Clinic
George Washington University

Mark Michels, Esq.
Lecturer in Law
Santa Clara University

Paula A. Monopoli
Sol & Carlyn Hubert Professor of Law
Founding Director, Women, Leadership & Equality Program
University of Maryland

Joe R. Reeder, Esq.
Greenberg & Traurig
Washington, DC

David B. Sarnoff, Esq., ACC
Director of Strategic Partnerships and Certified Executive Coach
Loeb Leadership
Principal and Certified Executive Coach with Sarnoff Group LLC

Aric K. Short
Professor of Law
Director of Professionalism and Leadership Program
Texas A&M University

Second, we want to greatly acknowledge the extraordinary editorial assistance provided by Sheila Sybrant. She helped each of the authors not only find their own voice, but also ensured that the manuscript eventually spoke with one voice, and a voice that was clear and concise. She nudged us along at times, forced us to better structure and organize our writing, and served on occasion as a tie-breaker when we could not agree. In a similar regard, we appreciate both the editorial assistance, reference, and fact-checking provided by our graduate research assistant Leah Faibisoff. We are grateful as well to Jessica Newman who provided invaluable guidance in the final copy-editing and polishing of the manuscript. The book is infinitely more readable because of their coaching and many contributions. Thank you as well to Lisa Shannon for excellent editorial assistance on the Instructor's Guide.

Finally, a thank you to the fine folks we've come to work with at Carolina Academic Press. Carol McGeehan, senior acquisitions editor, was an early supporter and champion and Ryland Bowman, managing editor, guided the book through the production process.

About the Authors

Donald J. Polden is dean emeritus and professor of law at Santa Clara University where he served as dean of the School of Law for ten years. He is a well-recognized authority on leadership education and development for lawyers and law students. He drew national attention to the need for more formal and research-based scholarship and curriculum development in legal education through the early creation of a law school course on lawyers as leaders. Professor Deborah Rhode of Stanford, another early pioneer of lawyer leadership education, referred to Don as "truly a founding father of the field of lawyers and leadership."

Don also is a demonstrated leader serving as dean of two major law schools from 1993 to 2013 and in promoting legal education within the American Bar Association and the Association of American Law Schools. His list of significant leadership roles includes chair of the ABA committee that established accreditation standards for more than two hundred law schools, leading dozens of law school accreditation teams, and serving as president of the Memphis Bar Association, to name a few. While at Santa Clara University, Don has served as director of the law school's Center for Global Law and Policy, responsible for ten international legal education programs, several of which he taught in while also lecturing on comparative law at universities in China and Hungary. Don is frequently called up to serve as a mediator, arbitrator, and judicial officer in many Santa Clara campus disciplinary proceedings.

Following service as Santa Clara's dean, Don has been actively engaged in teaching and scholarship, especially in the areas of leadership development, professional identity formation of law students and new lawyers, and lawyering skills and competencies. He also continues to teach corporate, sports, and antitrust law, and cofounded and led Santa Clara's nationally prominent Institute for Sports Law and Ethics. Don consults with law firms on leadership development of their lawyers, such as intellectual property law powerhouse Haynes Boone, as well as lecturing at the US Army's Judge Advocate General graduate program on leadership development of Army lawyer officers.

Don created and leads Santa Clara's Institute for Lawyer Leadership Education, which has conducted several national conferences and workshops on educating lawyers and students in leadership in the legal profession, including five leadership workshops for legal education hosted by Santa Clara from 2005 to 2013. He was instrumental in the 2018 launch of a new Section on Leadership for the Association of American Law Schools. This section includes over six hundred members, representing nearly one hundred law schools courses and programs. The section meets annually to promote leadership education in law schools, advance legal scholarship concerning law and leadership, and arrange programming. In 2020–21, Don served as chair of the section.

Don received an undergraduate degree in business economics from The George Washington University and his JD from Indiana University School of Law. During law school, he wrote for the *Indiana Law Review* and following graduation served as a judicial law clerk on both state appellate and federal trial courts. He practiced antitrust law, including participating in five federal jury trials, and he argued several cases in the US Courts of Appeal and the US Supreme Court. Don is licensed to practice law in the state of Iowa and federal courts.

Don has been teaching leadership for lawyers' classes for more than a decade and is a frequent speaker at national conferences and within law firms on leadership and the legal profession. He is the author of numerous law review articles on lawyer leadership, which have been published in the *Baylor Law Review, Santa Clara Law Review*, the *Hofstra Law Review*, the *Tennessee Law Review*, and the *Tennessee Journal of Law and Policy*. His antitrust scholarship has been published in the *Harvard Journal on Legislation*, and his work has been cited by the US Supreme Court. Don coauthored *Sports, Ethics and Leadership* (Routledge, 2017) and has authored several book chapters on lawyer leadership, employment law, and government regulation law. He is a recipient of the Edwin Owens Lawyer of the Year award given by the Santa Clara University Law School.

Barry Z. Posner is the Michael J. Accolti, S. J. Professor of Leadership at Santa Clara University and chair of the Management and Entrepreneurship Department in the Leavey School of Business, where he served for twelve years as dean. Barry has received the Association for Talent Development's highest award for *Distinguished Contribution to Workplace Learning and Performance.* He has been recognized as one of the top fifty leadership coaches in America, ranked among the most influential HR thinkers in the world by *HR* magazine, and *Inc.* magazine included him among the world's top seventy-five leadership and management experts.

Barry is the coauthor (with Jim Kouzes) of the award-winning and best-selling leadership book *The Leadership Challenge*. Now in its sixth edition, with over three million copies in print, the book continues to be a groundbreaking research study, combining keen insights with practical applications, and has been translated into twenty-two foreign languages. It is listed among *The Top 100 Business Books of All Time*, receiving book-of-the-year honors by the American Council of Health Care Executives and *Fast Company*, and the Critic's Choice Award from the nation's book review editors. Kouzes and Posner's *Leadership Practices Inventory* (*LPI*) has been called "the most reliable, up-to-date leadership instrument available today." The 360-degree online version has been completed by more than four million people.

Barry has coauthored other award-winning, inspiring, and practical books on leadership: *Everyday People, Extraordinary Leadership: How to Make a Difference Regardless of Your Title, Role, or Authority*; *Leadership in Higher Education: Practices that Make a Difference*; *Stop Selling & Start Leading*; *Learning Leadership: The Five Fundamentals for Becoming an Exemplary Leader*; *Turning Adversity into Opportunity*; *Finding the Courage to Lead*; *Great Leadership Creates Great Workplaces*; *Credibility: How Leaders Gain and Lose It, Why People Demand It*; *The Truth about Leadership: The No-Fads, Heart-of-the Matter Facts You Need to Know*; *Encouraging the Heart: A Leaders Guide to Recognizing and Rewarding Others*; *A Leader's Legacy*; *Extraordinary Leadership in Australia and New Zealand*; *Making Extraordinary Things Happen in Asia*; and *The Student Leadership Challenge*.

Barry is an internationally renowned scholar who has published over one hundred research and practitioner-oriented articles, in such publications as the *Harvard Business Review*, *Academy of Management Journal*, *Journal of Applied Psychology*, *Human Relations*, *Personnel Psychology*, *Journal of Selling*, and *IEEE Transactions on Engineering Management*. He has served on a number of public and nonprofit boards, such as the American Institute of Architects, Center for Excellence in Nonprofits, Global Women's Leadership Network, Sigma Phi Epsilon Fraternity, SVCreates, and Uplift Family Services.

He received an undergraduate degree in political science from the University of California, Santa Barbara, a master's degree from The Ohio State University in public administration, and his PhD in organizational behavior and administrative theory from the University of Massachusetts, Amherst. At Santa Clara he has received several outstanding teaching and leadership honors, including the President's Distinguished Faculty Award and the School's Extraordinary Faculty Award. Barry has been a visiting professor at the University of Western Australia, Hong Kong University of Science and Technology, Sabanci University (Istanbul), and the University of Auckland (New Zealand). He has made presentations and conducted leadership development programs for corporations across the globe, and been involved with leadership development efforts at more than seventy-five college campuses.

Index

F

G

R

S

T

V

W